DICHOTOMIES
OF THE MIND

DICHOTOMIES OF THE MIND

A Systems Science Model of the Mind and Personality

WALTER LOWEN
School of Advanced Technology
State University of New York at Binghamton
Binghamton, New York

With the assistance of Lawrence Miike, Consultant on Health Policy, Berkeley Springs, West Virginia

A Wiley-Interscience Publication

JOHN WILEY & SONS

New York   Chichester   Brisbane   Toronto   Singapore

Copyright © 1982 by John Wiley & Sons, Inc.

This publication is designed to provide accurate and
authoritative information in regard to the subject
matter covered. It is sold with the understanding that
the publisher is not engaged in rendering legal, accounting,
or other professional service. If legal advice or other
expert assistance is required, the services of a competent
professional person should be sought. *From a Declaration
of Principles jointly adopted by a Committee of the
American Bar Association and a Committee of Publishers.*

Library of Congress Cataloging in Publication Data:

Lowen, Walter, 1921–
   Dichotomies of the mind.

  Bibliography: p.
  Includes index.
   1. Psychology—Philosophy.   2. Intellect.
3. Personality.   4. Social systems.   5. Jung, C. G.
(Carl Gustav), 1875–1961.   6. Human engineering.
I. Miike, Lawrence H.   II. Title.
BF38.L68   150'.1   82-2611
ISBN 0-471-08331-3   AACR2

Printed in the United States of America

10 9 8 7 6 5 4 3 2 1

To Sylvia, Gary and above all, John

FOREWORD

This book will be important to people with diverse interests. First, it is a book for those who want a better understanding of people, both themselves and others. It gives insights of value to designers of products and to those in professions that deal directly with people, such as social work, psychology, and teaching.

This book, second, is for those looking for structure in the way people function intellectually. Walter Lowen models and classifies people's information-processing capabilities and presents a logical system of relationships among various human capacities.

Walter Lowen presents his theories in a manner that is a delight to read. His examples are easy to understand and make his concepts come alive. His work uses Carl Jung's as a starting point, but you don't have to be familiar with Jung's writings to appreciate what Lowen has to say.

I am an engineer by training. Walter Lowen's ideas have opened up, for me, whole new ways of looking at people; I now judge and criticize less. His system answers many of the questions of why people act as they do.

Walter Lowen's model of human capacities represents a landmark, and it will be both praised and criticized. It will certainly provide the basis for new discussions about people.

ROBERT S. BURCHI

IBM Systems Research Institute

PREFACE

The latest frontier to be conquered seems to be the search to understand the functioning of both the brain and the mind. I see this much debated distinction as simply the hardware and the software. The brain represents the physiology of the organ, how it is wired and ordered and how various parts of it are connected to inputs and outputs. The mind deals with the programs it uses to process information.

This view may be simplistic, but I have found it useful in my effort to develop an overall conceptual model that could serve as a framework to which I would link the ever swelling tide of new research findings reported in the literature. I felt strongly, as did many others, that to digest the minutiae and detail of new knowledge, what was missing was a single holistic model of both the brain and the mind.

This book describes that model and documents how the model evolved into a coherent and practical single representation called a profile. In the development of an abstract conceptualization that is to mold something as complex as the brain and its functioning as a mind, I had to draw on concepts from various branches of science. This should not be surprising since abstract concepts are the product of the mind and mirror its functioning.

The decision to explain this influence of borrowed concepts, assuming no prior knowledge of them and making the linkages of ideas explicit, has made this a bigger book than I would have liked. Some readers, familiar with certain concepts, can skip certain chapters. I have tried to signal the reader about this at the beginning of most chapters.

The book should be of interest to diverse audiences, since the model has implications for research in artificial intelligence and linguistics simulation, personality development and testing and career counseling, management and creativity, and ergonomics or human factors, to mention a few fields. Such a potentially interdisciplinary audience posed a problem in nomenclature. I have tried to define my terms, borrowed freely from psychology, the computer field, and other technical disciplines.

Those interested primarily in the psychology of personalities will notice the strong influence of Carl Gustav Jung and may want to concentrate primarily on the interpretive outcomes covered in Chapters 16, 17, and 18.

Those interested in modeling and simulation might use this book, as I have in graduate seminars, as a case study. Before any model can be analyzed or expressed in formal notation, it must be conceptualized, and that process seldom is documented.

Finally, and this is my own primary interest and I hope one exciting to others, the model might serve as a new systems approach to artificial intelligence. To those interested in these simulations of intelligent systems, the major focus should be on the model itself, including the description of the map of capacities discussed in Chapter 7 and its linkage to libido-induced flows discussed in Chapter 14.

I am indebted to many friends for their help, influence, and contributions; many of them are acknowledged in the body of the text. They include, but reach far beyond, Dieter Baumann, Jungian analyst; Stefan Bauer-Mengelberg, mathematician, lawyer, and conductor; Herbert Kramel, architect; Larry Miike, physician and lawyer; Gunther Borris, accountant; Robert S. Burchi, IBM; Rowan Wakefield, Wakefield Washington Associates; my students in experimental courses on this work; IBM's Systems Research Institute; A. M. Elijah of the Institute of Creative Development; and many friends and acquaintances too numerous to mention. Above all, my family—Sylvia, Gary, and John, to whom I have dedicated this book—played intensely active roles in the development of the model, and I thank them for their help and continuing encouragement.

WALTER LOWEN

Binghamton, New York
June 1982

CONTENTS

PART I

INTRODUCTION
AND PREVIEW

I marvel at the order in nature. Whenever some new secret of nature is revealed, what is uncovered is a new, beautiful, simple ordering scheme, be it the periodic table, the structure of crystals, the atom, or DNA.

I believe intelligence too has its explanation in some basic order. Further, I believe that intellectual inventions are simply mirrors of that order of the mind. The computer must therefore hold clues to how the mind functions, not because computers are like minds, but because minds looked into their own structures to do the conceptualizing. Mathematics is also such a mirror, and so are the rich conceptualizations of Jung's psychology.

This book is a combination of Jung's concepts, miscellaneous theories about the mind, principles of information theory and systems engineering, and my efforts to comprehend the diversity of personalities in which I've found myself immersed. It is written in the language of mathematics, computers, and psychology to construct a model of the organization underlying intelligence, and it uses that derived organization to explain human behavioral patterns.

I've been fascinated by my wife for nearly four decades. She is so totally different from me that I often wonder why our marriage has worked so well. Then there are two sons who are a peculiar mixture of us both. I have no trouble understanding the older one, but he is difficult for my wife to read. The younger one, whom my wife understands totally, is an unfathomable wonder to me. Clearly, it was he who triggered this work, for he wouldn't settle for a father who could not understand him. He became my teacher, introducing me to so many worlds of thought and people that I felt I was the only one in the family who knew nothing about people.

These personal puzzles were complemented by my professional experience in design. The insensitivity of man-made products to the needs of people has always irritated me: kitchens that are hazards, buildings that are insane, chairs that are torturous, cars that don't function except when empty of people in a showroom. The list is unending and is even worse with organizations than with things: social services that don't serve, universities that don't teach, task forces that can't accomplish what they set out to do.

My current interest is how people process information. My research in the late 1970s led to a rather complex model. Working in an academic environment afforded me the luxury of thinking unthinkable thoughts, crossing disciplinary lines, and venturing into speculation. This is therefore an unconventional book, which does not easily fit into a single discipline.

Why would I want to share such an odd and personal view with others? Because there is evidence, strong experiential evidence, not necessarily that the model is right in all details, but that the approach is right and produces results. In innumerable cases people who understood the model came away with a better understanding of themselves and a clearer insight into their interactions with others. I've seen the model used to improve the functioning of an organization, to improve product design, and to trigger exciting new research approaches to artificial intelligence.

All this is bound to make my model controversial, even spawning anger and attacks, because it dares to speculate in areas considered territorial imperatives to select disciplines. This has not deterred me. As the model grew, so did my insights, not only into how the mind processes information, but also into the writings of Jung. At times I feel as though every new thought I discover is territory over which Jung has already traveled. This too is not a help, for Jung has never been fully accepted in the United States. To many, his thought processes are too abstract and perhaps too difficult to comprehend. American science prefers rational pragmatism.

My advice to you in reading this book for the first time is not to worry about whether you can follow every step in its development. Just let the ideas wash over you, hold on to those that make sense to you or fascinate you, and ignore those that seem strange to you, for inevitably I shall lead you into some territories you'll find hard to swallow. One of these is the acceptance of one's "weaknesses" and the idea that weakness is the inevitable counterpart of strength. This is a view alien to our scientific-industrial society, which admits only to perfection. If you have weaknesses, the traditional view is to send you to school to correct them. As a consequence, engineers are berated because they write poorly, artists shamed because they are disorderly, and administrators accused of lacking imagination. All this is unfortunate and blind to human nature. The qualities criticized are innate, a consequence of the dichotomous organization of the mind.

A second alien idea is the introduction of typologies, with which Jung also dealt.* People just don't like to be put in a box and labeled. I argue that we do it anyway but with a cultural bias, which to me is far more intolerable. We label people by income, religion, education, race, sex—by a whole host of cultural classifiers that give us little insight into how their minds function. So view the model as a more rational alternative for dealing with the diversity of people we meet rather than as a distasteful psychological typology.

A-4

The alternative is to ignore differences in personalities altogether. Unfortunately, this is the operational norm for the technological component of society. Engineers are trained in first-order approximations; they view any system in relation to a reference system or prototype and then concentrate on the differences between the observed and reference systems. They call these differences deltas (symbolized by Δ). The net difference, even though it may be large, between one system and another (e.g., a Chevrolet and a Cadillac) is the sum of a lot of little deltas.

$$X = Y + \Delta_1 + \Delta_2 + \cdots + \Delta_n$$

The tendency is, of course, to transfer this approach to people, using as the reference the personality of the designer himself or herself.† Someone else is simply the sum of little deltas relative to

---

*Reference numbers are indicated in the margin, as here by A-4, and refer to entries in the bibliography.

†There is no evidence that behavioral traits related to this model are different for men and women. The culprit is the English language. In subsequent discussions I will avoid clumsiness in phrasing by using he or she interchangeably when an individual reference frame is needed.

$$me = you + \Delta_1 + \Delta_2 + \cdots + \Delta_n$$

$$me = you + 0 + 0 + \cdots + 0$$
$$me = you$$

him. If each delta, each individual difference, is considered inconsequentially small, first-order approximation dictates that all the little deltas can be ignored, netting out to no significant difference at all. The consequence is that the designer assumes everybody is just like him, so, if he designs something to suit himself, it'll be ideal for everybody else. We know only too well that this approach can lead to disaster.

So whether we like it or not, we must learn to deal with differences among people. The way to organize such differences to yield the most insights is through typologies.

A consequence of typologies is that there can be no such thing as the *optimal personality*. My model says that there are at least 16 different types of people. Each type of personality has definable preferences for processing information, and it is these preferences that I've been interested in exploring and making explicit.

Let me make one more introductory disclaimer. I offer no validation of the correctness of the model. Correlation studies bore me, and I leave those to others. Besides, I've seen too many well-correlated studies that lead to nonsense. I appeal instead to your experience in living and to your common sense. I've found that it is impossible for others to listen to my description without wondering how it relates to themselves. One just gets caught up in it, and my experience has been that many people find the outcomes simply uncanny. The model seems to have identified patterns of predictability in personalities that are far beyond what one would expect. In fact, it is somewhat frightening to me that the model works as well as it does. Those who use the model are ultimately the judges on subjective grounds, and I get far more confirmations than objections.

GLIMPSE

This is the first in a series of glimpses that are derived from the model. This one, which discusses how differently people talk, is an example of how one can sort out observed differences in people and use them to gain insight, understanding, and tolerance.

First of all, the 16 profiles that are developed show that everyone is either a talker or a listener, and everyone has a natural disposition toward one or the other. Talkers tend to interrupt; listeners almost never do. If talkers break into the conversation while a listener is saying something, *the listener stops in midsentence and yields the floor. If the same thing happens to talkers, they just talk louder or faster. They even talk when they know the listener is no longer paying attention. Rarely do they yield.*

But I plan to talk just about talkers, for there are tremendous differences among them, derivable from eight "talker" profiles. I am sure that you will recognize many of the differences.

There are articulate talkers and imprecise talkers, a consequence of whether or not people draw on the brain hemisphere that specializes in speech. Articulate talkers speak in completed, well-structured sentences, full of the precise words they need to express an idea. Imprecise talkers are driven by feeling, jumping around quite a bit, as when sentences have three different beginnings, none really completed. They also hunt futilely for words. Consequently, the listener must often guess what the subject might be. Here's an example of such a piece of conversation I overheard. "Honey, that's the thing about that kind of thing. You never know which thing. . . ." This is typical of feeling-driven, or what I call contextual *speech. It is usually spoken with lots of intonation and animation. And if you know the context, it makes sense. Such talking is full of "whatchamacallit's," "you know's," and, above all, "he's," "she's," and "her's," that seem to have no identifiable links.*

If you listen to an extended contextual conversation, you become aware of several intermixed streams of thought. They are all related contextually in the speaker's mind, but the abrupt manner in which the speaker jumps from one topic to another makes it seem incoherent. You have to listen to the whole stream to get the feel of things.

That is never necessary with articulate talkers. Their talking is well organized, as though they were following an outline to logically develop a complex idea. They rarely use "whatchamacallit's"; they always seem to find the words they need.

But there are sharp differences among the articulate talkers. Some, with a profile I call DETN, think in words. Coherent speech is thus an event concurrent with thinking. They are really explainers of their own thinking, as though they were thinking aloud. They are never at a loss for words and therefore like social events and talking on the telephone. What really matters to people with the profile DETN is the thought. In a related profile, which I call DEFN, the emphasis is far more on how things are said than on what is said. Such people orate, with far more color and richer tone. They do well on the stage or at the rostrum. They have a very effective, commanding, more emotion-colored speech, which is a powerful aid to preachers, actors, and diplomats.

These two examples are very different from people with another profile, DINT. I call them lecturers. They think in images and like to talk only when the image is clear in their heads. Then they give a complete description of the image. But they always have to think before they talk. Small talk is therefore difficult for them.

An interesting way to note the differences is to ask different types for directions. With some, you'll be sorry you asked. Others will respond immediately but correct their own instructions. And the lecturer will pause for a while before giving you a crystal-clear set of instructions so detailed you can't absorb it all.

This is just a small sampling of personality differences. When you really study the model in detail and see the many paths in which information can flow preparatory to speaking, you will develop a whole new appreciation of the richness of the English language. Just think of the many words we have for talking: talk, jabber, speak, lecture, argue, discuss, articulate, orate, profess, explain, describe, and so forth. Each word reflects a different way of processing information in the mind.

1

A PREVIEW

I'm primarily concerned with conscious behavior and information-processing, functions largely ascribed to the cerebral cortex. The cerebral
cortex is the uppermost layer of the brain, a crumpled sheet of just a few
layers of cells directly beneath the skull. There has been extensive physiological mapping of the cerebral cortex. There are no pain sensors in
it, so that once the skull cap has been removed in an operation, it is
possible to probe the cortex while the subject is conscious. One can
therefore ask the subject to describe reactions to electrical stimuli applied
with miniature probes. A subject might report that in response to a stimulus, a twitch was felt in the right big toe. By such means the major areas
of the cerebral cortex have been identified and mapped. The right and
left brain hemispheres show an amazing symmetry, with the right hemisphere controlling the left side of the body and vice versa. But in recent
years, in spite of such symmetries, surprising right- and left-hemisphere
specializations have been discovered. For instance, certain aspects of
speech are now recognized as such a specialization, usually found in the
left hemisphere of right-handed persons. But in spite of this very active
research, a great deal is not known.

As the cerebral cortex contains billions of cells with very complex
interconnections, it will take many more years of research before we
understand the functioning of the mind at such a cell-by-cell micro level.
My approach to the problem is from the opposite direction; it is a macro
rather than a microapproach. I'm interested in characterizing traits of
very large clusters of cells without any effort to identify them physiologically. In short, I'm looking for organizational principles rather than physiological details. Let me explain this difference in approach by analogy.

I can represent an organization with two kinds of maps. One is the
office layout, which shows who sits where. Every member of the organization can thus be plotted on the map. This is analogous to physiological
mapping of the cerebral cortex. Or I can draw a much more abstract
map, known as an organizational chart, where boxes represent no physical reality but an organizational hierarchy that shows how information
and functional responsibilities flow through an organization. There may
not even be a one-to-one mapping, since one individual might function-
ally wear more than one hat. It is this kind of mapping that is at the heart
of my model.

The most basic building block of the model is what I call a *capacity*,
and there are only 16 of them. A capacity must therefore reflect millions
of cooperating brain cells. Compared to scientific studies of the cerebral
cortex, my model is therefore very crude indeed. But even with only
16 capacities, the model gets very complex.

Let me describe these 16 basic building blocks:

Each capacity represents a large cluster of cooperating brain cells that,
when working together, carry out information-processing functions described roughly by the notations in the list. I have numbered them to help
us keep track of them. Each is described by a symbol and a word label.

1	⬚ Signal	5	! Sign	9	△+□ Combination	13	⟋ Strategy
2	= Match	6	⊙ Feature	10	Harmony	14	# Pattern
3	°/₁ Contrast	7	ﬨ Sort	11	Preference	15	Logic
4	—□— Control	8	‡ Routine	12	⦾ Association	16	Structure

I consider the symbol more powerful and appropriate than the word, as words have a way of delimiting, which is not right for such global capacities. For instance, the word "harmony," capacity 10 (⟶⟵), really has to do with felt esthetic judgments of whether things go together, balance each other, form a good fit, feel good. Any of these phrases would be equally expressive of capacity 10. I therefore recommend that you concentrate on the symbol rather than on the word.

Each symbol's vagueness or richness, depending on your point of view, is of course essential, since the 16 capacities have to describe a broad spectrum of cognitive behavior in billions of individuals. The capacities are therefore global in scope. Their descriptive powers derive from their subtle interrelationships, which I refer to as their *dichotomous* structure. Let me point out two essential aspects.

1. The 16 capacities contain all sorts of oppositional pairings. The most obvious is overall opposition, which makes capacity 16 the very opposite of capacity 1, 15 the opposite of 2, and so on.
2. The ordering of the capacities as suggested by their numbers also reflects a hierarchical import, which I refer to as *complexity*. Capacity 16 is therefore vastly more complex than capacity 1.

Let me breathe some meaning into these abstractions. The hierarchy reflects roughly the order in which capacities develop in a child. I refer to it as the progressive awakening of consciousness. From the viewpoint of survival, the very first capacity a newborn baby must deal with is capacity 1, denoted by a symbol like a traffic light or elevator signal (⬚). It is indeed the capacity to recognize a *signal*. The nervous system tells the baby that she is hungry. That signal must register in the child's consciousness; that is, the infant must recognize that she received that signal. Crying is sufficient indication to let us know that it has received such a signal, and the mother quickly learns to respond to that indication. In the absence of signals, the child can sleep. So the very simplest of all capacities is the capacity to recognize a signal.

The second capacity is denoted by an equal sign, intended to suggest the capacity to *match* (=); that is, the baby learns to recognize that some signal received was just like the signal received in a previous experience. The capacity to match, specifically to match signals, is absolutely essential to learning at the most primitive level. "This is the same as that" is quintessential for creating order out of experiences.

C-5,

Capacity 3 is essential for more refined ordering. The $^{o}/_{|}$ symbol stands for *contrasting* opposition. It is a vastly more sophisticated capacity in that not only are signals sorted out as "this is like that," but also as "this is the opposite of that"; that is, the child now not only recognizes signals for hunger, but also recognizes the signal "I'm satiated" as opposite to that of "I'm hungry." The child is increasingly capable of imposing a meaningful order on sensory experiences, matching like experiences, the precursors to synonyms, and opposite experiences, or antonymlike identifiers.

These capacities awaken in ordered steps, such as in Maslow's theory of needs, so that a new capacity cannot develop until the previous capacities have reached some minimal level of capability. Growth, very noticeable to the parent, thus comes in clearly discernible steps.

The leap from capacity 3 to capacity 4 is especially dramatic, for capacity 4 is not only a new capacity but also a kind of summary or integration of the previous three. It is the completion of a level of growth, what I call a *mode*. Capacity 4 is the ability to *control* ($-\Box-$). Here, control means essentially motor control in response to signals.

The remaining capacities awaken in a similarly progressive fashion. Of course, earlier capacities continue to grow; the child recognizes an ever richer set of signals, matches like ones, sorts out oppositional ones, and learns appropriate motor controls. At first the baby can only kick and grasp. Gradually he learns to reach, hold, and let go and to direct his kicks for a purpose.

As these capacities grow, a new set comes into play, uniquely linking eyes and hands. This is the awakening of the second mode, which is the stage in child development when a child learns to place blocks over a peg in proper order, sorting them by color and size. Such skills are precursors to more complex hand–eye skills such as tying a shoelace. This orderly progression of skills is described by the next four capacities, 5 (!), 6 (☉), 7 (ℕ), and 8 (‡).

Capacity 5 is represented by a *sign* (!). A sign is far more sophisticated than a signal but is related to it. If the mother waves her finger, meaning "no, no," the child learns to interpret that sign. A spanking may be in the offing, which generates a signal, pain, that the child can now link to the sign for "no, no" or "don't" or "danger." That is capacity 5, to identify signs. Not all signs are bad. Ceremonies, such as a lit candle, are signs, as are certain rituals that develop in family life.

As children are exposed to more and more signs, visual discrimination becomes essential. This is capacity 6 (☉), which I call *feature*, essence, or caricature. It is the ability to extract the essence from visual patterns, just as the cartoonist learns to convey what is essential with a minimum of lines. A curved-up mouth is the essence of happy; a turned-down mouth is sad; a tilted eyebrow is worry or surprise.

Capacity 6 deals with these visual discriminators and is later, as capacity 7 (⋈) awakens, applied to sort out things: "this is bigger than that, and I have five of these and three of those." Capacity 7 thus deals with *sorting* and counting.

All these capacities are essential precursors to another integrating capacity, number 8 (‡), which deals with *routines*, the little sequential programs to string together a sequence of motor instructions that the child learns, such as tying a shoelace or buttoning a shirt.

I think this is sufficient to give you an idea of what I mean by a capacity. So far, I have described half of the 16. These first eight capacities are ones that can also be observed in a dog or a monkey. I call the entire group *prelingual* capacities, essential precursor skills to language. Thus language begins with capacity 9, and as that awakens the child will rapidly surpass the dog in skills.

But let me stop here for a moment. I said earlier that the capacities are not only hierarchically ordered but also bear important oppositional relationships to one another. I call the most basic oppositional pair of subsets of the 16 capacities a *dichotomy*.

The dichotomies, which are derivable on mathematical grounds, give the most important insights into personality differences, and I therefore want to discuss them for a while. I have already mentioned one dichotomy, prelingual versus lingual. I call this the *language* dichotomy. It represents, mathematically speaking, a symmetrical partitioning of the universal set into two subsets, each with cardinality of eight. The power of the model stems from the fact that these 16 capacities lead to 256 oppositional pairings, an inordinately rich set of descriptors, which give the model, simple as it is, such incredible interpretive power. Dichotomies are very practical, because it is easier for people to describe themselves in terms of extremes than along a spectrum. It's a bit like playing the game of 20 questions; one can zero in on an answer rather quickly.

A quick view of some of the dichotomies can show you how they yield valuable insights into how people process information. But first, let me introduce some systematics.

I use the convention of listing the 16 capacities in an array of four columns. Each column represents a *mode*. The last capacity in each mode is an integrator of the previous three and itself and thus represents the completion of a mode.

Second, when we study orderings among the capacities, we use only their numbers, which not only serve as labels for the capacities but also describe their positions in the hierarchy of growth. The numbers are just a shorthand for identifying the capacities, which have very complex capabilities. Even their symbols and names are only summary labels for very complicated neurological information-processing functions. Review the list once more:

Mode		Mode		Mode		Mode	
1	Signal	5 !	Sign	9 △+□	Combination	13 ↗	Strategy
2 =	Match	6 ⊙	Feature	10	Harmony	14 ⊞	Pattern
3 ⁰/₁	Contrast	7 Ⅷ	Sort	11	Preference	15	Logic
4 —□—	Control	8 ‡	Routine	12 ⊙	Association	16	Structure

In this way the dichotomy of *language* can be visually shown as a symmetrical partition, of prelingual, on the left, versus lingual, on the right.

<table>
<tr><td>1 5
2 6
3 7
4 8</td><td>versus</td><td>9 13
10 14
11 15
12 16</td></tr>
</table>

this subset   versus   that subset
prelingual   versus   lingual.

Another partition could be:

<table>
<tr><td>1 5 9 13
2 6 10 14</td><td>this subset</td></tr>
</table>

versus   versus

<table>
<tr><td>3 7 11 15
4 8 12 16</td><td>that subset</td></tr>
</table>

I call this partition the dichotomy of *style*, with the oppositional attributes of contextual (C) versus detailed (D). Let me try to make this come alive through some personal examples.

As an initial guide, C and D can be equated with the computer terms "time sharing" and "batch processing," respectively. In brief, people seem to process information in two diametrically opposite ways or styles. Either they time share or they batch process; that is, they either do a lot of little things at one time, hopping from one to another and back again, or they stick to one ordered sequence from beginning to end. For instance, I'm a batch processor; my style is detailed. My wife is a time sharer; her style is contextual.

GLIMPSE

Typically my wife doesn't start cooking until I get home. So while she's busy in the kitchen, I sit in the living room reading. Suddenly, just as I'm in the middle of something interesting, I hear my wife calling from the kitchen, "Walter, please bring up a couple of onions from the cellar." Now what happens is that I didn't really listen. I simply filed an "interrupt" signal and kept right on reading till I got to the end of the article (completing the batch job). I would then walk into the kitchen and say to my wife, "What did you want?" to which I get the irritated response, "I forget, why didn't you answer me when I spoke to you?"

Now consider the case if my wife decides to get the onions herself. As she walks downstairs, her eye may fall on a plant that needs watering. So she detours to get the watering can right then and there, and then I hear her say out loud, "Gee, what did I come down here for? Oh, yes, the onions." Even then she may get sidetracked again. No wonder it took her much longer to get the onions than one might expect (time sharing).

This leads me to another aspect of C versus D, or the dichotomy of style. For instance, D style has a very good sense of clock time, and people of that type are punctual. In fact, they get upset at others who are not. Those tend to be the contextual types, who have a very good sense of rate rather than of clock time.

The dichotomy of style deals with fundamental differences in behavior, because it deals with two opposing strategies for finding a sense of security. The C style finds security in understanding the total context, whereas the D style satisfies the need for security through thoroughness and meticulous attention to detail. It is therefore not surprising that one can observe the difference in behavior at every turn. For instance, reflect for a moment on how your colleagues use their offices. Some shield themselves from interruptions by asking a secretary to hold all calls, by keeping their office doors closed, or through the orientation of their desks. Others, those who feel more secure if they don't miss anything and thus know all that's going on, follow an open-door policy. They like the phone to ring. They welcome people dropping by. Some are in fact hardly ever in their offices, since they spend most of their time in other people's offices.

This then illustrates how the dichotomies can be used as an organizing principle to sort out differences in behavior and thus give insight into how differently people process information. The list of criteria is very long, but the principle is always the same. Namely, each person seems endowed with two opposing ways of satisfying some goal or need, and

INTRODUCTION
AND PREVIEW

1	5	9	13
2	6	10	14
3	7	11	15
4	8	12	16

A-4

one of those two has to become dominant. Either one can predominate, but normally a choice is made.

The most telling and revealing dichotomies always involve some basic behavioral choices. Let me give one more example, a dichotomy that Jung labeled *attitude*. In the mathematical partitioning scheme, attitude involves the odd-numbered capacities versus the even-numbered ones.

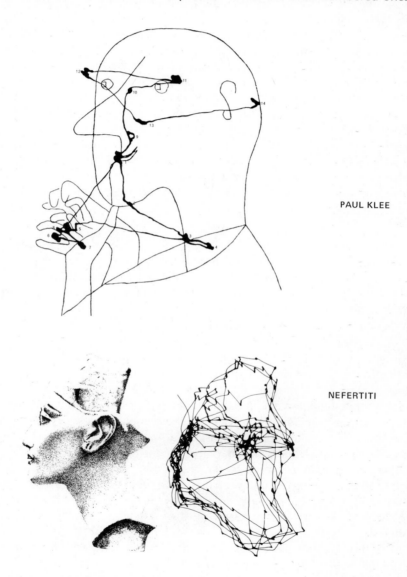

PAUL KLEE

NEFERTITI

EYE MOVEMENTS illustrating C-eye and D-eye information scanning. From "Eye Movements and Visual Perception." D. Noton and L. Stark. Copyright © 1971 by Scientific American, Inc. All rights reserved.

Jung labeled the two attributes of attitude extroverted versus introverted. They represent two opposing but equally successful strategies for survival. One is energy expending, that is, survival through aggression, like a shark; the other is energy-conserving, like a chameleon—in short, attack or hide, alter the environment or adapt to it. The behavioral consequences of this dichotomy are easy to observe. There are those to whom the external world is the only reality. They read reports of shipments, inventories, profits, and so on, and base their decisions on such external data. In contrast, there are those who, no matter how many computer printouts they get, follow instead some inner instinct that tells them, for example, that their operation is overextended and they had better pull in their horns.

These organizational dichotomies are reinforced by the dichotomous nature of inputs and outputs. Inputs come through our senses, and these sensory inputs also exhibit complementary opposition. It is most easily illustrated by the eye.

Notice that the eye traces superimposed on the picture by Paul Klee, in the upper part of the illustration, show a contextual trace, a kind of sketchy overview, whereas in the lower part of the illustration the trace of the bust of Nefertiti shows a systematic, thorough process of tracing out the image. We can thus assume the existence of a contextual or C eye as well as a detailed or D eye. Physiological evidence in the two regions of the retina, called the foveal and extrafoveal fields, points to such an assumption.

D-12

There is some evidence that similar pairings exist for other senses as well, and my model assumes such symmetrical pairings.

This complementary aspect of differences is even more pronounced with the outputs. I have organized outputs into four pairings: *body*, *hands*, *mouth*, and *intellect*. Body outputs result in physical action, such as playing golf. The two complementary aspects of body action, C and D, are *rhythm* and *control*, respectively, and both are needed for a good golf swing.

The hands also benefit from this complementary opposition. Consider the threading of a needle. One hand tends to *holding*, and the other to *manipulating*. Either one can be in control; you can either slip the thread into the eye of the needle, or you can guide the needle over the thread. The same pair complementing is activated in most hand tasks, be it sanding a piece of wood or plumbing, sculpting, or performing surgery.

Similarly, I have identified the two mouth output components to be *speech content*, mostly consonants, and *tone*, mostly vowels. The two intellectual outputs are *planning* and *conclusions*.

All these increasingly overwhelming details are most easily organized on what I call a map of capacities. The contextual capacities are linked into a C circuit, the detailed capacities into a D circuit. Inputs and outputs are appropriately connected. What we have then in effect is a network

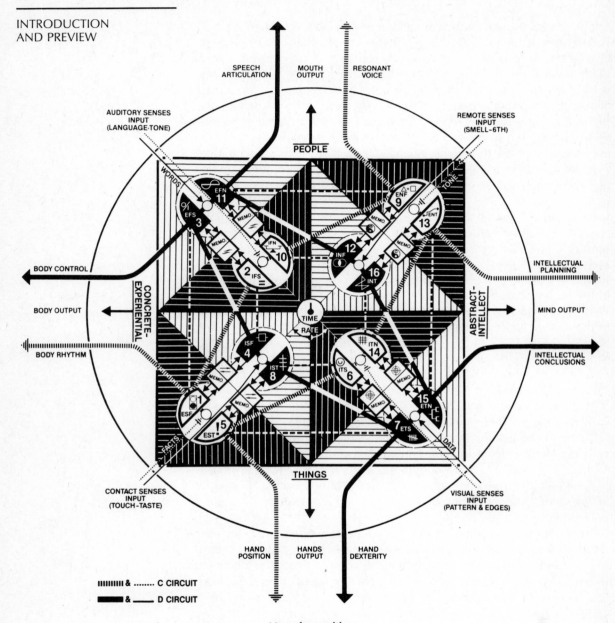

Map of capacities.

of information processors with inputs and outputs in which information can flow.

All these aspects are discussed and more fully explained in subsequent chapters. The aim here is to give you an idea of what this book is about. As the reading may sometimes be difficult, there is some benefit in knowing toward what end we're leading. It may also help you to know what got me into all of this.

Why did I choose these descriptions, this particular way of dividing up our conscious or recognizable activities, when there must be so many other ways? Well, there are really two reasons.

The first is simple pragmatism. It works this way: the order that emerges matches other organizational structures that have evolved quite naturally. One such example is the way academic institutions are organized. It served as one of the earliest clues.

Typically, there is a school of arts and sciences, with the three divisions of humanities, social sciences, and science. Disciplines in applied science and engineering are typically organized into a separate school; this insularity seems to persist, suggesting that arts and engineering have nothing to do with each other. The organizational separation of the technologies is even more pronounced, those schools usually being located on separate campuses. The story with the fine and performing arts is even more interesting. On many campuses, they live in a kind of shotgun marriage under the roof of the humanities. But there is always pressure for divorce, and the controversy in favor of separate conservatories rages on to this day.

One could rationalize such segregation by discipline on the grounds of intellectual snobbery. There is some of that, but I believe the more basic force is simply the nature of the personalities attracted to the various disciplines. It is simply natural to want to be with people who think as you do and whose styles and value systems are similar. When the value systems become drastically different, actual hostility and intolerance ensue. There is traditional disdain and jealousy between departments of English and engineering, for example. To an English professor, it is simply offensive to note how engineers tend to butcher the language. And engineers are not particularly gifted in or attracted to foreign languages. Consequently, there is not even a communication bond.

Unfortunately, campuses are notorious for such bickering and strife. It is very difficult, for instance, to find a science department curriculum that accepts credits earned in the theater department. In recent years societal needs, first perceived by students, forced academia to introduce interdisciplinary curricula in, for example, environmental studies, where biology, political science, and engineering faculties must work together. There are similar periodic episodes to introduce more liberal arts into engineering or some technology into the humanities. But sooner or later, people argue that the demands of their discipline preclude such luxuries. Whatever the rationalization, the clustering of like personalities in departments leaves its everlasting mark of exclusivity. There is also often a disdain for athletics, as though it were a corrupting influence on intellectual values. Athletes are at best tolerated in the classroom.

There is a strange love–hate relationship to all these oppositional pair-

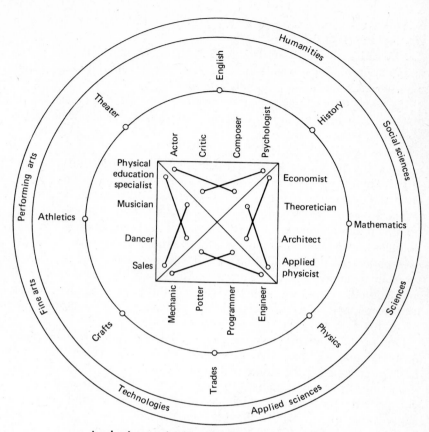

Academic organization related to map of capacities.

ings, which shows up so strongly on the map. English and engineering disciplines show up as opposites, as do physics and theater, history and crafts, and so on. The fascinating aspect of these oppositional relationships is that, although such pairs have a hard time doing business together, they often do interact in a recreational setting. It is amazing how many English professors are car buffs, how many scientists enjoy amateur acting or play a musical instrument, and how many mathematicians ride bicycles or even follow sports.

I can only conclude that the organizational structure of universities reflects, probably unconsciously, our dichotomous nature as formalized on the map of capacities.

The second reason I chose my method is more philosophical and personal. I am a firm believer in the view that our greatest achievements are but mirrors of our nature. It is not that we invent something new, but rather that we recognize a truth within us. This is discovery in the truest sense—uncovering that which is already there.

There are not only obvious copies of nature—pliers like our hands, cameras like our eyes—but also more sophisticated inventions, like servomechanisms and inertial guidance systems mimicking our nervous system. Perhaps most convincingly, all the directions we've built into computers—so-called programs and algorithms—form such an extraordinary match. Computers identify, compare, sort, order, classify, sequence, recall, control. All the most basic things computers do are things we have copied from our way of processing information. What better clue can I find than these external manifestations of our inner nature?

This then is the basic structure of the dichotomous model, a simulation of conscious information-processing represented as a processor network.

Now it is important to recall that embedded in this organization are oodles of dichotomies, or dualistic alternatives for reaching some goal, be it survival, security, or what have you. As individuals mature, they make these choices, because one or the other works better for them.

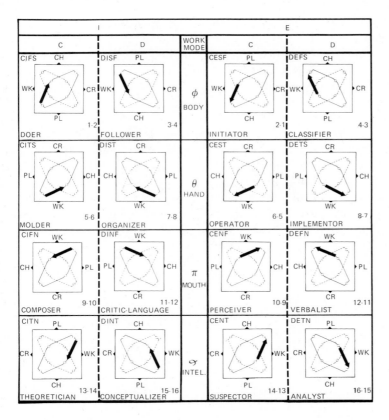

Basic personality profiles and mode orientations. E, extroverted; I, introverted; C, contextual; D, detailed; WK, work mode; CH, challenge mode; CR, creativity mode; PL, play mode; ———, dominant circuit; · · · ·, complementary circuit; a→b transaction shown with heavy arrow.

Once a preferential tilting occurs, reinforcement sharpens the differences. It is these differences that give each of us a unique personality. One cannot say that one choice would be better than another. They are just different, and it's better that we recognize the differences than to ignore them.

The tendency to ignore the differences is immense. For most of us, the experienced differences among people are overwhelming, so we do with them behaviorally what we do with people physiologically. If you look in an encyclopedia under "human physiology," you find a picture of a body that is nobody's and yet everybody's. It properly shows the head, arms, legs, where the heart and the liver are located, and how the muscles are distributed. But it is never the body of a fat, overly sedentary, flabby executive, or the body of a swimmer or a weight lifter. In fact, the word "people" does in words exactly what the picture does. It is an identifier that identifies nobody in particular and denies us a unique identity.

My model is designed to make those differences explicit. I call them *profiles*. I have identified 16 of them and show them in a diagrammatic shorthand.

Our objective is to read meanings into these schematic diagrams. Almost everyone falls into preferred patterns of behavior that are part of that person's nature and yet do not deny him or her the shadings and diversity necessary for a unique identity.

This subtle interplay between what we have in common and what is unique to us makes the story so complex. It leads us to discussions of libido, consciousness, roles, and a host of other subjects that are developed step by step, sometimes descriptively, sometimes through more technical formalisms. But you may lose sight of the most basic and all-pervasive organizational concept that's woven throughout this approach as you become immersed in the detailed discussions. So let me highlight it right from the start: I call it ambi-syn-anti.

2

AMBI-SYN-ANTI

(Both With and Against)

Ambi-syn-anti is the most pervasive structural concept underlying the organization of the intelligent mind.

A-4

A-3

E-2

Yin—yang

Anyone who has read C. G. Jung cannot escape the powerful role of the interplay of opposites in everything that is human. This principle is difficult to describe. Jung introduced the word *enantiodromia*, which means a "running counter to." But that is only a part of it. Jacobi referred to it as the law of opposites, writing, "For the psyche is a self-regulating system and there is no balance, no system of self-regulation, without opposition." That is a part of it, too.

Perhaps the closest to expressing just what I mean by the interplay of opposites is through the Yin—Yang symbol. "The dark half represents the Yang (standing for the active principle), the light half represents the Yin (the passive principle). However, each half includes an arc cut out of the middle of the opposing half to symbolize that every mode must contain within it the germ of its antithesis."

But even that is not exactly what I sense as the essential meaning. It is far more than just opposing poles, like male and female, even when I acknowledge the anima in male and the animus in female. It is more complicated and profound than that, and there simply seems to be no word for it in our language. So I've invented one.

Ambi-syn-anti is a collection of prefixes meaning "both together and opposite" or "both with and against."

In Western culture we have little room for anything that is not "either or." We tend to think of rich or poor, black or white, Democrat or Republican, Christian or Jew. To speak of a Jewish Christian—that is, to consider the merging of dichotomies—seems nonsensical. It is not that way everywhere; in Japan one can be Christian and Shinto, and in India one might be Hindu and Christian.

But in the fundamental essential of humanness, it is precisely the either *and* or that plays the key role. What makes our systems work, even the U.S. system of free enterprise, is competition *and* cooperation. It is both with *and* against.

The simplest example of ambi-syn-anti is a pair of hands. The two hands are not only mirror opposites of each other, but are opposite in their functions when they work together. One tends to holding, the other to manipulating (e.g., in threading a needle). The function of each hand is specialized and differentiated. Each acts in contrary fashion, yet each needs the other. As a pair, they can cooperate effectively because they are diametrically different, and a greater unity grows out of their opposition (the enantiodromia).

Furthermore, and this is part of the ambi-syn-anti principle, it is characteristic of a pair of opposites that one, and only one, is dominant; using the example of the hands, this would be expressed as right- or left-handed. We could speak of the "personality" of hands as holders and manipulators, or as types who excel either in steadying and positioning things or in manipulative dexterity.

I use the term ambi-syn-anti as an organizational principle that applies as one considers meta and microaspects of a system. Not only is each hand opposite to the other in a pair (metasystem), but there is also competition and cooperation within each hand (microsystem); that is, there is a pair of opposing poles within a hand—namely, the fingers and thumb—constellated as opposites, ideally suited to work with or against each other. Ambi-syn-anti holds at both the meta and microlevels.

My model of the conscious mind presumes ambi-syn-anti as a pervasive organizational principle that can be stated as follows:

For every whole thing

There is an opposite thing

And within every thing
There is a pair of opposites

So that opposites within opposite pairs
can interact

To make the original and its opposite
act as a new thing.

And

This ambi-syn-anti principle is the essential precursor of consciousness. I see consciousness as an awareness of the difference between the self and the rest of the world. Once this awareness has taken place, an arch pair of opposites has sprung into being: a person's inner world and all that which is external, separated by an envelope, the skin. The inner world, or the self, and the external environment stand in an ambi-syn-anti relationship to each other. For the self to survive, it is both dependent on and threatened by the environment.

Survival means not only recognizing the difference, but maintaining the proper balance between internal needs and external realities. I see the conscious mind as the organ charged with the responsibility to maintain that balance between the inner and outer world that is needed for survival.

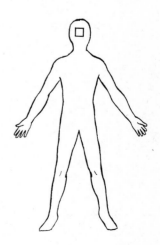

This balancing trick predicates, in my view, the structure of the conscious mind. Confronted with ambi-syn-anti challenges, the mind must possess a parallel structure to cope with them. This is the most fundamental assumption underlying my approach to the architecture of the mind and is reflected in my schematic representation of the conscious mind as polarized symmetry.

3

READER ORIENTATION

(On Dichotomous Modeling)

INTRODUCTION
AND PREVIEW

The mind and nervous system consist of billions of cells and complex interconnections. Viewed from such a perspective of detail, the complexity of "human nature" seems overwhelming. Any attempt to understand the mind at this level might be called the microscopic approach.

There is another approach, which I call macroscopic. It attempts to explain observable behavior by envisioning the mind as consisting of far fewer pieces—in short, to view it in less detail. This way, the complexity can be reduced to tractable levels. Such a process is known as *modeling*. The trick is how to best divide up the whole into useful pieces. Exactly what should the chunks be? It is as challenging as dividing up the sky. How shall we look at the zillions of stars? Can we simplify it by inventing a collection of them and calling it the Big Dipper? People of ancient days did exactly this. But was that a sensible collection of pieces? Will it help us understand the heavens? Would some other combination of stars have been more meaningful? These are the questions one faces in trying to model the mind.

There are really two kinds of approaches to the challenge. One is to look at the details and to describe which pieces might be combined into a macroscopic clump. The reverse approach is to start with the totality and divide it successively into smaller pieces as is done in geography, dividing continents into countries and countries into territories, states, counties, and so on. I use the latter approach. I avoid any look at details such as a nerve cell, its synapses, and all such microscopic anatomy and physiology.

Micro ←—Spectrum—→ Macro
Detail   Totality

As I deal with such coarse divisions, I need a coarse scale to describe what I have. The instruments or descriptors for measuring things must fit in scale. One would not measure a grain of salt in miles, nor the diameter of the earth in microns. Fortunately, such a scale exists in systems science. It is called *fuzzy sets*. Fuzzy sets are "sort of" descriptors. They point you in the proper direction but are not exact. It is a bit like someone pointing a finger at someone else, but you don't know exactly whether the one who pointed meant to lead your eye to the face or the hat or the nose.

Similarly the descriptors I will use for the pieces of the whole are not exact, but they are very powerful tools nevertheless. To interpret them requires a bit of imagination, just as you must fill in a specific context when someone points in a general direction.

This vagueness, which you must fill in, is an asset rather than a shortcoming. The interpretive vernier, or fine tuning, makes it possible to fit the incredible diversity of human nature under relatively few umbrella concepts. Were it not for that, either we would end up with a very complex model or a lot of people would be left out. Fuzzy sets dissolve this dilemma.

There is then available to us a useful tool to describe the pieces. But we have yet to decide how to divide the pie. What are the useful subchunks of the mind? Or, what kind of model might be most useful?

The model I have chosen is conceptual rather than physical. It is not based on the physiology of the brain; it is built on a concept, which I call ambi-syn-anti. This principle says to consider a pair of two things that are so different from each other that they form opposites pitted against each other. Yet, this very oppositional difference can combine to create a capacity greater than either one. The most obvious example of an ambi-syn-anti pair is man and woman. There are many other such pairs, such as staff and line responsibilities, strategic and logistic planning, or, as we have already seen, thumb and fingers. Such ambi-syn-anti pairs can do tasks together that neither one can do alone.

I decided that the model must reflect this ambi-syn-anti principle. This led to what I call a *dichotomous model*. Simply, it is a scheme for partitioning the whole into two pieces but more than once. Each division brings out a different ambi-syn-anti attribute. This approach is basically an organizing effort.

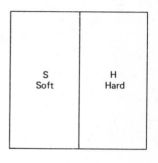

Suppose I run a salvage operation. All sorts of junk comes in. Somehow, I must organize it to find things. One way would be to use a dichotomous model. I might simply paint a line down the middle of the warehouse and sort soft things to one side and hard ones to the other. Clothes and sponges and dolls would end up on one side; tables, tools, and so on, on the other. Then I would take the whole again and divide everything I've got into two fuzzy sets, roughly small and large. Another dichotomous sorting might be according to color (redder or bluer) or to shape (rounder or longer).

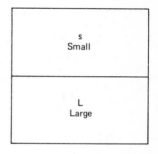

Suppose someone comes and asks for a toy fire truck. Well, it is hard, small, and red. The corner of the room that has objects with these attributes has far less to look through than everything I've got. I don't need to look at soft, small, and red or large and red or soft, large, and red. In fact, I need only to look at one-eighth of all I've got. That is quite a saving.

In fact, such a partitioning scheme is even more effective. If I should find myself in a pile of things classified as large, soft, and blue—the very opposite of what I want (small, hard, and red)—I know that what I seek is located diametrically opposite my present location.

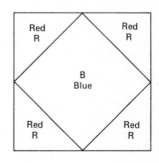

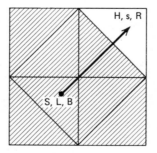

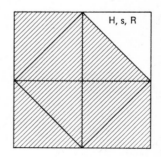

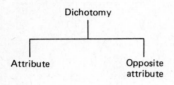

A dichotomous model thus is a very powerful organizer and one that fits ambi-syn-anti, since the organization is based on opposites.

The fuzzy set descriptors—large and small, hard and soft, red and blue—are called *attributes*. They "sort of" describe a thing like a toy fire truck, which has the attributes small, hard, and red. The criterion that divides a field into two halves is called a *dichotomy*; in the case of large and small, it is the size dichotomy. By definition, every dichotomy has two opposing attributes.

I can carry this process as far as is necessary. In the interest of keeping the model simple, it is wise not to go too far.

As part of this orientation, I must mention one other facet. I have viewed the conscious mind as an information processor. That is not the same as saying I envision the mind as a computer. The mind is far more sophisticated than a mere computer and acts and functions very differently. But its concerns are the same. Intelligence is also information. It is because of this that I find it helpful to borrow nomenclature from computer science and to use terms such as outputs, inputs, batch processing, and sorting. Don't let these scare you. The terms are self-descriptive. Inputs put information in. Batch processing processes information in a batch (it's like paying all your bills at one time). Take them literally, and the jargon becomes simple and useful.

In summary, my dichotomous model of human consciousness is a macroscopic model based on the ambi-syn-anti principle. The complexity of consciousness is simplified by means of dichotomies, which describe aspects of the mind by attributes. Several attributes taken together describe a subset of the mind with fuzzy set descriptors.

With the aid of these descriptors, we can learn what makes us tick: what our capacities are and what roles they play, what determines our personality, and how personalities clash and reinforce. In short, this simple model leads to all sorts of interpretable insights about human nature. That is my goal.

4

THE ARCHITECT AS ORGANIZER

(The Power of
Schematic Diagrams)

Eyes versus ears is a dichotomy. Thus some people would rather see pictures, and some would rather read words. The intent of this chapter is to encourage verbal persons to look at the pictures. You can skip this chapter if either you feel at home with diagrams or you despise them so much that you won't look at them no matter what they tell you.

INTRODUCTION
AND PREVIEW

E-1

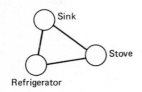

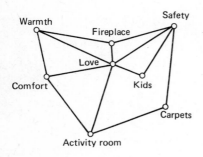

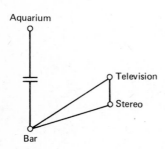

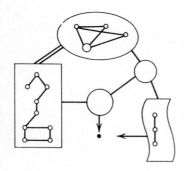

Architects are above all organizers of functions and spaces. The problems they face are similar to those I have set out to tackle. They are constantly faced with polarized demands and must organize poorly understood complexities.

Consider this stereotypical conversation with a client. "I feel the kitchen should be the center of the home, where everyone feels free to air problems and speak honestly. It should be a warm but efficient place, with easy access to the garage, the front door, the dining room, and the activity room. When I have guests, I want the kids out of sight, and a messy kitchen should also be out of sight. I don't want anyone in my kitchen when I'm cooking dinner, and yet I've got to know what my kids are doing."

Typically, architects think their way through such a mess of disorganized contradictory vagaries by drawing a structure chart, which is a symbolic diagram visually dramatizing relationships.

The lines in the diagram are not defined. They indicate symbolically that these three things are somehow tied together. The lines may represent the tracking of the steps you take; or they may simply mean that these three things involve food, so keep this area clean. The diagram is kept rather vague intentionally. All it must do is show relatedness and capture some essence of concern, so that more can be read into it than was originally intended.

The little circle, denoting whatever you are thinking about, need not always be a thing. It can represent any concern that merits organizational consideration. As shown, love, warmth, fireplace, activity room, comfort, safety, kids, and carpets form a meaningful set of things, places, and feelings whose interrelationships must be explored.

I show one more example, involving a television, a stereo, a bar, and an aquarium, to point out that architects can express in the diagram symbolic subtleties within the relationship diagram such as "Keep the liquor out of the fish tank," as denoted by the stretched out and interrupted line.

After architects have considered each small organizational problem, they link all these complexes into an organizational whole out of which, ultimately, a house develops.

It is in this sense that I use the phrase "architecture of the mind," and the diagrams in the margins should be viewed in this context. Technically, they are called *schematic diagrams*, for they represent the underlying schema.

Architects are not the only ones who use schematic diagrams. Such tools are common wherever order is sought or wherever symbolism can sharpen the organizational schema underlying complexity. Some, such as the organizational chart, have become classics.

An organizational chart, like a decision tree, reflects a hierarchical structure. It shows who is boss or how responsibility is divided. De-

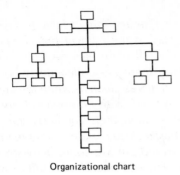

Organizational chart

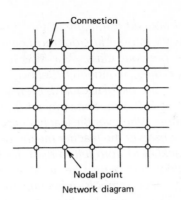

Connection

Nodal point
Network diagram

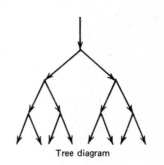

Tree diagram

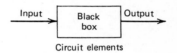

Circuit elements

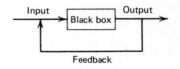

Feedback

pending on how you look at it—that is, how you interpret the symbols—it can also be viewed as a circuit, showing how information flows through an organization, either from the bottom up or from the top down.

All schematic diagrams show: (1) a structure, that is, an organizational schema, or (2) a circuit, showing channels of information flow.

When complexity in schematic representations is viewed as *structure*, the points (little circles or boxes) where lines connect and branch are called *nodal points*. In such a network diagram each nodal point is a symbolic representation of something significant: a boss, an office, a street intersection, whatever. The lines represent relationships, and the form reveals the organizational schema.

When such schematic diagrams are viewed as *circuits*, then the points in the net are called switches or processors or black boxes. That last term says, in effect, don't worry about what's inside; there is something there that controls inputs and outputs. The lines are the inputs and the outputs, depending on whether flow is into or out of the box.

This is enough. I took this excursion to encourage you to look at the diagrams. I understand only too well (as becomes apparent later) that different people find them helpful or annoying, but they are really just another language, symbols to denote a thought. It is a particularly useful language for dealing with complexities.

I use them, for they fit my nature and the task I've set for myself. That task is to discover what makes us tick, to discover, by means of a schematic representation, the architecture of the mind.

GLIMPSE

I've always found it fascinating to rummage, like an anthropologist, through places in which people met. There reside the vestiges of unknown personalities who left their telltale marks.

INTRODUCTION
AND PREVIEW

I noticed it initially in the classroom. The first thing I have to face as I walk into a classroom to begin my class is the leftover blackboard of the previous class. Who was in here? What were they dealing with? I can't help wondering. Believe it or not, there are colleagues who just don't use the blackboard. Even at 10 a.m. it's as clean as when the janitor left it at 7 a.m. Sometimes I find just words—with no apparent organization. Wherever the teacher happened to stand, there you find a remnant of whatever the teacher meant to emphasize. You certainly can't read the blackboard from left to right, for that would put Mussolini between Napoleon and Julius Caesar. Strange? Contrarily, I often find it full of well-organized symbols, reflecting an orderly development.

Observations like these make you very self-conscious about your own blackboards. Mine seem to be full of pictures, tables, and diagrams.

Blackboards are not the only telltale traces of personal traits. The uncleared dinner table in the restaurant can tell you a lot. You always can tell when a group of engineers was there. Not only do they always carry pens and pencils where others carry decorative handkerchiefs, but no paper napkin or even tablecloth is safe from their attacks. It is as though they can't talk without a pencil in hand. Their scribblings are incomprehensible boxes, circuits, and graphs decorated with Greek letters.

No less fascinating is the conference room after the storm. You can tell from the doodles how boring the meeting must have been.

It is in places like these that the mind leaves its imprint.

THE STATIC MODEL:
THE MAP OF CAPACITIES

Our objective in Part II is to develop the structure and interpretation of the map of capacities, the name I've given to the graphical representation of the 16-pole model. The structural approach was described in Part I, involving (1) symmetrical partitions, (2) ambi-syn-anti, which highlights opposition and complementarity, and (3) hierarchical nesting, which imposes a numbering order on the cells.

The map would be an empty structure if it were not possible to infer interpretive meanings that can be related to observed human behavior and behavioral theories reported in the literature. The key to these interpretive links is the symbol assigned to each of the 16 poles in the 16-pole model.

The most difficult challenge for me has been to reconstruct the thought processes that led to the specific symbolic (interpretive) assignments in the first place. It was a process that spanned years and involved a lot of trial and error, influenced by subconscious gestalts that surely were influenced in turn by Jung and my earlier research interests. Closure of this trial and error process occurred when the specific assignments presented in Chapter Seven indicated complete internal consistency with the four- and eight-pole models as well as with the body of relevant literature. In fact, to this date, I have not found any disquieting inconsistencies.

This effort to assign symbols to the 16 subsets is not as subjective as it may seem. I've chosen the approach of developing the 16-pole model in progressive stages precisely for the reason that it provides the most convenient way of explaining how associative links to the behavioral literature evolved in my mind. Involved were right-brained processes that, though rational and consistent, are very difficult to put into words.

The four-pole and eight-pole models are thus only convenient stepping stones to what really counts—the 16-pole model with its structural and interpretive aspects. If I have succeeded in this effort, the reader may be fascinated by the interpretive extensions that can be fashioned out of a symbol string. In fact, the four-pole and eight-pole models can be reconstructed as symbol subsets of the 16-pole model, and this view is often more satisfying and integrative than the progressive approach presented here. For readers attracted to this more integrative approach and examples of how new insights can be extracted from symbol subsets, Appendix A might be useful reading at this time.

5

THE FOUR-POLE MODEL

(An Introduction to Jungian Concepts)

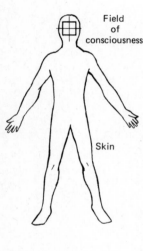

Field
of
consciousness

Skin

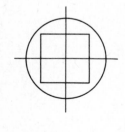

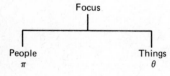

Focus

People
π

Things
θ

In this chapter I start to develop, step by step, what I call the map of capacities. It is in a most literal sense a map with an agreed-on orientation (like north being always at the top of the page). The map is partitioned (the way we divide a country into states) into so-called cells. Each cell has a name and ultimately a description.

The primary concern is the individual and especially that aspect of the brain which controls and determines conscious behavior patterns and uniquely human skills. This focus is graphically represented by the human outline and the little square in the head. In more abstracted form, I represent by a circle the envelope (skin) that contains the self. Everything outside the circle I call the external environment. The large square inside the circle I call the field of consciousness. It is this field that I want to partition by using dichotomies to uncover a possible conceptual organization.

We start with a dichotomy I call focus. Focus deals with items of interest in the external world on which the individual focuses attention. It divides that world into the world of *people* versus the world of *things*. The dichotomy of focus deals with these two opposing *attributes*: people and things. One could, of course, divide the world in many different ways. But this division into people and things is uniquely practical. It simply recognizes an easily observable difference among people. There are those who are people-oriented. They enjoy being with people and seek them out; they love conversation and care what is happening to others. They read the gossip columns and obituaries, they talk on the telephone for hours, and are happy only in jobs that involve contact with people, be the job in a shop, a classroom, or a church. In sharp contrast there are others who really are more at home with things. They tinker in their basements, work on their cars, are generally less verbal, and are more skillful with their hands. Focus, then, is the dichotomy that recognizes this opposing focus of interest.

I use a horizontal line, a kind of Mason–Dixon line, to divide the field of consciousness into an upper (northern) half, which contains those capacities ideally suited to deal with the world of people, and a lower half, which deals with the world of things. We are thus beginning the process of imposing a conceptual organization on the field, the very purpose we set out to accomplish.

To deal with an object in the external environment, whether a person or a thing, requires some interactions, which I call inputs and outputs. That's how our conscious mind knows that something or someone is out there. An *input* is therefore, in the truest sense of the word, an information flow from the external world into the brain. Diagrammatically, I designate such inputs by an inward-directed line piercing the envelope. Similarly, an *output* is an information flow from the self to the object in the environment. Such outputs may be transmitted through the voice, for instance, or through actions. In summary, focus focuses on the individual's involvement with things or people external to the self, and through inputs and outputs information is received from and emitted to the people and things of the external world.

Focus is in sharp contrast to a second dichotomy, which I call *approach*. Approach traffics in how the information received, be it from people or things, is internally processed. Again, there seem to be two major ways: *concrete* or *abstract*. By concrete, I mean to describe that large class of people who learn by doing, by concrete experiences. They say, "Don't explain to me how to drive the car, just let me try it and get the feel of it."

Others do the very opposite. They wouldn't dare try driving the car until they clearly understood what each pedal does and why a lever is moved first to that position. They learn by first forming an image or a concept in their minds. One notices this same disposition toward concrete versus abstract information-processing in a biology or physics class. There are those to whom the lecture makes no sense until they have been exposed to the laboratory experience. To them anatomy is actually the experience of dissecting the frog. They saw and felt the parts. Others wouldn't know what to do with the frog unless they had first grasped intellectually something of the system of organization underlying the study of anatomy.

Approach, then, is the dichotomy that recognizes that there are two opposing ways of processing information, identified by the attributes concrete and abstract. Concrete information-processing involves the body and touch and taste, since one actually comes in contact with the object of the experience. It's "getting into things" literally and physically. It's learning by doing, by repetitive experiencing, and thus by "conditioning." By contrast, abstract information-processing is basically cerebral, that is, thinking about it. It is not the real experience but some abstracted representation of it that is key, be it an image, a verbal description, a

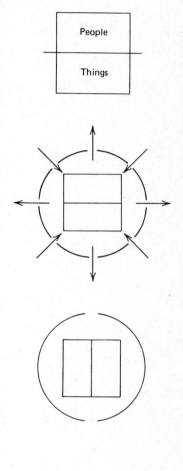

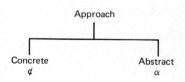

THE STATIC MODEL:
THE MAP OF CAPACITIES

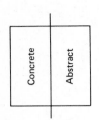

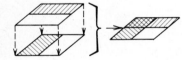

A-4

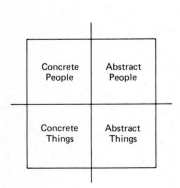

mathematical formula, or an organizational concept. It is clearly a vicarious learning, where no actual contact with anything real is required.

In the graphic representation, I use a vertical line to partition the field into the attributes concrete and abstract. By convention, the left half denotes concrete information processing; the right half, abstract processing. Tied to this orientation is the orientation of the body to the left and the intellect to the right, as is indicated later as the map of capacities becomes more developed.

The organization I am developing grows out of the successive application of dichotomies, which partition the original field of consciousness (the square) into two nonoverlapping (disjoint) halves. Partitioning, in the mathematical sense, also means that the sum of the two halves is equal to the whole.

It should be clear that one can have concurrently different partitionings. For political purposes, we might partition the United States into states (in fact, we do, except for the District of Columbia). For purposes of telephoning, we might partition the same area into area codes, which may or may not coincide with state boundaries. Or, for that matter, we have partitions by zip codes, football conferences, sales territories, and so on. All these partitionings can coexist; that is, we might describe a spot in the United States as being in the state of New York, area code 212, zip code 10016, and with a team that belongs to the North Atlantic Conference. The more partitionings we have, the richer the description and the more specific the location on the map.

In like fashion, I now consider the partition created by focus and approach concurrently. Graphically, this is done by what is called superposition, and we see that the two dichotomies have created four cells or quadrants. The one in the lower left deals with concrete, thing-oriented capacities; that in the upper left with concrete, people-oriented capacities; that in the lower right with abstract, thing-oriented capacities; and that in the upper right with abstract, people-oriented capacities.

These gross descriptions fit a classification scheme developed by Jung. During his clinical years, Jung worked with schizophrenics and noted some dramatic personality reversals, popularly referred to as split personalities. This ultimately led him to identify oppositional personality traits, for which he coined such words as *extrovert* and *introvert*. In his book *Psychological Types*, Jung develops, in a very scholarly fashion, his theory of personality grounded in the principle of opposition. He speaks of four major types, which he calls sensation type, intuitive type, feeling type, and thinking type. These four types bear oppositional relationships to each other such that intuition is opposite to sensation, and feeling is opposite to thinking. He referred to feeling and thinking as the judging (J) functions and to sensation and intuition as the perceiving (P) functions. The relationships among these four functions are often illustrated diagrammatically as shown.

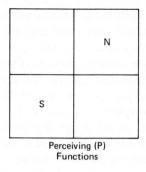

Perceiving (P)
Functions

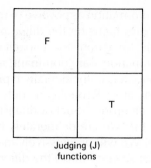

Judging (J)
functions

In building a model of consciousness, I now want to couple this Jungian classification scheme with the four quadrants obtained from the super-position of the dichotomies of focus and approach. In fact, I use the Jungian labels to identify the quadrants. The quadrant in the lower left, the one characterized by concreteness and an orientation toward things, is equated to the sensation function described by Jung and labeled S. The quadrant in the upper left of the map is labeled F for feeling. The quadrant in the lower right is T for thinking, and the one in the upper right is labeled N for intuition (I'm reserving the label I for introvert, a discussion taken up later).

This connection of the four quadrants to the four Jungian functions tremendously enriches the interpretive capabilities of the map. Capacities that organizationally belong to a given quadrant must be compatible with Jung's observation of the four basic types, described by the four Jungian functions.

The model-building approach, so common in science and engineering and especially systems science, tries to clarify differences by identifying variables. This means looking for some quantifiable measure such as temperature, which makes concepts like hot and cold explicit. That is not easily found in Jung's descriptions. Jung's approach was essentially that of an empiricist and based on clinical observations. He observed, conceptualized, and described. He did not quantify.

To bridge this gap, I want to suggest a variable that I call the *complexity index*, which takes on the values 1, 2, m (many and finite), and ∞ (infinite). Such quantitative associations are consistent with Jung's description of the four functions. Explicitly, the complexity index suggests that the sensation function (S) deals with "oneness" in contrast to the feeling function (F), which deals with "twoness" or duality. Put another way, the capacities assignable to quadrant S can be thought of as basic responses to sensations or sensory stimuli. Most basically, the S function says, "Do something," a simple act describable by the word "oneness." The capacities in the F quadrant act very differently, because they specialize in duality. Most basically, feeling capacities deal with like or dislike. They

Concrete People	Abstract People
F	N
S	T
Concrete Things	Abstract Things

Complexity Index

Sensation (S)	= 1
Feeling (F)	= 2
Thinking (T)	= m
Intuition (N)	= ∞

regard information as positive or negative, as good or harmful for survival. F capacities focus on the differences in observations and experiences.

People for whom the capacities with a complexity index of 2—the feeling function—are dominant, tend to see or prefer their world in black and white. It is coincidentally typical of American culture. You are either a Democrat or Republican, rich or poor. You win or lose in the competitive enterprise. Such a dualistic value system is typical of F.

Note that we are deliberately breathing meaning into the partitioning scheme. We will progressively make more and more explicit associations that must serve to make the differences among the partitions very sharp. So far, we have stated that the capacities assignable to the two left quadrants in the map are describable by focus, approach, and the complexity index. The quadrant labeled S deals concretely with things in a simple, action-oriented way. The quadrant labeled F deals concretely with people concerns according to the dualistic value system (like or dislike, good or bad).

Clearly, the N and T functions are more encompassing. I am suggesting that we associate infinity (∞), the ultimate in complexity, with intuition, the N quadrant. N deals with combining diverse experiences, possibilities and fantasies. There is no end to such speculations about the world of what might be. Note how opposite N is to S. S was 1, a simple, direct, almost obvious matter-of-fact response to a stimulus. N is the other extreme, ∞. It uses the stimulus to trigger the imagination to myriad possibilities. Put in people terms, S types are pragmatists; if they have a problem, they do something, some one thing. N-dominant types are the worriers, and dreamers; they don't need to be given a problem; they can invent their own. They live in the world of "what if."

This very dramatic contrast between S and N should not be surprising. It is a consequence of the dichotomous organization. In fact, the very idea underlying the dichotomous model is to bring out oppositional extremes. This is a very practical approach to take when dealing with anything as complicated as people. So it is important to describe not only a cell of a partition, but also its dichotomous relationship to the oppositional cell.

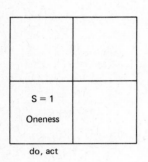

S = 1

Oneness

do, act

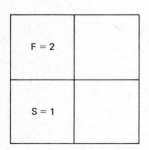

F = 2

Duality

choose, decide

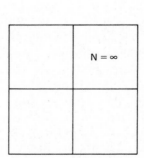

F = 2

S = 1

N = ∞

P functions

Possibilities

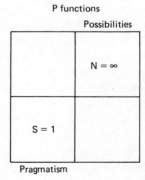

N = ∞

S = 1

Pragmatism

We have yet to elaborate on the thinking (T) function, which is the opposite of the feeling (F) function. Recall that F was associated with concreteness, a people orientation, and a complexity index of 2 (duality) as the value system or basis of judgment. (Both F and T are labeled the judging [J] functions by Jung). An F-dominant type reaches judgments by the dualistic choice of like or dislike, good or bad. Thinking is more complex, as indicated by the complexity index m (many); m is more than 2 but less than infinity and therefore finite. m is intended to suggest quantification—numerical, rational analysis. If F reaches a judgment by choice—that is, by selecting between good and bad—T reaches a judgment by evaluating many factors.

As an illustration, consider the process of buying a car. You might just fall in love with that "sweet job" in the center of the showroom. You would look at other car models, but deep down in your heart, you know which one you want. This process of selection is typical of the F judgment.

The T function operates very differently. Quantitative numbers like price, mileage, frequency of repairs, and depreciation become the dominant factors in reaching a decision. It is a rational, reasoned process for arriving at a judgment.

Actually, in buying a car one probably uses both processes, but what usually happens is that one process of digesting information is used to rationalize the true decision. If feeling is the real basis of choice, it is not atypical to hear the buyer say something like, "Gee, as much time as I spend in the car, it was worth the extra money." If thinking was the basis of the decision, the statement might be, "It's really not bad looking."

Focus, approach, and the complexity index are thus a shorthand for recalling key differentiating criteria, differentiations that bring out dichotomous relationships. You must recall, to aid in subsequent analysis, that S and N are very different from F and T. Yet within these two categories (perceiving [P] and judging [J]) S is the opposite of N and F is the opposite of T.

At this stage, when we are speaking of the four-cell model, we should get the deepest possible insight into the characterizing differences among the four quadrants of the map. I therefore must refer to the work of Mann, Siegler, and Osmond at Princeton, who pointed out an interesting temporal correlation with the four Jungian functions.

The correlations they found are consistent with the complexity index $(1, 2, m, \infty)$. Mann and her co-workers found that people for whom sensation is the dominant function relate most strongly to the *present*. What matters to them is the here and now, a single point on the time line. To feeling types, characterized by a complexity index of 2, the *past* is most meaningful. That is two points on the time line, one to the left of present. Feeling types have good memories, recall past encounters, and enjoy reminiscing. After all, their primary method of processing information is to reach value judgments based on past experiences. Was

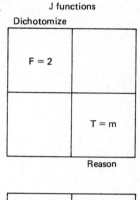

J functions

Dichotomize

F = 2

T = m

Reason

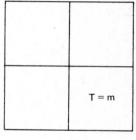

T = m

A-6

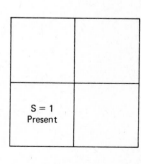

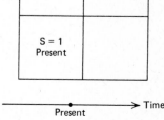

S = 1
Present

Time

Present

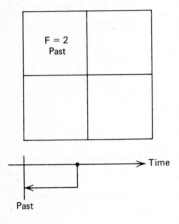

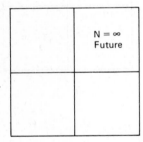

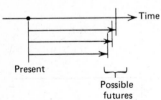

such and such helpful to my survival? Therefore, do I judge this now to be good or bad? That kind of functioning, typical of a feeling type, recalls specific, concrete, personal (people) experiences to build a recallable memory of value-classified (good or bad) experiences as a guide to making judgments.

To continue, Mann and her colleagues found N to correlate with the future. That too is consistent with the intuitive function. To deal with the uncertain future requires speculation, what I like to call "possibilitizing." There are, of course, an infinite number of possible scenarios for the future, consistent with the complexity index for N. Such possibilities projected into the future are of course not real and therefore an abstraction, the proper approach attribute for the intuitive function.

Very revealing is the correlation found by Mann, Siegler, and Osmond for the thinking function. They found that past, present, and future are of no interest in themselves to thinking types; they are interested instead in the temporal connections: how we got to the present from the past and what implications that has for predicting the future. This reflects a far more deterministic, rational process. I want to call your attention particularly to the idea of *sequential* information-processing revealed by Mann and her co-workers' findings. Interpretively, it is useful to associate the thinking function with the temporal characteristic of sequencing (from the past to the present into the future), the same type of concept that is so basic in computer processing of information. Current computers are described as sequential machines. That's not a bad description of the thinking capacities. Again, note the dichotomous contrast to the emotional (affect-driven) feeling type.

I hope you are impressed by the internal consistency of all the various descriptors. Let me summarize the associations suggested so far. Note that S and N are opposites in the P functions and F and T are opposites in the J functions.

| | Perceiving (P) Functions | | Judging (J) Functions | |
	S	N	F	T
Name	Sensation	Intuition	Feeling	Thinking
Focus	Things	People	People	Things
Approach	Concrete	Abstract	Concrete	Abstract
Complexity index	1	∞	2	m
Temporality	Present	Future	Past	Sequence

The oppositional relationship is accentuated in the mapping, where oppositional functions fall into diametrically opposite quadrants.

One last word about nomenclature. In lecturing on this subject, I've found that there is considerable confusion about the two Jungian terms sensation and feeling. To many people, the terms are too close in meaning, and they tend to get them confused. This problem is not helped by language usage, for we refer to feeling both in a tactile and in an affect or emotional context. I use the terms as labels strictly in accordance with the way Jung defined them. Toward the end of *Psychological Types*, Jung devotes a whole chapter to definitions of terms. I think you will find that reference to these definitions will remove any confusion about the labels.

GLIMPSE

If you want to get some insight into people, catch them off guard. Fathers are particularly interesting to watch. They flock to campus the first day the freshmen arrive, delivering their precious 18 year olds literally out of their protective clutches. Of course, there is that inevitable farewell when Dad is about to climb in the car and the youngster is on his or her own. Those are the moments to watch.

Some fathers shake hands while they deliver their last words of wisdom. Others hug and embrace, oblivious to the rest of the world. Some busy themselves with a last minute chore and let mother attend to the farewell, hiding their own emotions behind impatience. Some say goodbye to all the roommates whom they've just met but skip their own youngster, acting just like one of the boys. Some cry bitter tears without embarrassment.

What you see, of course, are the different ways the four functions find expression.

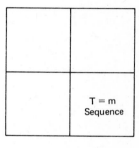

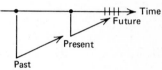

6

THE EIGHT-POLE MODEL

The 8-pole model is developed from the 4H–pole model by superimposing the attitude dichotomy. The style dichotomy, which represents the right brain versus left brain dichotomy, emerges as a fringe benefit, making input and output assignments possible.

46

THE STATIC MODEL:
THE MAP OF CAPACITIES

Four—pole model

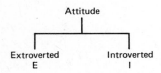

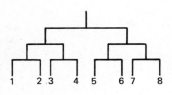

We have defined a dichotomy and developed a scheme for identifying opposite pairs. We have used two specific dichotomies, focus and approach, to partition the field of consciousness into four cells, which show on the map as quadrants. We have given these four quadrants names and labels—the functions S, F, N, and T—and we have found a rich set of associations for the labels, some related to a complexity index and some related to time. I call the map at this stage of development the four-pole model.

ATTITUDE

Our aim now is to extend the model to eight poles, and we will need a third dichotomy for that—that is, a partitioning scheme at the third level of the tree. The dichotomy we use is one Jung called *attitude*. Jung called the two opposing attributes of this dichotomy *extroverted* versus *introverted*. Before we delve into this, however, let's step back a bit.

We started the construction of the model with a large circle representing the human skin. The skin is the defining boundary that separates the external environment from the self. This is such a fundamental concept, at the very root of survival and identity, that it deserves elaboration.

I can envision myself sitting at the edge of a cliff overlooking a vast desert landscape. Before me is an incredibly empty sameness, miles and miles of sand, each square foot like any other square foot. But I must pitch my tent somewhere, so I pick a spot and pitch my tent.

The moment I do so, things have changed. Whereas before every square foot looked like any other, now those few square feet that are *mine* are different. They are different because there suddenly is an outside that is not mine, is unknown, and is potentially threatening. Once I'm sitting in my tent, every noise I hear is a potential danger sign. It is as though the existence of an outside, an external environment, gives purpose to my senses. It also gives the senses a direction. I might venture into the outside and use my senses to gather sticks and stones to build a fire, or I might sit inside my tent and use my senses to alert myself to potential threats. I use the environment aggressively to provide for my needs; that is, I intrude on and do things *to* the external, but I also defend myself *from* it. The mere existence of the boundary gives rise to both an aggressive and a defensive attitude.

These two aspects of attitude are so basic to survival that it is not surprising that the mind has special capabilities designed to enhance aggression and defense. One deals with acquiring, scavenging, and the other with conserving. Conserving means self-discipline, controlling your actions, to do with what you have, to not expend yourself, and to be unnoticed. The focus is directed inward on the self. Scavenging is directed outward. It means attack; go out there and do something to something. These are the basic forces underlying the dichotomy of attitude.

It is the existence of an outside, established by pitching a tent, that gives the senses a purpose—namely, to bring in information. It is attitude that decides how that information is to be used to control the self or the environment, the inside or the outside. This dualism has led to the specialization of capacities. Some capacities, such as noting the difference between something edible and something poisonous, are ideally suited for dealing with the outside world. Some capacities are ideally suited to focus on the self to adjust your behavior so you don't run out of food or freeze to death. If one draws mostly on capacities ideally suited to deal with things external, Jung would label such an attitude as *extroverted* or object-driven. If the capacities are those in the service of the self—that is, defensive and conserving—he would call it *introverted* or subject-driven.

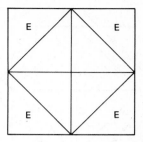

In popular usage, these terms have become distorted in meaning. It is an oversimplification to equate introverted with shy and extroverted with gregarious. The real criterion is whether the focus and interest are on things external or internal. There are managers whose decisions are essentially based on external factors: how many units were shipped, what the price of copper is today, and so on. And there are others who are guided by internal signals: I think we're spread too thin, I think we're overextended. There are many such examples. Some people dress in accordance with what is expected from them (an external force, be it a dress code or fashion), and others dress according to mood or desire for comfort. So the sense in which Jung used and I use the labels extroverted and introverted is whether the focus is on the external or the internal.

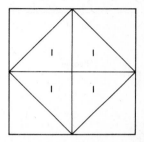

In constructing a map, it is therefore convenient to partition each quadrant such that we get an external (E) and an internal (I) cell. I use the E and I labels in conjunction with the function labels to identify the eight cells. We thus have ES and IS, EF and IF, ET and IT, and EN and IN.

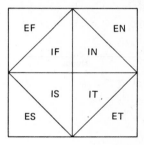

OUTPUTS

As mentioned, it is the flow of information from the outside as perceived by the senses (inputs) that feeds the conscious mind. This information is digested toward introverted or extroverted ends. Inputs are therefore useful to external as well as internal cells. Outputs, however, are always directed to produce some effect on the external environment. Since our map is to be taken literally, outputs should emanate from external poles. But just what input or output should be connected to which pole is not immediately obvious. Decisions such as these are critical in the process of model building.

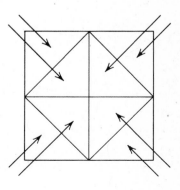

Recall that the four-pole model gave the map of capacities a basic orientation with people-oriented activities at the top of the map, things at the bottom, concrete on the left, and abstract on the right. At the very least, the input–output connections must be consistent with that orientation. This suggests the following general allocations:

47

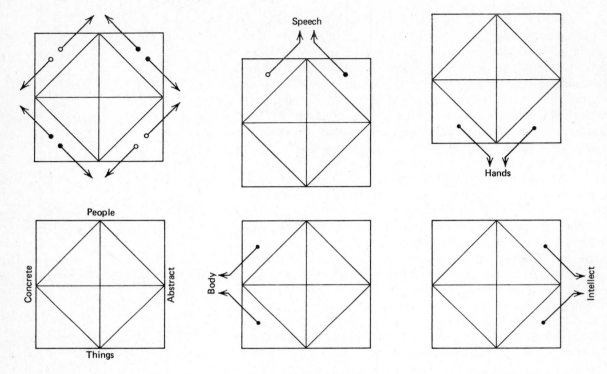

1. Speech and the related capacity of hearing should connect to the poles in the upper half of the map, since verbal communication is the major means for relating to other people (other people are part of the external environment).

2. The hands and eyes, also coupled capacities, should relate to poles mapped in the lower half of the map of capacities, since they are the ideal means for dealing with things. In other words, rocks don't talk to you, but you can fashion them into a tool with your hands.

3. Experiential capacities, mapped toward the left, must involve the body. How else could one get involved? So body action (in its most primitive sense, hunting, chasing, and so on) must relate to the capacities toward the left.

4. Perhaps the most difficult to see is the last assignment to be made: abstract outputs. What could that possibly be? I'm suggesting that an intellectual output is as much a design on the external environment as a physical act. The ability to formulate strategies—how to stalk an animal or how to use the environment for complex purposes, for example—is, in fact, what has made the human race master over larger external powers. So I assign the intellectual capacities of planning and of reaching logical conclusions as outputs to be connected to capacities on the right of the map.

Deciding what *input* to connect to what pole forced me to rethink a basic question: Are there really only five senses? It's not a silly question, for the idea of only five senses goes back to the Greeks. Maybe we're stuck on a concept whose time has run out.

It should be forthrightly stated that the symmetry of the dichotomous model makes five an unfortunate choice. The model cries out for inputs and outputs as powers of 2: 2^1, 2^2, 2^3, 2^4, possibly even 2^6. So, for purposes of building a model, it would be helpful if I could identify 2, 4, 8, or 16 inputs and outputs. This then was the motivation for the investigative detour I must describe.

The force that provided the missing clue was a convergence of what might best be called "loose ends."

P versus J Is Not a Dichotomy

Isabel Briggs Myers had been developing a test instrument to type people according to Jungian precepts. Yet there were aspects of the so-called Myers-Briggs Type Indicator that struck me as inconsistent in both interpretation and structure. One was the observation that the P versus J preference required different interpretations for extroverts and introverts.

B-2

This and other aspects led me to conclude that the P versus J opposition is inappropriate as a discriminator, because it is not a dichotomy in a mathematical sense. A true dichotomy must be equivalent to a symmetrical partition into two subsets in such a way that neither subset contains a pair of elements with opposite attributes. P versus J violates this rule since, for example, IN is the exact opposite of ES (since S is the opposite of N, and I the opposite of E), and yet both are contained in P. Therefore, P versus J is not a dichotomy.

This is an absolutely fundamental aspect of the dichotomous model, and it is therefore important to make this point clear and specific.

The eight cells with which we are dealing, namely,

$$\left.\begin{array}{l} ES \\ IS \end{array}\right\}S$$

$$\left.\begin{array}{l} EF \\ IF \end{array}\right\}F$$

$$\left.\begin{array}{l} ET \\ IT \end{array}\right\}T$$

$$\left.\begin{array}{l} EN \\ IN \end{array}\right\}N$$

can be organized by means of a so-called tree structure. Each pair of branches of the tree represents the two opposing attributes of a dichotomy. I illustrate this first by using the two dichotomies of approach and focus.

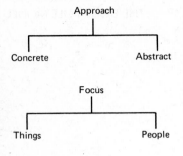

As noted in the four-pole model, approach divides the field of consciousness into the two opposing attributes of concrete versus abstract.

Focus divides the field of consciousness into the two opposing attributes of people versus things.

The two together create a fourfold partition labeled S, F, T, and N. This is reflected in the tree structure, with P and J also identified.

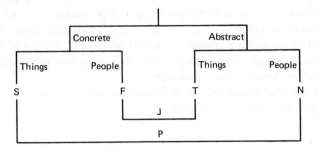

This representational scheme shows clearly that S is opposite N, since the attributes that describe S are concrete and thing-oriented, and those that describe N are abstract and people-oriented. S and N thus have totally opposite attributes. The same is true for F and T.

Let us carry this way of viewing things one step further to the eight-pole model by using the attitude dichotomy.

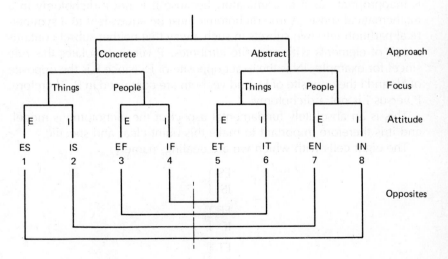

We notice four opposing pairs; for example, 1 and 8 or ES and IN. The attributes for ES are concrete, things, and extroverted; for IN they are abstract, people, and introverted—obviously opposite in every way. We can therefore make a list of opposite pairs, each pair composed of different combinations of cells into groups of four. For example, in the following diagram four dichotomies are shown (circled versus uncircled numbers).

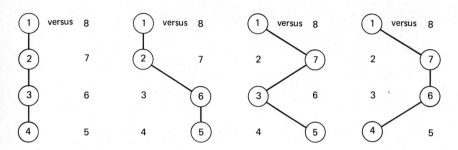

A true dichotomy must thus be a subset of four cells so chosen that I include only one of the opposing pairs. I cannot choose both 1 and 8 plus two other cells, because that particular set of four includes two elements with completely oppositional attributes. The P versus J partition would be 1, 8, 2, and 7 versus 3, 6, 4, and 5, which violates the definition of a dichotomy because 1, 8 and 2, 7 (and 3, 6 and 4, 5) are opposite pairs.

There are a number of legitimate dichotomies, four of which have been shown. Note that each subset of four (as well as its complement) includes only one element of an opposing pair. Either 1 or 8, 2 or 7, 3 or 6, and 4 or 5, but not both.

All the possible legitimate combinations can be developed by a schema known as a truth table:

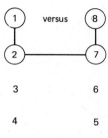

Cell Choice	Combinations															
	a	b	c	d	e	f	g	h	i	j	k	l	m	n	o	p
1 or 8	1	1	1	1	1	1	1	1	8	8	8	8	8	8	8	8
2 or 7	2	2	2	2	7	7	7	7	2	2	2	2	7	7	7	7
3 or 6	3	3	6	6	3	3	6	6	3	3	6	6	3	3	6	6
4 or 5	4	5	4	5	4	5	4	5	4	5	4	5	4	5	4	5

I have drawn these 16 combinations on the eight-pole model map. First, we should number the cells so we can actually account for all the combinations *a* through *p*. The numbering scheme, consistent with the oppositional relationship, is shown, and pairs of combinations are shown as numbered versus shaded.

There are eight possible combinations that satisfy the requirements of a dichotomy. These are all the symmetrical partitions there are, and, as expected, P versus J is not among them. There are, however, three that are familiar—approach, focus, and attitude—and five new ones.

We recognize the one labeled "*a* versus *p*" as the approach dichotomy; the one labeled "*d* versus *m*" as the focus dichotomy; and the one labeled

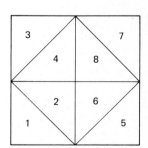

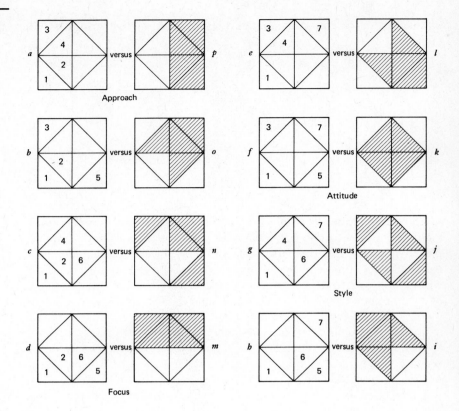

D-12

"*f* versus *k*" as the attitude dichotomy. The one labeled "*g* versus *j*" is a new dichotomy, which I have labeled *style*. I have given interpretive names to the four other dichotomies and call them "precursors to consciousness" (these are discussed later).

Now another loose end has to be brought into the picture. There has been in recent years a lot of activity in what has been called "split-brain" research. It is known that there are two brain hemispheres connected by the corpus callosum and, from physiological mapping of the cerebral cortex, that the left brain hemisphere controlled most right body functions and vice versa. In other words, there had developed a brain-hemisphere specialization, whereby the right arm, the right hand, the right leg, the right eye, and so on, were controlled by the left brain hemisphere. However, more interesting was the discovery of another kind of specialization of the brain hemispheres. When the corpus callosum was cut, either by an accident or in an operation, so that the two brain halves no longer were in communication with each other, certain impairments were observed, which led to the realization that one hemisphere specializes in speech. In most right-handed persons, speech resides in the left hemisphere.

I could not help wondering whether this right- and left-hemisphere specialization represented a pair of opposites that corresponds to the new dichotomy of style. In fact, the literature has pointed that way and alerted me to personality differences, which I call *contextual* (C) versus *detailed* (D). The differences are pronounced.

I observed that the class of people I call detailed (left-hemisphere dominant) is what C. P. Snow recognized as the scientific culture. Detailed people attain their sense of security from doing things systematically. In going from *A* to *B*, they are conscious of every detailed step in between. They proceed step by step, thoroughly, rationally, and sequentially, and they refuse to be distracted. They can do only one thing at a time, resembling what in the computer world would be called *batch processing*.

E-11

GLIMPSE

I recall years ago being in a dance class with several engineers and their wives. It was a fascinating study in contrast. The engineers learned the rhumba one step at a time. First they had to get the sequence of foot positions straight in their heads, so they would stomp like elephants from one imaginary footprint on the floor to the next one. They stared at the floor in full concentration until they had the sequence straight. Next they would focus on how to shift the body weight, and their hips would swivel like a dump truck with a broken spring, but ultimately they got that straight. And only then could they listen to the music and begin to co-ordinate the previously learned sequences into what might be called dancing the rhumba. It took time, but step by step they mastered it and became, in fact, fairly proficient dancers.

For most of the wives (who tended to be nonengineering types), this tedious process was extremely irksome. "Honey, quit staring at the floor and just feel the music," they would say, but it didn't help. The detailed mind could not deal with the totality of context until every detail had been drilled into consciousness.

Contextual types are the very opposite. Their sense of security comes from the *context*. They want to know everything that's going on at once and at the same time. They are what would be called *parallel processors* in computing. I call them *time sharers* (not quite the same thing), and contextual types like to do several things concurrently. While they hang on the phone, they scribble something on paper while the radio is blasting away and the secretary motions in the doorway. Every signal has meaning, and it is the convergence of them that matters, not the detail. They need to catch the *whole* sense of what's going on.

There is another aspect to contextual types in addition to time sharing. Contextual types talk in order to know what they are thinking: they speak first, then think. With detailed types it's the other way around; they must think before they can speak. For me, a detailed type, cocktail parties are truly painful experiences. Standing in a group of people, I never know what to say, because I don't know what the topic is. I don't know what to think about. Once I notice that they are talking about the weather, then it's a different matter. But my wife can talk about anything, for talk is not what is said, but how it's said. Conversation helps in reading the context, the mood of the total situation. After all, everything and anything relates to the context of the moment, so speech need not be directed or focused.

Observations such as these suggest that detailed correlates with directed speech and therefore the left brain hemisphere. After all, speech —composing or analyzing a sentence—is a sequential process. It is ordered rather than rate dependent. Whether I speak fast or slowly, the meaning embedded in the sequence of words does not change. Tone does, but tone or mood is a matter of context, not content.

D-11

In summary, then, I concluded that the dichotomy of style correlates with right- and left-hemisphere dominance rather than with perceiving versus judging. Furthermore, the dichotomy deals with fundamentally different ways of processing information: one is sequentially driven; the other is a parallel processor, ideal for context identification. Right- or left-hemisphere dominance leads to behavioral patterns so different that it is indeed appropriate to refer to it as style. In fact, I'm convinced that most human conflicts, in marriage and in business, result not from substantive differences but rather from differences in style. There is so little awareness of the differences in contextual and detailed styles that there is such a thing as intolerance of style. We simply presume that others operate in our style, and if they don't, that they're trying to irritate us. It just isn't so. Style is a dichotomy, a personality extreme, as fundamental as attitude, focus, and approach.

See page 14

D-12

To piece the puzzle together, I must bring in one more loose end. I refer you back to the preview chapter, where the traces of eye movements superimposed on the sketch by Klee and bust of Nefertiti reflected contextual and detailed vision.

To make the differentiation between the discriminating and contextual eye very clear, let me refer you to a common experience. When you are driving a car, your eyes operate contextually. You are not really looking at anything in particular. Your eyes are just generally scanning a large field of vision through the windshield. The eyes see nothing in deep detail, nor are you interested in detail. All you need for the task of driving is contextual information. Are you in your lane? Is there a curve ahead? You need to see a large field and receive some information but not detailed information such as the license number of the car a hundred feet in front of you.

View through a windshield

But suddenly something splatters on your windshield, and you focus your eyes on it: "Yes, indeed, a little yellow bug." You really have lost the field of view in front of you, just as though the road had disappeared. All you can see is that tiny bug with its red insides smeared on the windshield. It is a very different kind of vision, one ideally suited for discrimination and identifying a small field with a richness of detail.

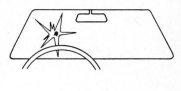

The contextual and detailed eyes carry out diametrically opposite tasks. It is not that one is better than the other. They are just different and are ideal for different situations. When you need to know a lot about a little, you draw on the detailed eye (foveal vision), which sees only a small field but a great deal of visual content in that field. It is particularly good at seeing edges formed by light and dark contrast. It sees colors and color-contrasted edges. For that type of vision to function, the various muscles of the eye must be well controlled. The eye must stay directed to that exact field of interest and must stay in focus. In such a case the eye is very disciplined.

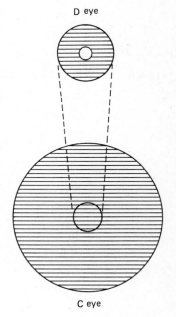

D eye

C eye

Contextual vision is just the opposite (extrafoveal vision). The roaming eye looks at blobs of interest rather than at edges. It looks at nothing in particular but sees relationships. How is that cluster of trees related to that house—or is it a barn?

Clearly, there are situations when one type of looking is more useful than the other. But a given individual is preferentially disposed toward one or the other. That is one reason why descriptions of witnesses at the scene of an accident will vary so dramatically. It is also why one person walking into a new room can tell you afterwards that he liked that blue still-life painting over the piano, whereas another can recall no specific picture but will note that all of them hung crookedly.

There is a parallel dichotomy to hearing. The D ear, or detailed ear, is particularly adept at recognizing consonants and pitch and can selectively focus on a sound pattern, such as recognizing the voice of a friend through the "white noise" in a crowded restaurant.

In contrast, the C ear, or contextual ear, hears tone particularly. It is a good alerting ear that, though it cannot make out the detail, catches the totality of the sound pattern.

INPUTS

This interrelated complex of thoughts and ideas led me to a new conceptualization of the senses. There are not five of them, but at least seven: taste, touch, smell, two seeing senses (C and D), and two hearing senses (C and D). But there is no reason to believe that the C and D dichotomy should not apply to taste, touch, and smell as well. This has led me to a different organizational conception of the remaining senses. I suggest, with an awareness of its speculative aspects, that there are *contact senses*, senses activated only by actual physical contact, like touch and taste,

56

THE STATIC MODEL:
THE MAP OF CAPACITIES

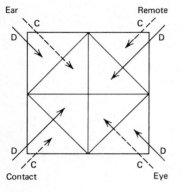

and *remote senses* like smell, where activation of the sensing nerve can be through diffusion over distances. Furthermore, I presume that both contact and remote senses occur as both C and D senses. One of these (a remote sense) might very well be what we call the sixth sense.

I am aware that there exist positional senses (proprioception and the semicircular canals of the ear) and an autonomic nervous system. We might view them as unconscious senses. But I don't want to get too literally tied to anatomy and physiology, so let me simply say that the sixth sense is a combination of all of the unconscious senses, giving us the capability to "feel the vibes."

This conceptual framework provides eight senses: a pair (C and D) of contact senses, a pair (C and D) of remote senses, a pair of eye senses, and a pair of ear senses—one input for each of the eight cells of the model.

Recall that for the outputs we decided that body outputs would be to the left, intellectual outputs to the right, speech to the top, and hands to the bottom. I therefore have assigned the inputs (senses) to the following poles:

1. Contact senses enter at the S poles.
2. Hearing senses enter at the F poles.
3. Remote senses enter at the N poles.
4. Eye senses enter at the T poles.

Finally, each external pole has two outputs. But I'm getting ahead of the logical development of the model.

GLIMPSE

Dichotomies are much easier to understand in the context of language. It's before or after, above or below, near or far, early or late, right or left, as though these were the only choices. There is an implied midpoint, such as now and here, but that is really the unmentioned reference point. What we don't seem to have in our language is a description for things like the position of a tire relative to the hub; a tire is both in front of and behind and above and below the hub. We might say it's around the hub, but we don't. We say it's on the hub or off the hub.

Right and left is even worse. The right side of the street depends on which way you are facing, so we say north or south, an unambiguous dichotomy.

You can't help wondering how our language would be if our cerebral cortex had three instead of two hemispheres and if each controlled and responded to three legs, three arms, three ears, and three eyes. Maybe then we'd have a before, a beafter, and an after; an above, an ablow, and a below; a near, a nar, and a far; and so on.

Nothing that is human seems to be able to escape our bifurcated symmetry.

MORE ON THE NATURE OF DICHOTOMIES

Dichotomies are basic to the concept underlying this model. Unfortunately, they are also the hardest to explain and the easiest to misunderstand.

Jung's juxtaposition of perceiving and judging is not a dichotomy in the technical sense in which I have defined it, because P and J each includes oppositional attributes. The key in my definition of a dichotomy is that a subset cannot include the opposite of any element in the subset. P and J do. Jung differentiated between what he called the rational and irrational functions. He considered feeling and thinking rational functions, that is, concerned with reaching judgments. The pair of functions F and T are therefore referred to as J (see Briggs Myers). But Jung is very explicit in stating that F and T are opposite functions, two opposite ways of reaching a judgment.

A-4

Jung labeled S and N the irrational, or perceiving, functions, called P by Briggs Myers. Again Jung points out that S and N are opposites, two different ways of perceiving. But J versus P is not a dichotomous choice.

B-2

The situation is very different with attitude and style. They are genuine dichotomies in the eight-pole model. It is valid to choose between the two attributes of each dichotomy. Is it extroverted or introverted? Is it contextual or detailed? These criteria are dichotomous differentiators. The differentiations are fundamental, and perhaps it is useful to elaborate on them a bit more. Let us review what we've said about the introverted versus extroverted qualities of attitude:

Attitude

Extroverted	*Introverted*
Focus on external	Focus on internal
Reality-driven	Model-driven
Object-driven	Subject-driven
Data-driven	Need-driven
Aggressive	Defensive
Expansive	Conserving

These descriptors make the most sense in the context of survival, which is the fundamental root underlying attitude. There are two ways to survive in a hostile environment. One is to behave like a chameleon, which can change its appearance to so blend into its environment that it can't be detected. That is an internally directed, conserving, defensive strategy for survival. This is in sharp contrast to the behavior of a shark, for whom attack is the best means of defense. It survives by aggression, with total disregard for the energy it squanders in the process. If it needs more energy, it simply goes out and gets it. Attitude therefore involves a true dichotomous choice: two opposite strategies for survival.

The dichotomy of style is similarly rooted in a fundamental concept: a dualistic optimization of how to cope, or what means to use to provide for *security*. The image that comes to mind is a lioness with her cubs. I see her lying lazily on her side, her eyes half-closed, with her cubs crawling all over her. She strikes a pose of benign tolerance. But make no mistake, she knows what's going on. Through her tactile senses, she knows where every cub is, and, should one stray too far, a paw or jaw will reach out and gather it back close to her. No matter how relaxed she may seem, her ears are perked as an alerting system to impending danger. The capacities she must fully use to provide security are those that maintain awareness of the total *context*: what the cubs are doing and what might be nearby that could be threatening. Dimensionally, her scale of concern is relatively small; it's what's in her immediate vicinity that matters, and within that area everything matters all at once. A change in the situation alerts her to danger; distraction is not an annoyance, for it is the unexpected that provides the early warning system. This is what I mean when I say that her sense of security depends on her contextual style. Context—the totality of the situation, the nearby macroworld—is all that matters.

When she is hunting, the situation is very different. Her sense of security comes from the assurance, the certainty, that once she attacks, everything is in her favor. She must win. Her job therefore is to optimize those skills crucial to the kill. All her energies are focused on one thing, the prey. Her stance looks like frozen concentration. Nothing can distract her. Her eyes stare in sharp focus, measuring the direction; her nostrils are fully focused, her muscles poised. And once she springs into action, nothing diverts her from the intended task. If, in her dart to kill, she passed an eight-course meal, the very end goal of her dart, she wouldn't notice it, for all her energies are focused on what she set out to do. It is this single-minded, batch execution of a task that I call *detailed*. It is a microprocess, which can succeed only if everything is focused on that single task. Security here—the certainty of success—depends on the single-mindedness of purpose, where every detail needed for the job is under optimal control.

It is in this sense that the dichotomies are fundamental: attitude in service of survival, style in service of security.

There are different words to bring out various aspects of the two attributes of style. I prefer contextual versus detailed to evoke the contrasting images just described. But there are others:

Style	
Contextual	*Detailed*
Right-hemisphere thinking	Left-hemisphere thinking
Parallel processing	Sequential processing
Time sharing	Batch processing
Rate sensitive	Absolute time sensitive
Macroprocessing	Microprocessing
Distributed	Single-minded

It is interesting to note from the dictionary that "context" derives from the Latin *contexere*, meaning "to weave together." Indeed, I envision contextual behavior as a kind of weaving. There is a given *structure*, the warp, consisting of a bunch of parallel strands of yarn running the length of the weaving. The weaver's preoccupation is with the woof, the strands that run over and under the warp. Now, the interesting thing in weaving is that you can stop at any time and pick up later where you left off. And it is never the same; you can change the patterns, the color, and the texture. The whole process involves many things that flow together into a rhythmic pattern, a rhythm that moves back and forth like the swing of a pendulum. It is a rate-conscious process unfolding before the weaver's eyes, where absolute time is meaningless. In the Far East it may take months to weave a carpet; the weaver may not know how much

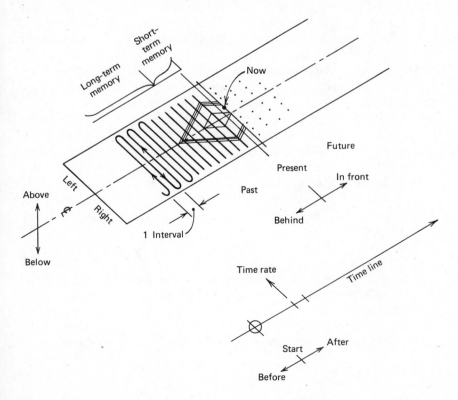

has been accomplished by March 31 but will have a good sense of whether it went well one day or not. The rate of progress is most apparent.

There is another aspect to the weaving analogy that is very powerful. Weaving is alertive. You see the patterns emerging and can foretell what should happen next. It is this predictive alertness to context that brings with it the recognition of the unexpected. If you pick up the wrong color for the next woof, you need not weave for three more yards before you know you have made a mistake; you know at once.

This alertness is also typical of contextual personalities. They notice changes in context and therefore are quick to perceive change and impending disaster. By contrast, the batch processor, working at a desk, might not even notice that the wastebasket is on fire, just as the lioness wouldn't notice the eight-course meal all ready for her.

This readiness to perceive change has a typical ambi-syn-anti paradox built into it, which often leads to confusion. Although the detailed types seem one-tracked, totally focused on what they're doing, they are far less rigid than the contextual types, even though they are the ones who so quickly notice change and adapt their processing to it. The key to this is the warp. Recall that I called the warp the structure of weaving. Take away the structure and you have nothing. So contextual types are very inflexible when it comes to basic things. In contrast, batch processors are inflexible while they're doing any one thing, but once they load a new program to execute, they can switch from one thing to something very different. We might say that contextual people are flexible in what they are doing but not in how they do it. And detailed people are controlled or rigid while they are doing any one thing, but utterly flexible in whatever task they tackle.

If this seems confusing, perhaps an example will help. Let us say a couple, a woman (C type) and a man (D type), had planned to go out to dinner with friends right after work and then go to the theater; a program has been set for the evening. Now assume that one of the many daily disasters occurs; the car has a flat tire, she can't find her purse, the baby-sitter is late, the kid is screaming. The D type will be upset; in fact, he'll yell at everybody and make things worse. The C type calmly picks up the phone, calls the friends, and suggests they eat after the theater. Period. In other words, C notices the change of total context and takes corrective action. The D type only knows his program got botched, and he's at a loss as to what to do.

Now take a more fundamental issue, such as an impending divorce or a death in the family. The basic structure in which the C type operated has been destroyed. She is uncompromising and inflexible. But to the D type it merely means one routine has come to an end, and he's about to start another.

Language is inadequate to describe such ambi-syn-anti dualisms. Who is the flexible one? Well, all one can say is that it's complicated.

You will notice that (by design) I introduced certain sex biases. I connected "she" to contextual and "he" to detailed. That is, of course, factual nonsense. Male personalities are as often C as D. I suspect, however, that the C versus D dichotomy may well have evolved out of an earlier sex-based dichotomy.

The way I visualize it is that eons ago and probably in lower species of animals, the brain had much more redundancy in its organization. However, once socialization began—that is, some cooperation between male and female—skills learned by one sex from the other improved survival skills so vastly that some redundant capacities were no longer needed. It is in this way that Jung's archetypes of animus and anima make sense to me.

I visualize an archetype as a remnant of past organizational structures of the mind. It is as though male and female were once an organizational dichotomy, which, as the brain evolved, became less functional. But the remnants are there and still play an important role in unconscious processes such as dreaming. It is in this sense that Jung's archetype of anima means the femaleness in the male, his capacity to express and understand tenderness and nurturing qualities. In our culture these are frequently clearest in unexpected contexts, such as a man's feelings for his automobile. It's his baby. Animus is a similar collective archetypal assertive force operating in the female.

A-5

The point of this discussion is that genuine dichotomies, which can be identified out of set theoretical considerations, interpretively always carry with them some very fundamental issue such as survival, security, and reproduction. Dichotomies, in the sense in which I have defined them, are therefore far more than merely some observable oppositional pair. They are basic.

POLES AND CIRCUITS: THE MODEL AS AN INFORMATION-PROCESSING NETWORK

In developing the model so far, the dichotomies have been used as a tool for conceptualizing the organization of the field of consciousness. It has helped sort out what capacities to map in a given location. The resulting organization was a key to speculating how inputs and outputs might be connected to the various capacities. We might call this a nonconnected or "nonwired" model.

With inputs, outputs, and capacities, it is more appropriate to view the model as an information processor. This raises the question: How does information flow in the eight-pole model? The next step we are about to take is analogous to superimposing a network of roads on a geographical map that indicates states, counties, and cities.

I envision, in the center of each cell, a theoretical construct that I call

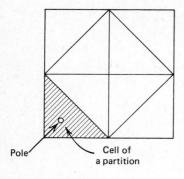

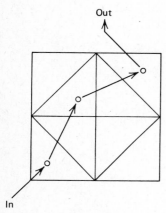

Pole   Cell of
a partition

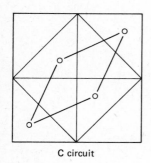

Out

In

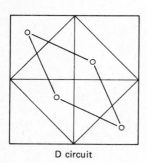

C circuit

D circuit

a pole. The relationship of a pole to a cell is analogous to the relationship between a county and its seat of government. A cell is a limited region encompassing a collection of brain cells.* A pole is a reflection of what this collection of cells actually does or accomplishes. A pole is therefore the information processor reflecting the collective activity of the cell. It can be thought of as the region's computer center.

Poles do not work in isolation. They receive information from somewhere, process that information according to their specialized capacities, and pass this processed information on to some other location, where the same sequence takes place. We should therefore envision the eight-pole model as a network consisting of eight interconnected computer centers, with inputs and outputs from and to the external environment.

Because of the fundamental difference in operation, I envision the poles in C-designated cells as tied together in a time-sharing network and those in D-designated cells as tied together in a batch-processing network. I refer to these as the C and D circuits, respectively. Each pole in the C circuit gets a time slice of attention. The C poles must therefore deal with operations that can be executed quickly, such as pulling yarn through a warp of a weaving. But the process can be repeated over and over again at arbitrary intervals in quick succession. The poles in the D circuit, however, carry on more complex processing functions, which, once started, must be completed. They operate in a batch mode.

A typical process might be as follows. Information is received by the eye. The incoming information is preprocessed. That means that the light stimuli are transduced to electrical impulses, or signals, and sorted out in a format the appropriate pole can process. The pole receives the incoming signal, regards it as a data string, and processes that data according to its specialized capability. The processed data may have been a sorting to identify only those parts of the image where the pattern changed from light to dark, that is, to recognize an edge. This transformed information string will then be sent on to some other pole, which may specialize in comparing that edge pattern with previously experienced edge patterns stored in its memory. The second pole's job is then to identify decoded images.

At this stage we need not be concerned with the details of what goes on. I simply want to establish that poles in the same circuit tend to work in cooperation with one another. I call such a coupling of two poles in the same circuit a *transaction*. A transaction is usually the first level at which one can recognize an observable human skill, such as identifying an image or recognizing a tune. A lot more is said about transactions later; now I only want you to understand that the line connecting two

---

*Note that "cell" is used as a mathematical term to describe an element of a set and is used in brain cell as a biological term. The word "cell" thus denotes two very different things.

poles, with an arrow at one end of the line designating the direction of information flow, is the code for designating a transaction on the map of capacities.

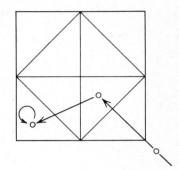

We see later that transactions can be linked into a chain in the same way that a trip is planned with the aid of a road map. Go from Boston to New York on Interstate 85, then continue on Interstate 80 to Pittsburgh, then trace your way back to Boston in the reverse direction. I call such a sequence of transactions a *metaprogram*.

Let me summarize some key concepts covered in this section:

1. We use a dichotomous partitioning scheme to delineate cells.
2. We then focus on a pole in the center of each cell as the abstraction that captures the functioning of that collection of brain cells represented by the cell. A pole is an information processor, whether you think of it in terms of biology or computer simulation.

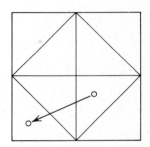

3. The poles are interconnected in a network. Most basic to this network are two distinct circuits, C and D, which link contextual and detailed poles together in separate circuits. As we see later, the C and D circuits are not the only connections between poles.
4. The information flow, in a specified direction from one pole to another, is called a transaction. A transaction corresponds to an identifiable human skill.
5. Transactions can be linked, describing a more elaborate sequence of information-processing steps. This is called a metaprogram.
6. An interpretation of the network-processing functions in computer terms is called a simulation.

GLIMPSE

You too must have had experiences where, for instance, you passed by the automobile rental place and decided to pop in just to ask whether it will be open Christmas day. As you walk in, you see a long queue of people, so you decide to walk up to the head of the line and say, "Excuse me, will you be open Christmas day?"

You usually get one of two responses from the attendant. The response you hope for probably would come from one who has a telephone nestled between her shoulder and her ear while she's punching stuff into the computer. She'll look up ever so briefly, say "of course," and without missing a beat goes back to her phone and terminal. Clearly a contextual type.

But you might encounter the opposite type. He will either ignore you totally or become flustered, slamming down his pencil and turning to you to say, "Sir, will you please go to the end of the line? Can't you see we're terribly busy?" He'll mutter a bit more as he tries to regain his composure and go back to where he was. He might even get angry, press "cancel," and say to his customer, "Ugh, some people. Now let's see—we'll have to start all over. You wanted a compact for what day?"

7

THE SIXTEEN-POLE MODEL

(A Complete Description of the Map of Capacities)

The previous chapters introduced concepts and traced the development of ideas that led me to the conceptualization of the 16-pole model.

Although the 16-pole model is but the next logical extension of the eight-pole model, it is a uniquely different model of the mind. What carries over is, primarily, the modeling methodology, whereby, as in the eight-pole model:

1. *Each cell is partitioned symmetrically once more.*
2. *New dichotomies are systematically uncovered.*
3. *Interpretive meanings are attached to cells and dichotomies.*

It is this last step that becomes complex in the 16-pole model. In the earlier chapters we could draw on the insights of Carl Jung, for his conceptualization of four functions, each with two attitudes, fits the eight-pole model very well. But the 16-pole model goes beyond Jung's structure, and we must look elsewhere for interpretive clues.

One of these, mentioned in the previous chapter, involves the idea that poles are tied into circuits. This means one has to explore not only the connections, what might be called the hardware of the brain, but also that which is flowing in these circuits, which might be called the software of the mind.

Exploration of the software aspect uncovered a dilemma that centered around ambiguities and misinterpretations of what Jung meant by superior, auxiliary, and inferior functions. To build a consistent model, this dilemma had to be resolved.

As to the hardware aspects of the model, one would expect to be able to find physiological parallels that would lend credence to this modeling approach.

I plan to discuss these two aspects before I continue with the systematic description of the 16-pole model.

THE SOFTWARE ASPECT

The interpretive dilemma of the superior versus inferior function

The conceptualization of a circuit, triggered by the discovery of the style dichotomy, suggests that there is a flow (of information) driven by some potential difference. It is natural to assume that such a flow is from the superior to the inferior function. This raises the question of how one identifies the superior function. Jung is not very specific about that point.

B-1, B-2

Malone and Briggs Myers recognized the dilemma and chose interpretations that are just the reverse of what I concluded they must be. The issue is a fundamental one, with consequences that affect the modeling and interpretation processes.

The difference in interpretation stems from the fact that I envision typological behavior as a consequence of natural libido-driven flow; that is, a given personality type has a natural potential field that superimposes libido differentials on the field of consciousness, leading to preferred flows of information. The major (most conscious) flow between pole pairs is what I call the *characteristic transaction*. The direction of information flow is from the data pole to the processing pole. I call the data pole the *driver* pole and the processing pole the *characteristic* pole.

Driver pole
16

Consider, for example, the characteristic transaction for the profile DETN, which runs from 16 to 15 (16 → 15). Pole 16 (⪦) is then the driver pole, and pole 15 (⪦) the characteristic pole.

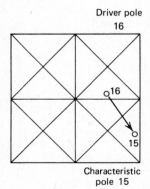

Characteristic
pole 15

Also note that pole 16 lies in the N function and pole 15 lies in the T function.

Now the gist of the matter is this: which of those two functions, N and T, is the superior function and which is the auxiliary function? Briggs Myers, for the case DETN (which she calls ENTJ), labels T the superior function and N the auxiliary function. I label them the other way around.

The difference is not trivial. As I see it, the difference in interpretation stems from the fact that the characteristic pole is always the more obvious one. It is certainly the pole others see. This is particularly true of extroverts. Others see not only the processing (how people deal with information) but also the outputs resulting from such processing. What the outsider does not see is the incoming data and how they are perceived, what they trigger, and how much attention they demand. That is a very private, invisible inner process.

Let me be specific about this. No one knows what you take in through the ears. Others may see you sitting in the restaurant while someone at your table is talking, but no one knows whether you are wrapped up in your own thoughts or listening to the person talking, to the background music, or even to the conversation at the adjoining table. Even if it is established that you are listening to the person speaking at your table, no one can know what you hear. The speaker may be talking about a cruise she took to the Caribbean. The data you may select to process as you listen may be her enthusiasm about the trip, the specific places she went to, or the boat she was on. The stream of words will have to be selectively related to your personal construct, and no one knows what that is. The outsiders see only the net results of your selective listening and processing, such as if you finally break in with an output to say: "I'm so glad you had such a good time," "Which place did you like best?" or "How many days were you on the boat?" Through your response, people see only the processing or characteristic pole. In the case of DETN, that is the T pole, and therefore they assume that T is dominant and characteristic of you. Thus they assume T is the superior function.

Actually, the characteristic (responsive) behavior is a consequence of what the driver pole decided to pay attention to. The driver pole is the one that determines the outcome and is therefore far stronger. In fact, it is the pole with the larger libido, and that is why information flows from 16 to 15. I therefore consider the driver pole to be the one in the superior function. For DETN, then, I consider N to be the superior function, and T the auxiliary function. DETN personalities know that. Although they may seem very logical to others, they are really intuitively driven, and their greatest weakness is not feeling, but sensation.

It is also interesting to note that, in my experiences with the Myers-Briggs Type Indicator, the score for the auxiliary function is almost always larger than that for the superior function.

In summary, the position I have taken is that the superior function must have the greatest libido. This shift in perspective affects the interpretation of profiles.

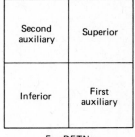

For DETN

THE HARDWARE ASPECT

Linking the 16-pole model C and D circuit interpretation to the physiological organization of the cerebral cortex

I have had to progress from the four-pole to the eight-pole to the 16-pole model in somewhat disjointed fashion. Ideally, I would have liked to develop the poles first and then the circuitry to complete the map of capacities. But the discovery of the style dichotomy, with its clear implications for circuitry—that is, one of the basic "hard-wire" connections of the model—made at least a preliminary discussion of circuitry unavoidable at the eight-pole model stage. I recognized the existence of transactions at the eight-pole stage before I had available the formalisms of the 16-pole model, which identifies links in a rational and systematic way. Thus I also decided to introduce a concept directly related to the C and D circuits, the pole interactions within the C or D circuit, or transactions (I have a lot more to say about other types of pole interactions shortly).

What I mean by hard-wire connections is rooted in an earlier assertion that C and D are equivalent to the right and left hemispheres of the brain. The equivalence of the map of capacities to the physiology of the cerebral cortex is developed by means of the following six diagrams.

Diagram A shows a typical view of the cerebral cortex. Left brain hemisphere (LBH) and right brain hemisphere (RBH) are labeled. Superimposed on the LBH and RBH are some wiggly lines that demark (according to Ridley), gross regions that fit the Jungian functions. These gross regions, which are not quite the same as the frontal, occipital, parietal and temporal lobes, are labeled F, T, S, and N in each hemisphere.

F-4

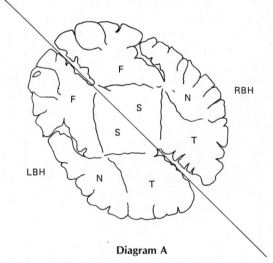

Diagram A

In diagram B this top view of the cerebral cortex in the same orientation has been schematized. Each hemisphere has been made circular, the boundaries defining the four regions F, T, S, and N have been made severe, and the corpus callosum has been exaggerated, clearly showing it as a bridge between the two hemispheres.

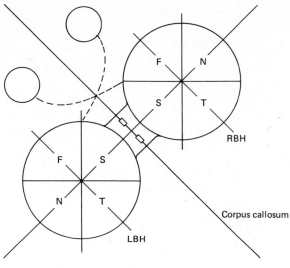

Diagram B

Diagram C depicts how information travels in the network of brain cells. A pulse emanating from a neuron travels along the axon and, if it jumps the synapse, is picked up by a dendrite of another neuron, which in turn can trigger a new pulse that travels on as a sequence of events. That sequence can be visualized by the far simpler schematic representation shown at the bottom of the figure.

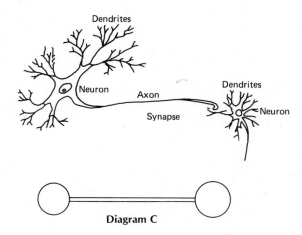

Diagram C

In diagram D I show one each of two classes of such information-flow events. The one shown in the RBH is within a region (called mode link), and the one shown in LBH crosses a boundary from one region to an adjacent one (a transaction).

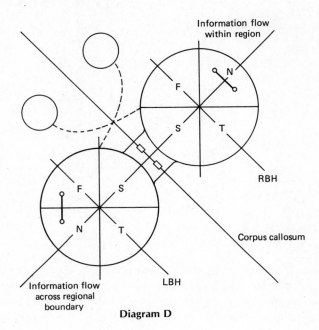

Diagram D

Diagram E depicts all the possible cases: one channel in each region and one channel crossing every boundary.

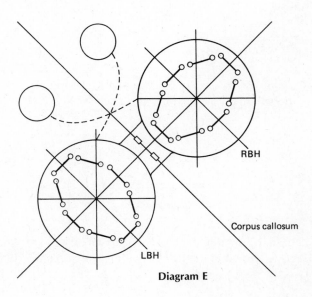

Diagram E

And last, in diagram F I have folded the LBH onto the RBH through a hinge along the axis of symmetry to yield the familiar map of capacities.

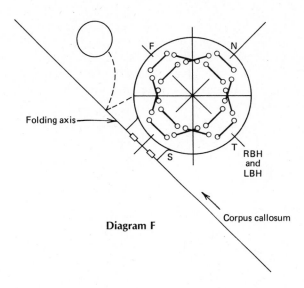

Diagram F

FORMING 16 POLES

I took so long before plunging into the 16-pole model because the complexity of the model increases enormously. But we should now be ready.

To go from the eight-pole model to the 16-pole model, we simply divide each cell down the middle. The ES cell, for example, now splits into ESF and EST cells, meaning that portion of the ES cell facing toward F and that portion facing toward T. In a similar fashion, all cells are labeled: ES becomes ESF and EST, IS becomes ISF and IST, and so on.

Eight—pole model

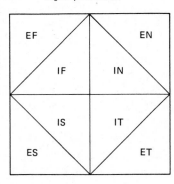

16—pole model

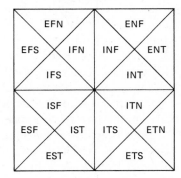

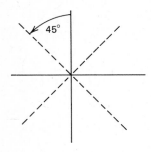

C-5, C-2, C-1

TWO NEW DICHOTOMIES EMERGE

Next, in a fashion similar to that discussed with the eight-pole model, we generate a truth table to help us identify new dichotomies. The truth table has 128 columns (which are not presented here). Sure enough, the previously identified dichotomies of focus, approach, attitude, and style emerge, plus two new ones very basic in their symmetry. They are shown diagrammatically and indicate a diagonal line of symmetry. In fact, one might view the map as having a new pair of reference axes created by a 45° rotation of the original axes.

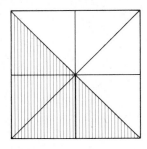 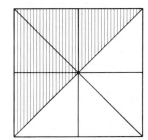

The key question this observation raises, of course, is: What is the significance of these new dichotomies that give rise to a new orientation grid? The answer did not come easily and is again a result of the influence of several loose ends.

One such idea that somehow seemed to fit the context of the model is what might be called *discontinuous growth*. By this I mean that things develop in steps like a staircase. There are lots of models like that in physics and psychology; dislocation theory, important in the growth of crystals, is one example, but perhaps better known is Maslow's hierarchy of needs. Clare Graves and Arnold Gesell developed similar models in other contexts. All show this stepwise growth: a period of instability and tremendous reaching out followed by a period of stability and integration. The next step cannot begin until the previous one has been completed. In short, these models say that growth progresses in steps; in other words, it is *hierarchically ordered*.

It would be helpful here to elaborate a bit on Gesell's model. He describes vividly how children struggle to master a given set of skills and how difficult they seem to the mothers while in such a stage. This brings to mind, for instance, that trying period in babies' lives when they insist on feeding themselves, no longer accepting the spoon-shoveling routine. Of course, in the process the plate lands upside down on the floor, and there is more spinach on the mothers than in the children. But it is a necessary struggle, and it is inevitably followed by a delightful stage when children can do quite a few things on their own. But that happy interlude comes to an end, and new aggravations ensue. Some new skill seems to be awakening, and the child is ready to tackle it no matter whether mother is ready for it or not. She may well lament, "What happened to my darling 3 year old?" And so it goes, step by step to higher and higher plateaus, to increasing challenges, sophistication, and complexity. In fact, *complexity is the key*. Complex skills are built out of simpler skills that have been mastered.

THE 16 POLES ARE HIERARCHICALLY ORDERED

This kind of reasoning led me to the conclusion that the 16 poles are hierarchically ordered and that the two new, so highly symmetrical dichotomies give the clue to such ordering. The outcome of this searching is captured by the numbering system associated with each pole. It is a hierarchical numbering that goes from the simplest capacity to the most complex.

The hierarchical ordering of the poles progressively from 1 to 16 is most apparent from the tree structure and the polar plot. The tree structure reveals that there are four dichotomies, hierarchically ordered. This hierarchy of dichotomies defines progressive opposition from pole 1 to pole 16. For 1 and 2, the first three levels of dichotomies are identical, but the fourth level is the opposite. For 1 and 3, the first two levels are identical, the third level is opposite, but the fourth level is identical. For 1 and 4, the first two levels are identical, the third level is opposite, and the fourth level is also opposite. The relationships between pole 1 and the rest of the poles become progressively more opposite as we move to 16, so that finally, 1 and 16 are completely opposite; that is, they differ at all four levels of dichotomies (0000 versus 1111).

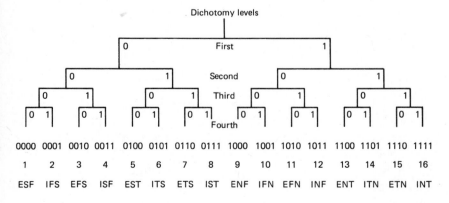

Our numbering system reflects the four dichotomies that result in a 16-pole tree. For example, pole 1 (ESF) is represented by 0000. If we examine the tree, we see that:

THE STATIC MODEL:
THE MAP OF CAPACITIES

First-level dichotomy (0000)	1–8 versus 9–16
Second-level dichotomy (0000)	1–4 and 9–12 versus 5–8 and 13–16
Third-level dichotomy (0000)	1–2, 5–6, 9–10, and 13–14 versus 3–4, 7–8, 11–12, and 15–16
Fourth-level dichotomy (0000)	Odd numbers versus even numbers

On the map of capacities, these dichotomies are as follows:

First-level dichotomy:

Second-level dichotomy:

Third-level dichotomy:

Fourth-level dichotomy:

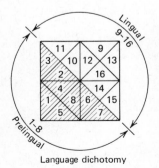

Language dichotomy

We recognize the third-level dichotomy as style and the fourth-level dichotomy as attitude. The first- and second-level dichotomies are the new ones that emerge from the 16-pole model.

The first-level dichotomy, which I call the *language* dichotomy, partitions the 16 capacities into *prelingual* (1 through 8) and *lingual* (9 through 16). It is the 9 through 16 set of capacities that makes humans uniquely human. Capacities 1 through 8 can be identified even in dogs, but children must grow through them before they can deal with linguistic conceptualizations.

The language dichotomy thus reveals the most fundamental hierarchical structure out of which humans and their language evolved.

The second dichotomy, which I call the *concept* dichotomy, is more closely tied to humans as cultural beings. It divides the capacities into a *natural* (1 through 4 and 9 through 12) and an *acquired* (5 through 8 and 13 through 16) set of capacities. By natural I mean innate capacities that emerge even if no disciplined learning is imposed. Children will ultimately learn to use the toilet and will develop speech whether they go to school or not. In fact, the natural capacities show up as preschool skills. Children can recognize a tune and may even laugh at dissonance, and they can understand picture books and fairy tales. But they cannot read, do arithmetic, and deal with logic and geometry without a disciplined learning effort. The acquired capacities are culturally learned by learning the algorithms that chain natural skills together into more complex forms.

The third- and fourth-level dichotomies are style and attitude, respectively, dichotomies extensively described in previous discussions.

Let me summarize where we stand. We have discovered two new dichotomies, language and concept, which are the key to hierarchical ordering of the poles from most simple to most complex. We reflect this hierarchy by assigning to each pole in the 16-pole model a number as well as a name, as follows:

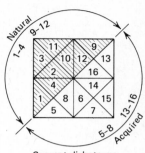

Concept dichotomy

1	ESF	⊡	versus	⪤	INT	16
2	IFS	=	versus	⊣ᴄᴄ	ETN	15
3	EFS	°/|	versus	⌗	ITN	14
4	ISF	–□–	versus	↗	ENT	13
5	EST	!	versus	⊙⊙	INF	12
6	ITS	⊙	versus	↶	EFN	11
7	ETS	ℕ	versus	⊼ᴛ	IFN	10
8	IST	‡	versus	△+□	ENF	9

In the table and in its alternative representation as a tree, polar plot, or map, you also find a symbolic identifier, which I discuss next.

Language					Concept					Style					Attitude			
1	5	9	13		1	5	9	13		1	5	9	13		1	5	9	13
2	6	10	14		2	6	10	14		2	6	10	14		2	6	10	14
3	7	11	15		3	7	11	15		3	7	11	15		3	7	11	15
4	8	12	16		4	8	12	16		4	8	12	16		4	8	12	16

Array

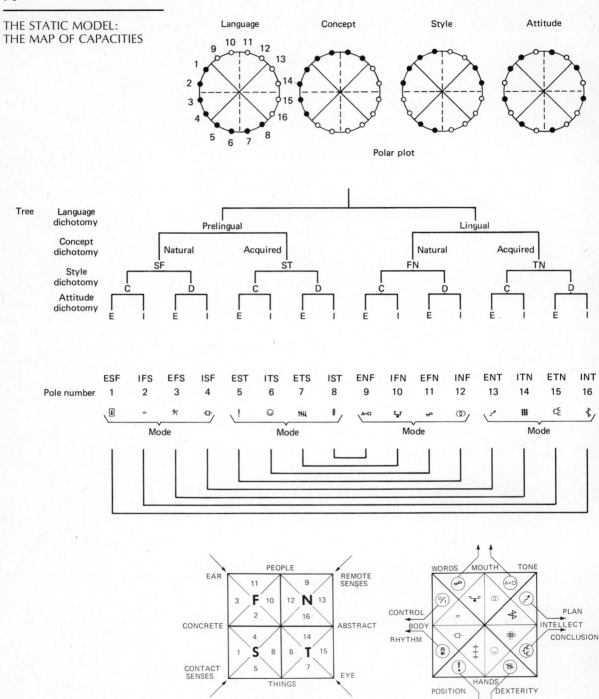

Map of capacities.

The symbol associated with each pole is my shorthand for describing a functional interpretation. The symbols were laboriously selected by trial and error. They had to satisfy all the criteria we have discussed so far: fit the meaning of Jung's functional description, fit complexity, and satisfy all the dichotomous relationships that come into play. The symbols are thus incredible information compressors, which words are not. The pages that follow make this abundantly clear.

I describe the poles in hierarchical order and in groups of four. Each group corresponds to a *mode*, formed by the overlay of the two highest-level dichotomies, language and concept.

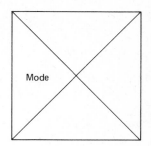

The Concrete Mode (poles 1, 2, 3, and 4)

Pole 1—ESF ▣ Signal. I've stylized a light signal as it might appear on an elevator. Its purpose is to register recognition. If the light signal is on, it tells you that the system has recognized that the elevator has been called. I also associated this with the simplest act of being alive. To survive, a child must first recognize the signal that it is hungry and indicate its recognition by some response such as crying. Noticing that something is happening and responding to it are certainly the most basic aspects of being alive and functioning.

Signal, lying in the S quadrant, is a simple act of oneness. It is also clearly sensation-driven. It says simply, "I noticed."

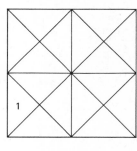

ESF ▣

Pole 2—IFS = Match. I've selected the equal sign as the symbol to denote the simple process of matching. Again let us visualize what's going on by referring to an infant.

One sensory signal alerts the child that it is hungry, a slightly different one tells it that it is full, yet a different one that it is cold, and so on. At first all these signals tell the child simply that something is going on, that it is alive and that it notices it is alive. But it does not know what to make of this barrage of information that reaches the brain. But with the matching capacity alive, the child has a means for creating some order out of the signals. It does this by relating incoming signals to past experiences. This is the first step in learning.

Experienced signals are filed in memory. With the matching function awake, the child can now compare a current signal to past experiences and determine whether it has experienced that signal before. Not only will it know now whether a signal is new or old, but it has also stumbled onto a process for sorting out different signals simply by noting that some signal was just like that one and not like any of the others. (This experience, by the way, is vital and exciting to an observant scientist—the discovery of something new.)

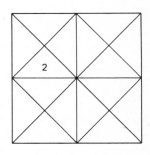

IFS =

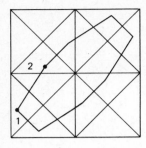

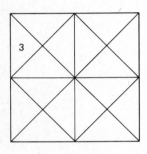

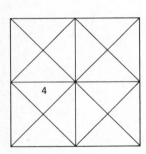

EFS $^\circ/_|$

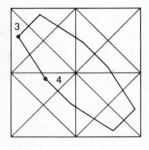

D-8

Through the matching of signals with past experiences, so typical of F types, the child evolves the capacity to identify and, through that, to prepare itself for conditioning. Hunger, crying, mother, and comfort become a connected sequence because the matching capability of signals provided a means for recognizing a structured context. It is the beginning of the awareness of context. Note that poles 1 and 2 are indeed in the C circuit.

Pole 3—EFS $^\circ/_|$ Contrast. Once signals are matched to create context, the next capacity in the hierarchy of growth is to differentiate, to recognize the difference. I chose the symbol 0 versus 1 to label this ability to dichotomize, to recognize that there are two signals—one pleasurable, one painful—and that one is the opposite of the other. Note that EFS, as with IFS, lies in the feeling function, which deals with duals (twoness). F also deals with judgments. It is the beginning process for ordering things by simply classifying a signal, an experience, and so on, as 0 or 1, or good or bad, or harmful or helpful. It is the most fundamental aspect of value and control so vital for survival. Together with matching, it provides even more power to sort things out so that signals can be discriminated and ordered.

Pole 4—ISF –□– Control. Pole 4 has already reached significant sophistication. Not only does it know the differences between opposing extremes, but it also links them together to effect a desired outcome. For a symbol, I've chosen the black box with inputs and outputs, a simple control device. Recall that for an infant the simplest task is an overwhelming, conscious challenge. The child will grab a finger if it is placed in its hand, but it cannot relax its grip. It must learn how to let go of something; that is, it must learn to direct its motor commands (an S specialty). An infant will practice such acts over and over again. It may by accident find the right ear with the right hand and has to struggle for days before it can do the same at will. Basically, control means motor control, the simple act of doing, which is typical of S.

Poles 3 and 4 involve complex processing routines. To deal with dichotomies means searching a memory file consisting of two separate and disjoint lists. Motor action, no matter how simple, involves dozens of muscles, all of which must work in proper coordination and sequence, a very complex act that Lessac calls the "organic instruction." A single organic instruction activates all the appropriate commands to a selected set of muscles. Each organic instruction, be it grasping a rattle or sticking it into the mouth, must be experienced, identified, practiced, and stored in memory for future recall. Such elaborate information-processing rightfully belongs in the D circuit, where there is time to execute the complicated sequence of events. Poles 3 and 4 are part of the D circuit.

Poles 1 through 4 form an important cluster of poles that I have called a *mode*. These four poles often work together and serve as command centers for body, or gross motor, activity. They control body movement directly and through that provide the chief vehicle for exploring the environment. When they all work together, the child seems coordinated, able to walk and climb and get into things.

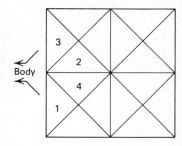

Capacities 1 through 4 are therefore also the keys to *concrete* behavior, or learning by doing. We see later that these capacities take on dominant roles in the athlete, the dancer—anyone for whom the body is the most highly developed instrument.

The Thing Mode (Poles 5, 6, 7, and 8)

Pole 5—EST ! Sign.   Note in the map of capacities that poles 5 and 1 share the ES cell. They form a pair of poles that I call a *superpole*. Therefore, poles 5 and 1 must share many attributes—be quite similar to each other—yet form a complementary contrast. In short, they must exhibit ambi-syn-anti characteristics. Signal and sign bear such a relationship to each other.

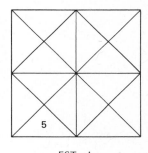

EST   !

A-5

Jung has written extensively on signs and was particularly preoccupied with the difference between signs and symbols. According to Jung, a symbol like the swastica or a cross of the church is always related to an archetype, whereas a sign is simply a label that stands for something.

A sign is thus a shorthand for something more complicated. In algebra Σ and Π are signs, and it takes chapters in a book to explain what they stand for. A hand signal to a dog to sit is also a sign and is understood by the dog just as clearly.

Note that the group of capacities 5 through 8 belongs to that attribute of the concept dichotomy which deals with *acquired* concepts and skills. It is a more complicated group of capacities, where complex skills are built out of simpler ones. In this sense signs are simply labels to bring into being a more complex set of operations. In computer language it would be equivalent to calling a subroutine by name. The job of pole 5 is to keep track of the labels. It is the librarian of complex tasks. Pole 5 is thus an efficient identifier of complex experiences, thoughts, feelings, and concepts. In terms of simulation it involves a substitution, a very quick process, appropriate for the C circuit.

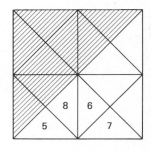

We see pole 5 in action when we hunt for a word or try to recall someone's name. It acts much like stock clerks, who must know the label before they can store or retrieve anything. If they work in a pharmacy, their whole world is labels, the identifying signs that distinguish one pill from another. Without signs the world would be utter chaos.

E-10

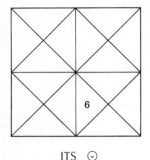

ITS ☉

○ ○ ○ ○ ○ ○ ○ ○ ○ ○
○ ○ ○ ○ ● ● ● ● ○ ○

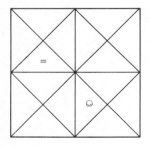

Pole 6—ITS ☉ Feature.   Shannon articulated two key concepts in information theory. One concept is that information comes in discrete binary units called "bits." A second idea is that information can be expressed as a probability, or, put another way, information is a measure of surprise. If your daughter is expecting a child on May 1 and, due to modern medicine, you know that it will be a girl and delivered by cesarean section on May 1, a telegram announcing the birth of a girl is hardly new information. The outcome was predictable.

A more concrete example is how a television screen works. The picture on the tube is generated by a series of dots sequentially energized on the screen. It is as though a machine gun were sweeping the screen, line after line, firing blanks or bullets. Each blank generates a black dot, each bullet a white one. The instruction to the gun, actually firing electrons rather than bullets, is a sequence of "on" and "off" commands.

on , on , on , on , on , on , on , on , on , on
on , on , on , on , off , off , off , off , on , on

The first line, all "ons" is not very interesting. The set of commands will simply produce a blank (white) line on the screen. If all the lines on the screen were the same, there would be no information. The second line has two points where the signal changes from "on" to "off" and from "off" to "on." These are the places where the image changes from white to black and from black to white again; that is, these signals define the edge where something is happening.

From an information point of view, the instruction set to the electron gun might have been, "In generating the next dot, always do the same as in the previous dot *unless* I send you instructions to change." This helps make the point that in image processing it is the edge where a change occurs that is rich in information; in other words, edges, recognized by contrasts (i.e., where a change occurs) are the real sources of information.

It is in this sense that I have called pole 6 *feature* and denoted it by a symbol that shows the key features of a smiling face. It is an important means for recognizing visually received images. Like matching (pole 2), it is also an identifying capacity, but one that relies on the eye rather than on past experiences.

This process can be used to produce a silhouette or just the outline of some more complex image. It is thus an example of information reduction. No one does this better than the caricaturist, whose eye is trained to select that key feature that conveys the identifying essence. With John L. Lewis it was the eyebrows; with Richard M. Nixon it was the nose and the jowls. It is in this sense that one must think of pole 6. It has the unique skill to extract the essence or key feature from a visual image.

Pole 6 is the second pole in the thing mode, just as pole 2 was the second pole in the concrete mode. And indeed poles 2 and 6 share many similarities. In fact, pole 6 can be thought of as simply a more sophisticated matching pole. It matches features instead of just signals. So it must first extract the feature. Thus ITS is an information extractor. It can extract the essential information by first reducing the amount of information it has to deal with. First it reduces a whole field to lines of contrast or edge effects. Then it extracts that subset from the simplified line image that is the key feature.

Pole 7—ETS ⋈ Sorting. Pole 7 lies in the T quadrant and deals with "many." I envision pole 7 much as a systematic, computerlike processor that can sort things through its ability to count. Fed properly preprocessed information, it can establish that it has five of these and nine of those and three of some other, and that the proper order should therefore be first 3, then 5, then 9.

ETS is thus an orderer of quantified information. It is a capacity we constantly draw on, whether we're figuring out whether to get off at the next subway stop or setting the table for dinner.

It is important to conceive of all the poles as very broad, basic capacities. The quantitative sorting specialization of pole 7 must not be too narrowly interpreted. There is, of course, no end of examples; for instance, whether to use singular or plural or how to find something in a file both involve substrate processes that involve pole 7. As it lies in the D circuit, it should not be surprising that pole 7 deals with aspects of grammar. Recall that the D circuit corresponds to the left brain hemisphere, which specializes in speech and other sequential processing activities.

Pole 8—IST ‡ Routine. By routine, I mean any fixed, ordered sequence of events, literally like a computer program. Pole 8 says, in effect, do this first, that next, and so on. Much of what we learn is routine, such as how to tie a shoelace. Just think how much practice it takes before a child regards that routine almost as a single organic instruction, which, once begun, almost automatically flows to its conclusion. Writing the letter "A" is also such a routine. With experience, routines become less complicated and so automatic that, once the routine has been initiated, we no longer need to think about it; in fact, we don't. Consider your routine in the shower. Do you really know whether you wash your left leg first or the right one? Chances are that it's always the same.

The function of pole 8 is to construct, memorize, and execute routines. It is therefore a great economizer of conscious actions and an important orderer or systematizer. Obviously, routines can be complicated and lengthy, the kind of process that is better suited for the batch processing D circuit.

Poles 5, 6, 7, and 8 also form a subset of processes that are relatively simple, yet more complex than that of poles 1, 2, 3, and 4. Poles 5 through 8, which deal with capacities such as identifying objects and

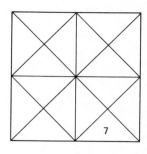

ETS ⋈

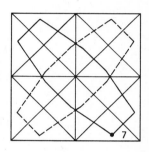

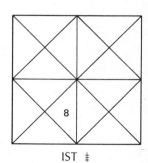

IST ‡

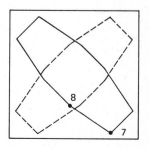

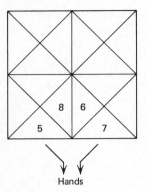

Hands

actions by labels, recognizing them, counting and executing routines, are processes that require discipline. They are learned capacities requiring much repetition, even though the capacity to learn these skills is already there or "prewired" in the brain. Subset 5 through 8 is found by the superposition of the language and concept dichotomies, which form the *prelingual* and *acquired* mode (the thing mode). Children must activate these capacities before they are ready to talk.

Before we proceed with the description of the remaining poles, let me remind you that a host of relationships must be satisfied. Every pole from 9 through 16 must exhibit some oppositional relationship to the poles already discussed. Each pole pairs up with different poles already mentioned in various ways defined by dichotomies, functions, complexity, and superpole relationships. The symbols and interpretations assigned to the poles are therefore anything but arbitrary. It is easier to digest all this interpretive information if, in thinking about these even more sophisticated poles, you refer to the relationships of the poles already discussed.

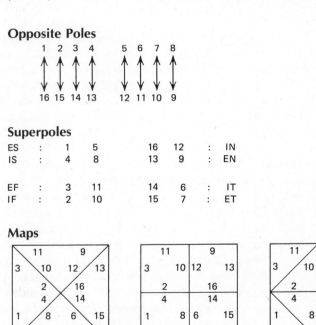

Opposite Poles

1	2	3	4		5	6	7	8
16	15	14	13		12	11	10	9

Superpoles

ES	:	1	5		16	12	:	IN
IS	:	4	8		13	9	:	EN
EF	:	3	11		14	6	:	IT
IF	:	2	10		15	7	:	ET

Maps

Modes   Functions   Superpoles

The People Mode (Poles 9, 10, 11, and 12)

Pole 9—ENF △ + □ Combination. The symbol for pole 9 was selected to suggest the combination of two dissimilar things. Combining is the key capacity for building more complex constructs and ideas from simpler ones. But the symbol is more than just combining. It suggests combining odd elements that might not normally be thought of as belonging together.

Koestler cites the marvelous example of Archimedes's breakthrough. Archimedes was preoccupied for weeks with a problem posed by the king; namely, how much gold was in his crown. One day when Archimedes stepped into the tub to take his bath, he noted how the water level rose as his body sank into the water, and he hit upon the idea of measuring volume by displacement. It is this kind of intellectual capacity to connect two apparently unconnected things that is characteristic of pole 9. Fantasies, imagination, scenarios, and possibilities are all the results of this kind of combining. It's at the root of intuition, the quadrant (N) in which pole ENF lies.

Note that pole 9 lies opposite pole 8, and note that routine is the very opposite of imagination and intuition. Pole 9 deals with the new, something not thought of before. Pole 8 deals with the old, an ordering of known things and a conditioning of old experiences. Poles 8 and 9 are opposite elements of what Jung called the perceiving functions. We see now that P can be interpreted as two ways of dealing with information, one aimed at predictability, the other at surprise. Both involve a linking, pole 8 by sequentially chaining events into a flowchart-like routine, pole 9 by linking dissimilar elements into some new meaning.

Koestler also gives a fascinating explanation of humor. Humor is an intriguing subject, and one can indeed categorize humorists by the pole they draw on most. Some build images; others' forte is to attach funny labels to common experiences; and many, such as Victor Borge, draw on pole 9 to bring together elements of differing contexts. The laugh comes always at the juncture when surprise is most strongly sensed.

Pole 9 is a very sophisticated pole, at the root of new ideas and concepts, for it deals with contexts. It is also a very quick process and entails exactly what is meant by a "flash of insight." It is a natural candidate for the C circuit.

Pole 10—IFN Harmony. IFN forms, together with pole 2 (IFS), the IF superpole. Recall that pole 2 stood for matching, symbolized by an equal sign (=). IFN is a more sophisticated matching; it deals with harmony and balance, an emotion-driven skill (F quadrant). IFN addresses the question of whether two things fit together, whether they form a pleasing pair. It is far more than saying this equals that; it says this and that balance each other, they fit, they harmonize. It is a value judgment—not categorized by merely pain or pleasure—but a value judgment of a bigger whole.

As to opposition, recall that pole 7 lies opposite pole 10. Pole 7 was the sorting pole. It reached a judgment by counting, that is, it makes a *quantitative* value judgment, saying that this is more than that. Pole 10

D-6

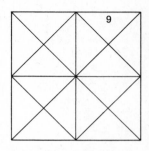

ENF △ + □

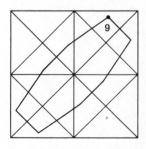

8	9
‡	△ + □
Old	New
Predict	Surprise

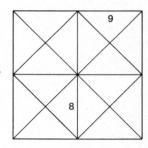

‡ versus △ + □

9 in C circuit

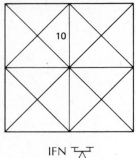

IFN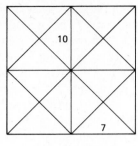

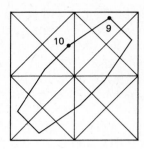

IFN ⊥̄△ versus ⋈

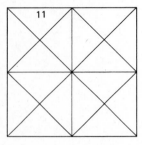

EFN ∽

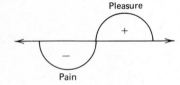

Pleasure

+

−

Pain

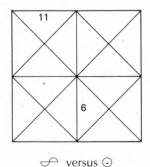

∽ versus ⊙

makes a *qualitative* value judgment; it says that this goes better with that; I like this better.

Pole 10 works closely with pole 9, since they are adjacent poles in the same (C) circuit. I have a great deal more to say about this powerful cooperation of the "combining" pole 9 and the "harmonizing" pole 10. As we shall see when we interpret transactions, it is the harmonizing of combinations that creates music and poetry.

Pole 11—EFN ∽ Preference. EFN also lies in the F quadrant and therefore has to do with value judgments. It is also the more sophisticated half of the superpole EF, whose other half is pole 3, EFS. Recall that pole 3 dealt with contrasting, basically sorting things out as either pleasurable or painful. EFN works similarly, but it can deal with gradations of pain and pleasure. Its world is not merely black and white but a continuous spectrum of dark and light gray. It is a more sophisticated way of making choices because vastly more information is being processed. The symbol is meant to represent a wave going from all bad, through sort of bad, to neutral, to sort of good, to marvelous.

It is useful to contrast EFN with its opposite pole 6, ITS. ITS, the feature (⊙) pole, scans ordered and disordered bit strings to extract the crucial information. EFN scans all information and orders it along a spectrum from unacceptable to ideal. In short, it places relative values on information, which is more properly called *preference*.

Pole 12—INF ⊚ Association. Pole 12 is crucial to language. Like pole 9, it is a pole in the intuitive quadrant and also concerned with combinations, but with combinations as associations. It basically looks for what two different things might have in common.

The symbol associated with pole 12 is called a Venn diagram, a tool used in set theory. It is a diagrammatic way of indicating certain characteristics of subsets. For those unfamiliar with Venn diagrams, let me elaborate a bit. Consider, for example, the members of some college outing club. Let us say half of them are freshmen and half of them are women. We might let one circle stand for all the freshmen and the other

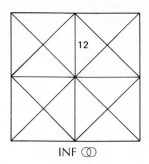

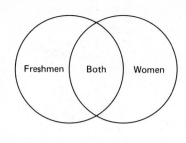

INF ⓪⓪

for all the women. The region where the two circles overlap, the intersection, identifies those club members who are both freshmen and women. That subset identified by the intersection shares two attributes and points out that there is an association between freshmen and women.

Words also share attributes. Mother and love have something to do with each other. In fact, we extract meaning from a word by detecting associations with other words. This is what underlies the construction of a thesaurus.

The INF pole deals largely with symbols. Words are, of course, also symbols. The main job of this pole is to keep track of associative relationships—that is, to assign words to sets, which include other words as well. The meaning of a word is then extracted from these set associative relationships.

Let me give just one example to make the connection between sets, associations, and meanings clear. Early in a child's linguistic development, words are largely labels (signs) that stand for objects. This is why children learn nouns first. The child may have a dog at home and learns to label it as Fido. Later, the child may point to another dog and call it Fido, only to learn that it is called Poo, which is another doggie. Then, on some subsequent trip to the zoo, the child may point at a goat and call it doggie. Ultimately, the child learns that there is a large superset called animal. A subset of it is called dogs, and that subset contains subsets of poodles, terriers, and so on, with names like Fido and Poo. This is a simple example of how we learn the meanings of things through associative connections. This sophisticated task is handled by pole 12, a pole in the D circuit dealing with speech.

It should not be surprising that the opposite of pole 12 is the sign (!) pole 5. Again, both fall in the P functions, which deal with information but tackle very different aspects. Pole 5 is more like a dictionary; it keeps track of the labels. Pole 12, like a thesaurus, worries about what these labels mean through associations with other labels.

Poles 9 through 12 should be regarded as a group. Working together and being in themselves very sophisticated, they are especially powerful in any linguistic context. There is only one level of complexity beyond these, the last four poles to be described.

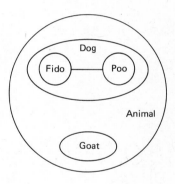

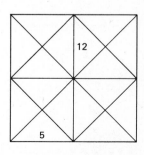

! versus ⓪⓪

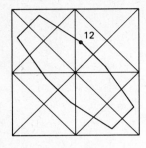

12 in D circuit

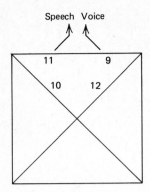

Speech   Voice

11   9
10   12

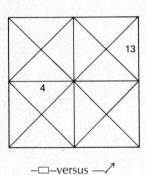

ENT —↗

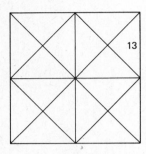

—□—versus —↗

ITN #

The Abstract Mode (Poles 13, 14, 15, and 16)

Pole 13—ENT —↗ Strategy.   ENT is the other pole of the EN superpole. As is true with ENF, ENT also deals with combining, the generation of possibilities out of odd elements, but ENT links them into a sequence that constitutes a plan of action or *strategy*.

ENT belongs to that group of abstract poles which copes with making complexity manageable. Conceiving a strategy for dealing with such complex tasks is what ENT specializes in. It is also an attempt to control, just as its opposite, pole 4, does, but on a vastly more sophisticated plane. In computer jargon one might say that ISF (pole 4) is like a statement, a line of code, a single control instruction. ENT is more like "top-down design" for a very complex programming task.

There is also something unique about the strategies ENT generates, as though it were throwing them out as trial balloons, more than willing to try some amended strategy next. It can do this quickly, being in the C circuit. One must therefore regard a strategy as simply a more complex sequence of possibilities. It is the part of consciousness that constantly plays the game of "what if." It is the mind's way of preparing for the yet unknown, the very opposite of control in the absolute sense. There are no absolutes in ENT's world, only possible schemes for proceeding. It is a key capacity for anyone entrusted with planning.

Pole 14—ITN # Pattern.   Pole 14, though it works closely with its adjacent pole 13 in the C circuit, is very different. Being in the thinking quadrant, it is logic-driven and responsive to visual stimuli. Its job is to detect patterns in a complex display of information. It is a more sophisticated way, a quantified way, of telling one thing from another, seeking identification and clarification through contrast. Its opposite, the EFS pole (pole 3), does this very simply through dichotomies, dealing with only two things at a time. ITN will take a rich *array* of information and look for differentiating criteria. Is it tall and thin or short and fat? Is it symmetrical or not? Is it a repeating pattern? In short, it tries to extract and recognize useful classifying features from a pattern. If EFS is like Boolean arithmetic, ITN is like matrix algebra.

One cannot interpret pole 14 too narrowly. Patterns exist not only in images, but also are hidden in events, in data, even in tax returns. In fact, a tax examiner uses his power of detecting abnormalities in patterns to identify suspicious returns. Patterns are the clue to order and disorder, and, in the broadest sense, ITN is thus the pole that measures the entropy of information.

This last group of poles satisfies the attributes of lingual and acquired. Such modern-day preoccupations as playing the stock market, digesting printouts of management information systems—that is, reaching decisions with data-base organized information—would be impossible without the ITN capacity. And it has to be learned.

Pole 15—ETN 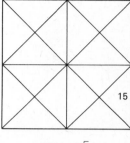 **Logic.** Nothing is more symbolic of ETN capacities than the modern digital computer. It surely is the product of people who think logically. Contrary to what some computer people think, it's just one kind of thinking capability, a very batch-oriented, detailed, logical, quantitative, complex form of decision making. But this is the specialty of ETN. It eats data and sorts them according to some logical binary schema.

ETN

As should become second nature, ETN is a close relative of ETS; both are part of the same superpole. ETS is also a sorter but far more primitive because it lacks the logical criteria for sorting. Given quantified data, ETN makes logical, rational decisions. The process is well replicated in the computer and therefore may not need further elaboration.

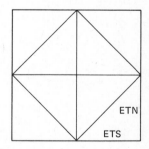

Pole 16—INT 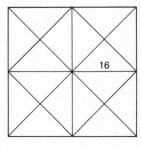 **Structure.** A structure is very abstract, but I must mention that I mean structure in the sense of gestalt, some hidden schema that gives systems form, meaning, and a framework of reality in this internal representation. Structure deals with the underlying order and connections that make the whole seem larger than the sum of its parts. It is what is behind anything complex, such as a theory in physics, a Shakespearean line, a symphony, a government, a building, a thought, an idea.

Piaget and Chomsky really deal with structures in their attempts to provide insights into psychology and linguistics. It is in this sense that INT deals with abstract concepts.

Structures are also a way of combining things, but in the sense that systems theory looks for structures that explain the relationship between elements of the system that give it a certain behavior. Gestalt is really a better word, for it suggests the underlying skeleton that gives form.

INT is a holistic capacity; it can function only when it looks at the

INT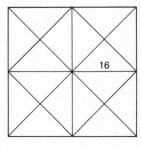
C-3, D-5

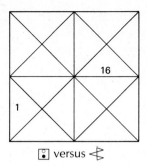

whole. It is at the opposite extreme of pole 1, the simple signal. Pole 1 says, "There is something there." Pole 16 says, "What is underneath it that makes it give out signals?"

Postscript to the Discussion of Poles

I know that words are inadequate expressions of ideas. The 16 poles are very vivid and alive to me, each one unique, each holding a predictable relationship to others. It takes time to digest the previous pages to the point that the words are no longer words, but living ideas.

Clearly, some poles will be easier for some people to understand than others. But it is important that the reader has some grasp of these specialized capacities. They are the building blocks for far more fascinating insights yet to come.

The functioning of the poles should become clearer as we go on, for we can tie them to examples all of us have observed. You may want to reread sections and use these descriptions of the poles as a dictionary.

I presented the poles in numerical order because that is the way they were ordered by the highest-level dichotomies of language and concept and because it makes looking them up easier. I could have ordered the presentations by functions; in fact, much of the preceding discussion involved functional similarities. All poles in a given function have certain

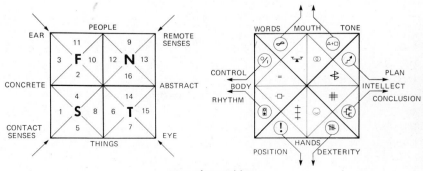

Map of capacities.

things in common. The S poles—signal and sign, control and routine—all deal with identification and motor-linked action. The N poles—combine and strategy, association and structure—deal with possibilities perceived through symbols and with linguistic concepts. The F poles—contrast and preference, match and harmony—deal with value choices and optimization, as though one were interpreting a wave form. The T poles—sort and logic, pattern and feature—deal with logical ordering and image analysis.

MEMORIES AND CLOCKS

Next, for a bit of relief, let me take an excursion into memories and clocks. It is not essential to the understanding of the model, and my original reason for addressing this component of the model was to develop the idea of computer simulation, or artificial intelligence, in some detail. I now believe that this is too great a task to cover in this basic conceptualization of the map of capacities. But again, I'm getting ahead of the story.

Any system capable of learning, any intelligent system, must have memory. The research literature gives hardly any clues as to how memory might be organized. The most frequently cited statement is that memory might be distributed, possibly in the middle layer of the cerebral cortex.

I had to make some speculative assumptions in constructing the model. My main criterion was to make allocations consistent with the model as delineated so far. Initially, I assumed that each pole had its own memory but ultimately decided that internal and external poles—for example, ESF and ISF—might share a common memory. Such memories are shown as a box between poles on the map of capacities. The connecting arrows denote that either pole can insert information into or recall information from memory.

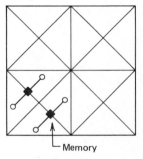

└ Memory

The key questions are: What kinds of information are held in memory, and how might the memory be organized? I give only a cursory description here.

Memories in the S Quadrant: ⇄
The symbol stands for push–pull, which suggests a basic instruction to a muscle to contract or relax. Lessac has named a complex of such instructions to a specified set of muscles an "organic instruction." Organic instructions cause motor activity: in the case of SF, body or gross motor activity; in the case of ST, mostly hand or fine motor activity.

It is easy to visualize how an instruction set that sends push–pull commands to specific muscles might be constructed. It is likely that such instruction sets have a programlike organization whereby complex move-

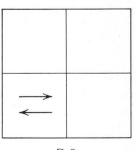

D-8

ments are assembled out of simpler instruction sets. Such an assemblage, such as to walk, would be an organic instruction. One can see in a child how laborious and highly structured the process is. Certain skills must be mastered before more complex ones can be attempted. Clearly, there is a lot of trial and error as well as feedback, a process reminiscent of program debugging.

Let me cite one specific example observed in Lydia. Lydia, barely 1 year old, was right-handed. One of the games Lydia and her mother had fallen into was to place a large earring in the shape of a big "O" over Lydia's right ear. Lydia would reach for it with her right hand, remove it, and promptly show off that she got it. One day, Lydia had a spoon in her right hand when the mother placed the earring on Lydia's right ear. Well, there was no choice except to use the left hand to retrieve the earring on the right ear. But that motor routine had not been used before. First, the left hand reached for the left ear, only to detect that such a move was false. She then tried to reach over her head, but the arm was not long enough to reach the right ear. It took lots of tries, but she finally figured it out, and this procedure became the new favorite game. When it became boring for Lydia, one could be sure that the program was debugged and stored under some organic instruction in memory. Thereafter, only the sensory stimulus on the right ear was necessary to call up the proper organic instruction.

It is worth noting that every motor sequence has to be learned by practice: how to find your mouth (perhaps one of the earliest organic instructions), how to grasp and let go, how to sit up, how to walk, how to go down steps, how to blow your nose, how to ride a bike, and so on. These are the kinds of control, routine, and identification instructions that are stored in the push–pull memories.

While I was preoccupied with symbols, I came across a marvelous handbook of them. The editors had compiled almost every reasonably standardized symbol you could think of—symbols used in mathematics and astrology, those on labels and road signs, welding symbols and map symbols, even symbols hobos use to communicate with one another. Interestingly enough, the editors made a special point to state that they had never found a symbol for push or pull. That's why I had to invent one. Perhaps push and pull are so basic that we've dropped the idea from consciousness.

E-4

Memories in the F Quadrant: ≈
I've invented another symbol to describe what goes on in the memories of the F poles. The symbol is ≈ and in colloquial language is best called *vibes*. It is meant to denote a wavelike characterization of a value. Its meanings are obvious if I give only three examples:

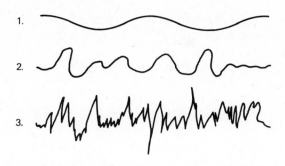

1.

2.

3.

The first wave clearly suggests something soothing, quiet, comfortable, and harmonious. The second wave is interesting, livelier, but still pleasant. The third wave form suggests irritation, chaos, erratic unpleasant disharmony. I assume that experiences are stored in memory with some such wave characterization to denote the value of the experience, to attach a perceived value to what is so aptly called vibes. Some people are better at catching vibes than others, having the ability to read the tone of a voice, to read between the lines, and to perceive the ambiance of a situation and its aesthetic content.

Beyond that, I envision F memories to be organized in two complementary memories, a kind of dual synonym—antonym organization. After all, F has a complexity index of 2. F memories can thus find opposites very easily. Good evokes bad, large evokes small, as has been amply demonstrated in association tests.

Memories in the T Quadrant: ⊕

I envision the T memory as a matrix structure symbolically represented by ⊕ . The T memory deals with images and sortings, and therefore it seems reasonable to envision some reference grid and assume that all information is classified by references in that grid. Large would mean distant from the origin. Small would be close to the origin of the Cartesian axes. Equalities and similarities, even scaling, could be easily determined.

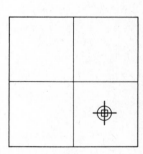

Memories in the N Quadrant: ☯

Last, I must explain the N memories. I envision the organizational basis of this memory to be symbols of an archetypal nature. For this reason, I've used the ancient symbol of the yin-yang to identify the character of the memories.

As suggested earlier, I envision the organization of this memory as a complex Venn diagram, where every entry in memory has a number of archetypal symbols such as ○, ∘, △, □, +, and ⊶ associated with it. Each archetypal symbol points to a large associative set, and several symbols

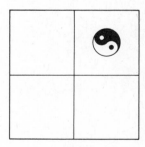

indicate intersections of sets. Such an organization seems ideal for poles whose functions specialize in meanings, abstract concepts, and new ideas.

You can become aware of some such functioning when you are looking for a word on the tip of your tongue. It's like rummaging through an identified subset. A very similar process occurs when you see someone on the street, and you know you know the person but can't place him. So again you rummage through possible associations of where you last saw him: was it in church, or in the grocery store, or at Antonella's party? Clearly, the structure of such a multifaceted organization for poles with a complexity index of infinity is more complex. But the combinatorial nature of sets permits tremendous richness with few variables. The possible classifications behave as power sets, that is, as 2^n. With only 10 symbols, over 1000 unique classifications are possible.

One more symbol deserves comment.

Clocks:

There is something archetypal about the overall form and symmetry of the entire map of capacities. I thought I constructed it strictly out of logical and pedagogical considerations. But who knows what hidden forces which are the true masters of our creations, lie in the unconscious? Something very basic is clearly at work.

For instance, it was pointed out to me on more than one occasion that the map bears an uncanny structural resemblance to the format of astrological charts used in the south of India. There have also been many who have said, for reasons they themselves do not comprehend, that there ought to be something in the center. One student, Michael Aigen, actually wrote a paper on the subject, suggesting that the center must be the soul, some godlike force. This reminded me of some fascinating references that at the time seemed too wildly unscientific, though fascinating, to be useful.

One of these, the article in "Fields within Fields within Fields," ingeniously linked brain waves, time, and God into a single conceptual framework. This triggered the idea that, as in the heart of every computer, the map too needs a clock. The symbol in the center is there as a reference to the absolute time of the D circuit, and the rate acumen of the C circuit is symbolized by the pendulum's ticking.

So much for memories and clocks. With them, we have all the pieces of the map of capacities: a field, functions and cells, a basic orientation provided by dichotomies, poles, memories, inputs, and outputs. All that remains is that we put it all together; we must now delineate the connecting circuitry that permits information to flow in specified paths.

F-1

E-5

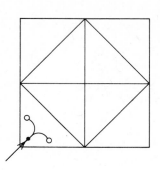 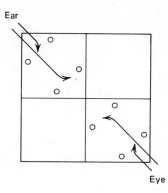 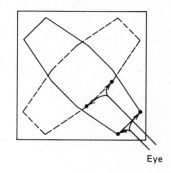

Ear

Eye

Eye

CONNECTING INPUTS AND OUTPUTS TO THE 16-POLE MODEL

Inputs

All inputs carry information from the external environment to a circle at the center of each superpole. The circle represents a preprocessor that directs transformed bits of information to each pole for further processing. In the model eyes and ears have been assumed to be an opposing pair, with eye inputs connecting to the T poles and ear inputs connecting to the F poles. We mentioned earlier that both visual and auditory information carry a D and a C component, so these components must be directed to appropriate poles. Detailed visual information is directed to poles 7 and 15 for sorting and logical processing. Contextual visual information—spatial relationships of a large field—are sent to poles 6 and 14 for feature recognition and pattern analysis.

A similar specialization effect occurs with auditory inputs. Detailed auditory signals, consisting largely of speech content—that is, consonants—are sent to poles 3 and 11 for initial dichotomous sorting. Tonal auditory signals, like inflection and emphasis and interval timing, are directed to poles 2 and 10 for value matching.

In a similar way the contact senses of touch and taste are sorted out according to detail and context and sent respectively to poles 4 and 8 for D information and to poles 1 and 5 for C information. These sensory inputs provide important information for identification and motor feedback, respectively.

Lastly, the remote sensory inputs involving smell and a possible sixth sense, some acute perceptive skill to read vibes, are connected to poles 9 and 13 and to poles 12 and 16 for interpretive analysis—that is, to suggest associations or combinations.

The preprocessing can play a significant role. It is known, from detailed studies of the frog's eye, for example, that considerable data processing,

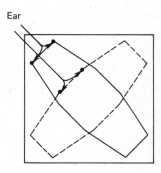

Ear

Remote senses

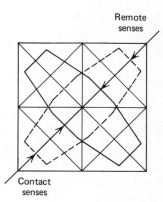

Contact senses

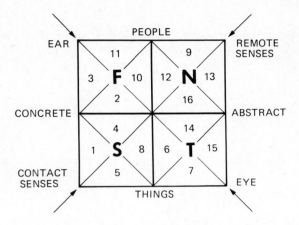

through suppressor and reinforcer perceptrons, occurs before signals reach the brain. An example would be what I postulate as an "express flag." It identifies selected incoming information as emergencies for survival and sets switches for quick action. For instance, something flying toward your eye triggers an immediate action to close the eyes, bypassing any complex analysis of the information. The express flag says, in effect, "Don't bother to analyze what is flying into your eye, just protect yourself." The instinctive scare reaction when we hear a sudden sharp noise may or may not be explainable in such a way, for instincts may involve other parts of the brain as well.

One way of testing whether the assignments of inputs to poles is reasonable is to examine the functioning of the model if a blind or deaf person (or both) were to be simulated by the model. Such an analysis would involve other parts of the circuitry not yet discussed, but the outcome is affirmative.

Outputs

The output connections (see the completed map of capacities after the next section on internal circuitry) were largely dictated by the orientation of the map and served as a dramatic example of ambi-syn-anti, for the juxtaposition of outputs is such that C and D poles always contribute as an opposing and complementary pair. There are four such output pairings with dichotomous orientations; body to the left, mind (intellect) to the right, hands toward the bottom, and mouth (speech) to the top.

The D component of the body output comes from pole 3 and gives precision and control to body movement. The C component of body output emanates from pole 1 and contributes to body rhythm. The two combine to provide body coordination. Anyone who has played golf, danced, or bowled knows how crucial both components are. In most

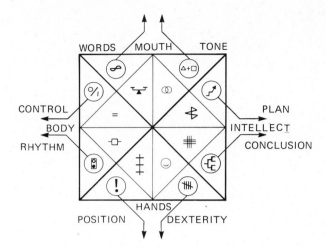

amateurs one or the other is stronger, so they may have a beautiful golf swing but are poor on the putting green or vice versa.

Opposed to the body is the mind, with two intellectual outputs: a conclusion emanating from the logical D pole 15 and a plan emanating from the strategy C pole 13. Both are needed for intellectual work, and mathematicians and chess players know only too well that it's faulty outputs in one or the other that may do them in. Either they don't see their way through the problem well enough, a planning output, or they fall into false logic, an improper conclusion.

The complementarity of hands manifests itself as dexterity and positioning skill. Positioning, or the directives to orient and place the hand properly in three-dimensional space, comes through pole 5, a pole in the C circuit. Dexterity, which involves a very detailed set of motor activities, emanates from pole 7 in the D circuit. The hands work together on most tasks yet do very different things in ambi-syn-anti fashion. Whether you hammer a nail, tighten a bolt, cut a piece of wood, or write on a pad, one hand tends to holding and positioning and the other tends to manipulating.

By output of the mouth, I mean the production of voice as in speaking and singing. Voice, or, better, what Lessac calls "vocal life," also has two components. One is produced by the shape of the sound chamber, the shaping of the mouth cavity through the control of facial muscles, involving jaw, lips, and tongue. These contribute to articulation, the production of "t" and "s" sounds, for example. There is also a resonant component that produces a tonal quality. The first effect is emitted by the D pole 11, the second by the C pole 9. Both are involved in speech. In fact, as we shall see, both also involve the adjacent regions of the body and the mind. Only the hands play no direct role in the production of speech. Rather, they form a separate language (body language), usually

D-9

anticipating vocal speech. (More is said about this in the discussion of the manifestations of the conscious and the unconscious.)

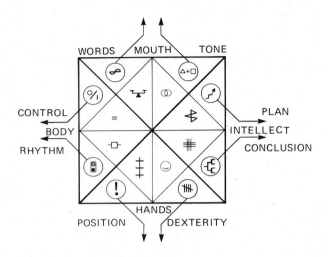

INTERNAL CIRCUITRY DERIVED FROM A COMPETITION–COOPERATION MODEL

In the eight-pole model, all the detailed superpoles must be tied together through a D circuit, and all the contextual poles tied together in a C circuit. The link between adjacent poles in a specific circuit was called a *transaction*.

However, it is not at once obvious what the internal connections of the more complicated 16-pole model should be. I developed a matrix to answer that question rationally and systematically. It explores the interrelationships of the poles on the basis of competition and cooperation.

The matrix shows aspects that are at play in any political situation. Consider, for instance, a committee of the Senate addressing a legislative issue. It is likely that the senators are divided on a number of issues. Should the program be self-supporting or financed with taxes? Should legislation favor the poor or apply across the board? Should it be implemented through existing free-enterprise systems or through a government agency? Furthermore, not all these issues carry equal strength. One senator may yield on some issues but not on others.

But politics is a collective process. So a given senator may want to form a coalition with other members of the committee. Who should be approached first?

It stands to reason that he will select that member who shares most of his views, especially those views on which he does not plan to compro-

TRANSACTION (T)
CROSSLINK (X)
MODE LINK (M)
LOOK AHEAD (L)

		00--				01--				10--				11--					T X M L
		00	01	10	11	00	01	10	11	00	01	10	11	00	01	10	11		
		1	2	3	4	5	6	7	8	9	10	11	12	13	14	15	16⁻		
00	00 1																	1	2,3,5,9
	01 2																	2	1,4,10,6
	10 3																	3	4,1,11,7
	11 4																	4	3,2,8,12
01	00 5																	5	6,7,1,13
	01 6																	6	5,8,14,2
	10 7																	7	8,5,15,3
	11 8																	8	7,6,4,16
10	00 9																	9	10,11,13,1
	01 10																	10	9,12,2,14
	10 11																	11	12,9,3,15
	11 12																	12	11,10,16,4
11	00 13																	13	14,15,9,5
	01 14																	14	13,16,6,10
	10 15																	15	16,13,7,11
	11 16																	16	15,14,12,8

Cooperation/competition matrix.

mise. The two together can then decide who else to bring into their confidence.

The matrix represents a systematic way of doing exactly the same thing. The players are poles, not senators. The issues are attributes of dichotomies; the strength of an issue is reflected by the level of the hierarchically ordered dichotomies. All this information is contained in the binary code for each pole, which was determined from the dichotomous tree structure. The matrix simply compares each pole to every other pole and notes the extent and level of agreement (basis for cooperation) and extent and level of opposition (basis for competition). For instance, pole 1, represented by 0000, has nothing in common with pole 16, represented by 1111. They are, in fact, in total disagreement on every issue and therefore in opposition to one another. But pole 1, 0000, and pole 2, 0001, share

x = disagree
y = agree

0000
1111
xxxx

0000
0001
yyyx

97

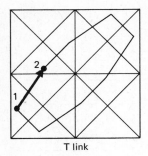

T link

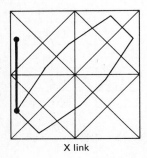

X link

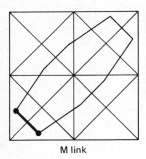

M link

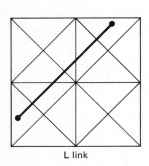

L link

the same attributes of the first three dichotomies; they have a great deal in common. It is this commonality that binds them together and makes it natural to establish close communication.

In the matrix I have singled out those combinations of poles that share three of four attributes. Interestingly enough, they always bear the same relative relationships to each other on the map of capacities. I have therefore given these linkages names.

I have labeled the two strongest links T and X. Poles in both links share the two highest-level attributes, and, in addition, T-linked poles always share the third-level attribute and X-linked poles always share the fourth-level attribute. *Both T and X always fall within the same mode.*

T stands for *transaction* and links a pole to its nearest neighbor in the same mode and in the same circuit (C or D). For the example of pole 1, the transaction is the connection from pole 1 to pole 2.

X stands for *crosslink* and identifies the link to the nearest pole in the same mode and with the same attitude (extrovert or introvert) but in the opposite circuit. In the example shown it would be the link from pole 1 to pole 3.

The other two links have been labeled M and L. Poles in both links share the two lowest-level attributes and one other. *Both M and L always link a pole in a given mode to a pole in an adjacent or opposite mode.*

M stands for *mode* link. It connects the given pole to the other half of the same superpole but lying in the adjacent mode.

L stands for *look ahead* and is a kind of spy in the midst of the opposition. The look ahead is always linked to the pole in the same circuit, on the same side of the diagonal (language or concept dichotomy) on the map, and with the same attitude (extrovert or introvert). It is, relatively speaking, the weakest link and is, primarily for reasons of readability, not shown on the map of capacities.

The T and M links serve as the main channels for information flow through the C and D circuits. The X and L links serve as feedback channels suppressing interfering information flows or not suppressing information flows that provide complementary or reinforcing capabilities.

There is one more link of interest that I call the *memory* link. It is

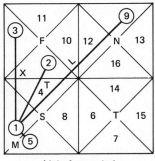

Links from pole 1

weaker than the previous four in that it shares only two attributes, those of the first two dichotomies (language and concept). For pole 1, it is the link to pole 4.

In this fashion all the linkages for all the poles can be explored and mapped. This has been done on the complete map. *The transactions and mode links combine to form the C and D circuits. The crosslinks combine to form the interconnections between the circuits* and play the vital role of coordination through feedback.

One cannot help noticing certain similarities between this circuitry and what is called a "Wheatstone bridge" in electrical engineering. The analogy to circuits is unavoidable in other respects. For any given pole, the links act as vectors; that is, they have a direction, as though current were flowing from one pole to another, driven by a difference in potential between poles. We shall see that this potential is analogous to the term "libido" as used by Jung, who defined it as psychic energy. (More is said about this later.)

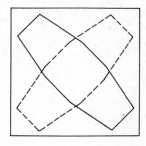

A-4

GLIMPSE

I know how boring it is to read about 9 linked to 10 and how meaningless that seems. It reminds us of assembly-line workers putting together a television set or an electrician splicing a ruptured cable. What a tedious job!

But hating the details of connections or linkages does not diminish their importance. Just think how upset you are when the telephone is dead, or the light won't go on when you flick the switch, or when, as is often the case with adopted children, we don't know who our parents are. The popularity of the book and television special Roots *was a marvelous example of the power of linkages, for the specification of connecting links is all a family tree is.*

Linkages are also at work when we meet someone from Istanbul and we say rather hopefully, "Do you happen to know my good friend Hizir in Istanbul?" Even though we don't know the details of the linkages, we've learned that there is a reasonable probability that we are linked through a network of acquaintances.

What is increasingly called infrastructure *is the establishment of linkages. One thinks about such things only when they're missing, such as when the transportation workers are on strike or if you want to install your color television in a developing country.*

Links may be boring, but we can hardly function without them. If we really want to understand how we function, then we must make the effort to trace the linkages.

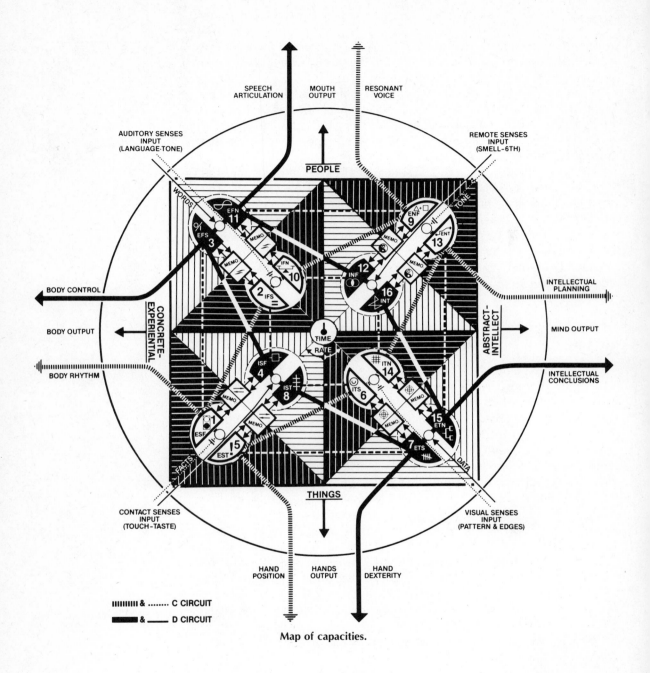

Map of capacities.

POSTSCRIPT

The construction of the map of capacities is now complete. We have identified the pieces and how they are organized. The result is a map of 16 poles, tied into a complex network, with inputs and outputs communicating with the external environment. The map also has a defined orientation. I urge you to review the completed map of capacities in view of the explanation of it as covered in this chapter. To fully appreciate the map's power one must develop a feel for the interrelationships among poles.

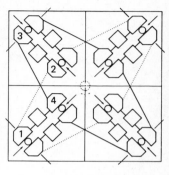

The map is as yet static. Not until we define differentiated libido—that is, differences in the strength of poles—can we envision the system as a dynamic flow of information through the network. We define these differences through personality profiles. I envision what I call a profile as an overlay on the map of capacities that brings out the dynamic aspects of the (information) system.

We now begin to breathe life into the map.

8

TRANSACTIONS AND
THEIR INTERPRETATIONS

In this chapter you gain insight into how the symbols can be used to extract interpretive meanings. The technique of constructing symbolic sentences serves as a first glimpse at personality differences and the coupling of capacities with professions. Some may find this chapter tedious, for it cannot be read easily like a novel. You may therefore choose to skim the chapter now to get the essential ideas and come back to it later, using it as a reference manual.

We'll be talking increasingly about the incredible diversity of people, which, after all, makes each of us a unique individual never totally known to others and not always known to ourselves. This mystery of who am I and who is he or she is, in many ways, the greatest game we play and is an unending topic for poets and philosophers.

Psychology deals with this subject, but this is not a book about psychology. This is a book grounded in systems science, a field basically concerned with order. Our approach is thus not rooted so much in psychological theory as in discovering whatever order there might be in diversity. The tool for uncovering such order is the map of capacities.

The model contains 16 possible transactions (from 1 to 2, from 2 to 1, from 3 to 4, from 4 to 3, etc.). Each can be equated to an identifiable human skill. One objective of this chapter is to develop a logical methodology for interpreting each transaction and thus become familiar with these 16 basic building blocks of human skills. The labels chosen for the transactions suggest an occupational association. They also form natural groups and pairs.

A transaction always involves two poles in the same mode (concrete, abstract, people, or things) and in the same circuit (C or D). Because of the nature of the circuits, one of the poles is always an external pole, and the other an internal pole. One of these two poles is always the more energetic pole (the driver pole) and thus acts as the information *source*, or the supplier of data to be processed. The relatively weaker pole (the characteristic pole) of the pair serves as the *processor* of information. A transaction thus consists of two poles and a link, with information flowing from the data pole to the processor pole. This flow is identified by placing an arrow on the link near the processor pole and directed toward it. If the arrow suggests an information flow into an internal pole, we call the transaction *introverted*. The reverse flow is called an *extroverted* transaction.

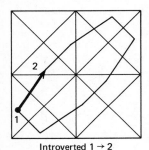

Introverted 1 → 2

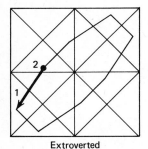

Extroverted
2 → 1

One transaction dominates because it is the most natural and competent and the preferred one. This is certainly true in mature, well-individuated personalities. This most dominant transaction characterizes that whole personality so definitively that I have called this transaction the characteristic transaction for that profile. Since there are 16 transactions, we can expect to derive 16 profiles from the model.

Recall that I had concluded that observable personality traits in a given individual are more like the characteristics of the processor pole, even though the data pole has the greater energy (libido). This implies that our nature is revealed more by how we do things than by what we deal with. I therefore also referred to the processor pole as the *characteristic* pole. It is characteristic of our nature.

Because of its importance, each characteristic transaction has a name in addition to its numerical notation. The name of the characteristic transaction also serves as the name of the profile associated with it.

Further, the name of the characteristic pole is used together with the circuit (C or D) in which it lies as the profile or characteristic transaction name.

For example, if 1 → 2 is the characteristic transaction, we will single out the processing pole, 2, and note that its name is IFS. Transaction 1 → 2 is in the C circuit. We combine these two labels into CIFS, the name of the characteristic transaction for 1 → 2. Thus a profile name always identifies both the circuit (C or D, or style) and the characteristic (processing) pole.

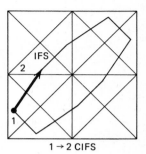

1 → 2 CIFS

Transaction Interpretation (Prelingual)

Transaction		Verb		Noun
1 → 2	2 =	to match to equate	1 ⊡	the signal the cue the sensory feedback the touch the kinesthetic perception
2 → 1	1 ⊡	to signal to alert to notice to sense to accept	2 =	the match the likeness the duplicate the equality the synonym
3 → 4	4 —□—	to control to do to link to effect to execute	3 °/₁	the opposite the negation the antonym
4 → 3	3 °/₁	to dichotomize to contrast to categorize to oppose to negate to counter to judge to like or dislike	4 —□—	the control the action the motion
5 → 6	6 ⊙	to recognize to differentiate to contrast to capture	5 !	the sign the label the identifier
6 → 5	5 !	to identify to label to sign	6 ⊙	the caricature the feature the contrast the characteristic the visual essence
7 → 8	8 ‡	to systematize to codify to make routine to temporally order to list to organize	7 ₪	the sorting the count the number the quantity the order the elements
8 → 7	7 ₪	to sort to itemize to count to order	8 ‡	the routine the schema the program the sequence

THE STATIC MODEL:
THE MAP OF CAPACITIES

Transaction Interpretation (Lingual)

Transaction	Verb	Noun
9 → 10	10 — to harmonize / to balance / to weigh / to empathize / to feel	9 — △ + □ — the possibility / the scenario / the fantasy / the worry / the guess
10 → 9	9 — △ + □ — to combine / to envision / to imagine / to guess / to intuit / to fantasize / to compose / to assume	10 — the balance / the harmony / the disharmony / the esthetics
11 → 12	12 — ⊕ — to associate / to relate / to mean / to interpret / to imbue	11 — the preference / the selection / the choice / the quality
12 → 11	11 — to prefer / to select / to choose / to evaluate	12 — ⊕ — the association / the meaning / the set intersection / the semantics
13 → 14	14 — ⊞ — to pattern / to recognize / to see / to characterize / to imagine / to arrange / to design / to spatially organize	13 — the strategy / the plan / the sequence
14 → 13	13 — to strategize / to plan	14 — ⊞ — the pattern / the image / the clue / the regularity / the shape / the feature / the theme / the arrangement / the spatial relationship / the regularity / the idea
15 → 16	16 — to structure / to construct / to conceptualize / to theorize	15 — the logic / the syntax / the reasoning / the decision / the order
16 → 15	15 — to logically order / to reason / to decide / to evaluate / to compare	16 — the structure / the gestalt / the concept / the essence

The profile name also gives the attitude of the profile. In the example CIFS, it is introverted. It also identifies the first auxiliary function (F for CIFS) and the superior function (S for CIFS), in that order. Lastly, it identifies the concrete mode, since it contains the functions S and F.

Let us review this with one more example, DETN. It identifies a particular profile whose characteristic transaction has ETN (pole 15) as its characteristic or processing pole. It is a transaction in the D circuit and must therefore be the transaction 16 → 15. Since the end number 15 is odd, this must be an extroverted transaction. This is also evident from its name (DETN). Pole 16 lies in the N function; pole 15 lies in the T function. Thus the transaction is in the abstract mode (T and N). But we also know now that the flow is from 16 to 15 (16 → 15), or from N to T. Sixteen is therefore the pole with the higher libido (potential) and is in the superior function N. Pole 15 thus lies in the first auxiliary function (T).

The notation scheme is therefore very rich in information and works as described for all characteristic transactions or profiles.

A linguistic algorithm is used to interpret the meaning of a transaction. The data pole is regarded as a noun, for it identifies the subject of what is being processed. The processor pole is taken as a verb to describe the action process performed on the data.

The previous table lists such interpretive phrases for all 16 transactions. This is followed by a more detailed discussion of each of the transactions starting with DETN, 16 → 15.

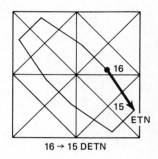

16 → 15 DETN

Transaction 16 → 15—Analyst (DETN). Consider transaction 16 → 15. Note that the information flows from pole 16 to pole 15. Pole 16 is therefore the data pole and pole 15 is the processor pole. Now let us identify the poles:

From pole 16: INT, structure ⦀.
To pole 15: ETN, logic, ⦀.

Note that the transaction is to an external pole and is therefore extroverted. Also note that pole 16, the data pole, is to be treated as a noun and pole 15, the processor pole, as a verb. We can therefore construct the simple phrase, "to logically sort a structure."

You will notice that I had to take some liberties in constructing the phrase since logic is not a verb. The phrase should really have been, "to ⦀ the ⦀," where the symbols are shorthand for richer descriptions of the poles. Translating ⦀ as a verb could therefore have been "to logically sort" or "to process logically" or any such verb phrases that do justice to the functioning of pole 15. The translation for ⦀ as a noun could also have been gestalt, concepts, and the like.

The translation process is therefore not a matter of pure substitution but one of catching the essence of what the two poles do in their verb and noun relationships. It is inevitable that a sentence so constructed will always seem very abstract and general. This must be so, for the description must cover a large class of specific skills. It is therefore useful to reflect

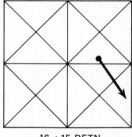

16 → 15 DETN

on the constructed sentence to search for a more meaningful term that characterizes the particular transaction.

To logically sort structures or to logically process concepts or interrelated information bits, where the information provided consists of structured concepts, is captured by the word *analysis*. "To analyze" really means to apply logic to structured data and ideas. We see then that transaction 16 → 15 could be labeled as that skill which deals with analysis or diagnosis. It is the skill used by scientists, lawyers, physicians, and so on, when they analyze or diagnose a situation. Analysis is a very sophisticated skill, which is not surprising when one considers the hierarchical position of the poles. Analysis requires linguistic (lingual) ability and discipline (acquired) to master. It is an extroverted activity. People who are interested in analysis or diagnostics tend to focus on the external world, be it the patient or the scientific data.

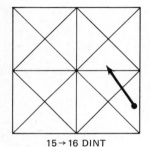

15 → 16 DINT

Transaction 15→16 —Conceptualizer (DINT). The methodology should become increasingly clear as we go through the translation process for all the transactions. Let us next consider the reverse process, 15 → 16. Here logic pole 15 provides the data, and concept pole 16 does the processing. The translation algorithm is thus "to $\nleqslant$ the $\dashv_{\mathsf{E}}^{\mathsf{E}}$," which in words could be "to structure logically sorted information" or "to find a structure that makes sense out of logically sorted data or information." This introverted process is well described by the word "conceptualize," which I use as a name for transaction 15 →16.

Notice that pole 16 is an internal pole, which is bound to do something subjective—that is, process so as to reflect the internal state of the subject. But it deals with external data supplied by pole 15. The inputs to pole 15 are visual and detailed. Consequently, the conceptualizing is likely to involve visual information-processing, the kind of activity typical of an architect or a physicist to whom visual images are powerful tools.

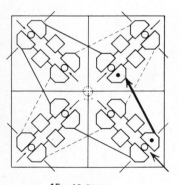

15 → 16 DINT

I shall proceed in a similar fashion with the information-processing descriptions of all the transactions, but, before I continue, I want to alert you to certain aspects.

1. The result always describes a human activity that can be identified with an occupational skill or a profession. Since I've chosen to describe the transactions in inverse hierarchical order, I discuss the intellectual (abstract) professions first. This simply reflects that poles 13, 14, 15, and 16 are part of the intellectual (abstract) mode.

2. In interpreting transactions, it is useful to note the style and attitude of the transaction. This helps fill in important interpretive information.

3. Note that the process is always the same; namely, the more energetic pole is identified as the data source and interpreted as a noun, and the other pole, the one at which the arrow points, the processor pole, is interpreted as a verb.

The Intellectual Mode

16 → 15	Analyst Extroverted Detailed batch processor
15 → 16	Conceptualizer (tends toward visual) Introverted Detailed batch processor
14 → 13	Suspector Extroverted Contextual
13 → 14	Theoretician Introverted Contextual

Elaborating on the last two transactions in this group completes the discussion of the intellectual mode.

Transaction 14 →13 —Suspector (CENT).   Note that both poles 14 and 13 are in the C circuit and that pole 13, the processor pole, is extroverted. The symbolic sentence for the transaction is "to —↗ the #" or "to strategize the pattern"—that is, to find a strategy that will help explain the pattern in the data. Loosely translated it says, "How should we proceed in light of the patterns noted?" This is an activity typical of the detective, or the suspector. Clues are of interest only if they form a pattern. The pattern in turn suggests a strategy for unraveling the mystery. This kind of skill is required not only of police detectives but also of lawyers, mathematicians, investment brokers, and football coaches. "Suspector" is used as a key word to recall the intellectual activity of formulating a plan triggered by observed patterns. It is an intellectual, intuitive process guided by observation, and is an activity highly dependent on context.

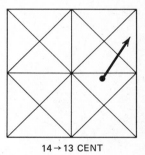

14→13 CENT

Transaction 13 →14 —Theoretician (CITN).   Transaction 13 → 14 is the reverse of transaction 14 →13 and can be translated as "to # the —↗" or "to find the pattern given strategies." The phrase suggests a search for some regularity that explains a particular sequence of events. It means coming up with a theory, some internally imagined pattern that unifies the occurrence of certain possibilities. It is an internalized, abstract, intellectual activity.

The descriptions given may at first seem confusing because the differences among the four transactions in the intellectual mode seem relatively small, and indeed there are tremendous similarities among them. That is the way it should be, for these four transactions belong to one mode and therefore bear an ambi-syn-anti relationship to one another. They tend to complement one another.

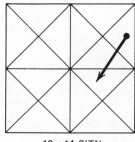

13→14 CITN

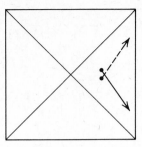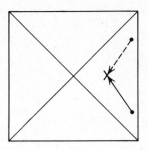

Consequently, the two extroverted transactions, the analyst and the suspector, are two sides of a coin, both concerned with problem solving. The two introverted transactions, the conceptualizer and the theoretician, also form a complementary pair in service of understanding. Note also that these pairs consist of one detailed and one contextual transactions, but both have the same attitude. This same pattern will be apparent in the subsequent modal groups of transactions.

THE VERBAL MODE

The verbal group consists of the four transactions that lie in the people-oriented mode:

12 → 11	Verbalist
11 → 12	Critic
10 → 9	Perceiver
9 → 10	Composer

Transaction 12 →11 —Verbalist (DEFN).

Extroverted
Detailed
"to ↜ the ⟨⟨⟩⟩"

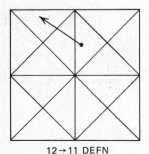

12→11 DEFN

This can be translated into words to say "to prefer the meanings" or "to select the best word to express what you mean to say" or, in short, "to express," "to be articulate."

This is a typical example of a detailed transaction. It presumes that a thought connected to meanings exists and that the job is to find the best words so the thought can be articulated. It is conscious speech formulation where the emphasis is on conveying information content. It is a people-oriented activity, or at least one directed at people. This process is vital to the orator, lecturer, actor, preacher, diplomat, writer, editor—to anyone involved in an activity where effective expression is important.

This transaction has some peculiar overtones stemming from the fact that what matters here is not what is said but *how* it is said; that is, the focus is not on concepts but on expression. This is what made me choose verbalist as the label. A really great verbalist (orator) can make something trivial sound meaningful. It deals simply with the skill of choosing words to convey a meaning irrespective of the value of the meaning. Perhaps it should be described as verbal dexterity, which is so important to speech writers, phrase-makers, and spokespersons. Have you ever listened to briefings by State department representatives? They are very conscious of word selection and say no more than they intend to convey.

The verbalist transaction is therefore basic to speech. It is the transaction that generates a carefully selected string of words. It is interested in effects and communicative results and thus is typically extroverted. The transaction typifies people who would rather speak than listen.

GLIMPSE

I don't mind sharing an embarrassment with you. We are a loud family. At the dinner table everyone tends to talk at once, and at times it is frustrating to try to tell a story.

We didn't really know that. Each one just started talking louder than the next, and occasionally accusations flew across the table that someone was interrupting all the time. My wife seemed to be particularly guilty, though she denied it.

One day, when one of my sons brought home a new tape recorder, we decided to hide it under the table and settle the argument once and for all. We then told my wife what we had done and that its aim was to prove to her how she was always interrupting. So we gathered around to listen to what had just transpired. Guess what? It was I who did most of the interrupting, but no one was flawless. We're just a family of mostly talkers, as the profiles point out very clearly.

This is not a rarity. Recently I was asked to analyze a working group in industry. There were nine people in all, eight talkers and one listener, who was the manager of the group. That insight alone explained a lot.

Transaction 11 →12 —Critic (DINF).

Introverted
Detailed
"To ⓪ the ⌒ "

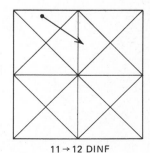

11 → 12 DINF

This means to extract the right associations and therefore meanings from expressed preferences or carefully chosen words. The reverse transaction of 12 → 11 is introverted and indicates a far more careful listener than speaker. Transaction 11 → 12 emphasizes extracting meaning from a carefully selected string of words with preferential overtones. It involves very astute, critical listening, with exacting interpretation that notes the differences in meanings in words like lied, falsified, distorted, misinterpreted, and misunderstood. The exacting nature is typical of detailed transactions.

It may be helpful to mention that this transaction is vital to a host of professionals, including speech therapists, voice coaches, theater critics, political analysts, interviewers, copy editors and opera singers. The transaction typifies those who would rather listen than speak.

Transaction 10 →9 —Perceiver (CENF).

Extroverted
Contextual
"To △ + □ the ⊤△⊤"

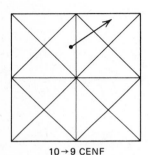

10→9 CENF

Literally this means to combine or make possible the balances or imbalances. It is a contextual skill of noting harmony and dissonance and guessing what might be behind them, reading between the lines and being perceptive. This seems an uncanny skill to many detailed people. For instance, in interviewing a very bright, attractive candidate for a job, the perceiver might vote against the applicant on the grounds that the person is an alcoholic. "How in the world did you know that?" someone might ask, and the response might be, "Well, it was written all over him." The perceiver noted aspects that were not in harmony with others and ultimately leaped to the conclusion that alcoholism could account for the dissonances that seemed out of context. As one would expect, it is a capacity that is intuitive, deals with vibes, and is strongly contextual.

The skill typified by the perceiver transaction is vital in many occupations, including business, personnel work, counseling, psychiatry, and interior decorating, to mention a few.

Transaction 9 →10 —Composer (CIFN).

Introverted
Contextual
"To ⊤△⊤ the △ + □"

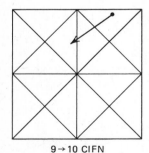

9→10 CIFN

This can be translated as "to harmonize the combinations." Transaction 9 → 10, the last of the verbal transaction group, is a contextual but introverted activity and typifies the poet and the composer. The combinations to be harmonized might be the words to form a poem, the notes to form a musical composition, or the people who, if invited to a party, would get along harmoniously. The composer transaction deals with envisioning combinations that work well together. It truly is devoted to creating balance out of combinations of possibilities.

The possibilities could be negative—that is, potential disasters—and in this sense the transaction also represents worrying. If the son of parents characterized by 9 → 10 transactions goes on a trip, for example, they immediately begin to envision combinations of misfortunes that harmonize with their fear of losing their son.

The introverted nature of this transaction also relates it strongly to spiritual values. The combination of 2 and ∞, the two complexity index numbers associated with this transaction, contributes to this. It tries to reduce the ultimate complexity of God to a simple good or bad dualism. A favorite subject of this transaction is therefore spiritual concern as opposed to religious concern. It is really fascinated by the possibilities for good and evil. The transaction is therefore typical of human sensitivity, with a warm, concerned artistic quality that comes from the preoccupation with vibes. Harmony, after all, is noted by the character of the vibes. The composer is therefore very sensitive to "vibes" and preoccupied with them.

Again, it is important to look at the complementary relationships of this group of transactions. Transactions 12 →11 and 10 → 9 form the extroverted pair. This combines the orator with the perceiver. If you think of the diplomat, you will immediately recognize the interrelationship of the two skills. The ability to perceive the situation would be a tremendously useful complement to have in order to phrase a statement, and it works the other way as well. For the skilled interviewer, a properly phrased question would contribute tremendously to perception-rich responses.

A similar complementary relationship can be expected for transactions 11 →12 and 9 →10. Critical listening helps the composing process, which is why it is so important to have music performed and poetry recited. And, conversely, an awareness of composition helps criticism. The two transactions together heighten each other's skills.

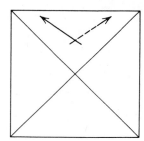 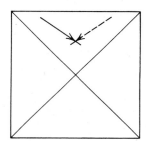

THE FINE MOTOR MODE

The four transactions in the fine motor group are:

$8 \rightarrow 7$ Implementor
Extroverted
Detailed

$7 \rightarrow 8$ Organizer
Introverted
Detailed

$6 \rightarrow 5$ Operator
Extroverted
Contextual

$5 \rightarrow 6$ Molder
Introverted
Contextual

These descriptive labels may be too narrow, but they do seem to conjure up the right images.

Transaction $8 \rightarrow 7$ —Implementor (DETS).

Extroverted
Detailed
"To ℕ the ‡ "

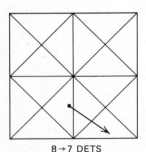

8→7 DETS

This can be translated as "to sort the routines" or "to create some order given routines." To me, this conjures up old-fashioned handbook engineers whose job is to create some ordered effect, such as designing a conveyor belt in a packing machine. Their calculations of speed, pulley sizes, stresses, and so on, are the routines they use.

But this image gives too narrow an interpretation. It might be better to emphasize the extroverted, action-oriented nature of the transaction: its dependence on pen and paper (eye–hand coordination); its detailed, orderly nature; and the requirements for discipline and preoccupation with things. So my original choice, the engineer, has been replaced by "implementor." There are managers who operate just as engineers do, even though they are dealing with people. Bureaucracies fit this transaction too.

Transaction $8 \rightarrow 7$ is the very opposite of the transaction $9 \rightarrow 10$. I call this oppositional transaction the *hidden agenda*. This is discussed further later, but right now the contrast helps clarify transaction $8 \rightarrow 7$.

Transaction 9 →10 is the composer, the transaction that looks for harmony in combinations. That is exactly what the implementor hopes to accomplish but in a different way. The skills of the implementor are such that more systematized ordering procedures must be drawn on to achieve that end. It is therefore described by the very detailed processes of routine and quantitative ordering.

Transaction 7 → 8 —Organizer (DIST).

Introverted
Detailed
"To ‡ the ⋈"

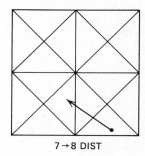

7→8 DIST

This is translatable as "to routinize the sorting" or "to systematize." Transaction 7 → 8 is an introverted activity dedicated to efficiency and order, the characteristics you hope to find in a good secretary, a good librarian, or a good bookkeeper. For some people it is extremely difficult to generate or invent routines that can handle sortings. It's an organizational, conceptual skill that every good programmer must have.

People with this systematizing and organizing skill value method as a means to an end. How things are done matters to them, not just what is done. They like order, sequential processing, neatness, and efficiency. It is as though they were saying, "I want to remove all this clutter to free myself for good perceiving," which is their hidden agenda. To them it is what's out of place that is the important focus of interest. The efficient maintenance of order is therefore essential.

The transaction is associated with all the expected attributes. It deals with things. Hands, eyes, and touch are important; it pays attention to detail. It is typical of the fine motor mode and finds outlets in activities such as filing, weaving, and office managing.

Transaction 6 → 5 —Operator (CEST).

Extroverted
Contextual
"To ! the ☉"

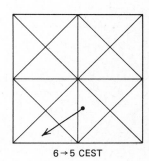

6→5 CEST

"To label the feature" is a sensation-oriented skill, preoccupied with active identification. It is a skill crucial to the surgeon, the machinist, and the automobile mechanic. Consider the surgeon as the classic example. To me, an operation is just a bloody mess; but to surgeons it is important to differentiate, to tell one nerve bundle from another, to identify this tendon, that artery, that fleshy organ. To them, it is anything but a bloody mess; it is a highly differentiated arena of contrasting elements in which they must maneuver. Identification, location, sensation, feel, touch, and control are vital stimuli for guiding the scalpel with precision. The automobile mechanic uses the same conscious skills: sensation-rich, good hand—eye coordination, and excellent sense of hand position.

Transaction 5 →6 —Molder (CITS).

Introverted
Contextual
"To ⊙ the !"

"To feature the sign" is an introverted transaction, and the information source is likely to have a rich input source, in this case from the contact senses. This information is identified—that is, labeled—and then processed to extract essential information. Although this sounds very abstract, it is in fact what the artisan, craftsman, or sculptor has to do. Sculptors and carpenters get their data from touch as their hands run over the surface of the work piece. They must sort out the signals they get to identify where the surface does not meet their expectations, where it is too rough, too thick, or not sharp enough. Only in this way do they know what actions to take next. The transaction is a tactile scanning.

The four transactions in this group most often work together in pairs, yielding hand—eye coordination skills most usefully applied to things, such as a camera. Things might even include a person, as in the case of a masseur.

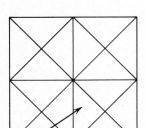

5→6 CITS

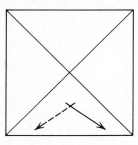

THE GROSS MOTOR MODE

The last group of transactions, the gross motor group, involves the four most basic poles. The transaction list is:

4 → 3	Classifier
	Extroverted
	Detailed
3 → 4	Follower
	Introverted
	Detailed
2 → 1	Initiator
	Extroverted
	Contextual
1 → 2	Doer
	Introverted
	Contextual

Again, the labels should not be interpreted too narrowly.

Transaction 4 →3 —Classifier (DEFS).

Extroverted
Detailed
"To °/₁ the −□−"

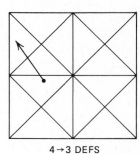

4→3 DEFS

This means "to dichotomize the control" or "to make a dichotomous choice about aspects that control a situation." In the most literal sense, control means motor control of the body. In a more generic sense, it means control of actions, which in turn influence the external world. Politicians are good examples of this transaction because they are especially interested in manipulating external events and because they are constantly faced with dichotomous choices. Should they announce their candidacy now? Should they accept that speaking engagement? Should they respond openly to reporters' questions or say, "No comment"? A lot depends on their skill in making the proper binary choice of data that affect control.

Some athletes also face similar tasks. In baseball the batter must decide whether to swing or let the ball pass. The incredible concentration a weight lifter exhibits before picking up the dumbbell is another example—and an extreme one, because all the body control choices have to be executed in but an instant.

This skill is also typical of the anthropologist involved in an excavation.

Transaction 3 →4 —Follower (DISF).

Introverted
Detailed
"To −□− the °/₁"

This translates as "to control the dichotomies" or "to respond with appropriately controlled actions to a situation whose success or failure depends on your actions." This transaction has to do with "follow the leader." It is a very service-oriented, rather than an initiating, skill.

The nurse is an excellent example. Stored in memory, as a consequence of training, are a host of do's and don't's: keep the patient warm or cool, keep the head low or high, make the patient vomit or don't make the patient vomit, and so on. And clearly the nurse's job is to effect precisely controlled conditions, to act in accordance with clear-cut instructions. The transaction therefore is typical of following instructions.

A musician playing the cello does the same thing. The instruction may come from the printed page or from the conductor, and execution above all involves control.

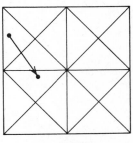

3→4 DISF

THE STATIC MODEL:
THE MAP OF CAPACITIES

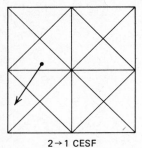

2→1 CESF

Both 4 → 3 and 3 → 4 transactions, though very different, require attention to detail and are therefore typical batch processors.

The last two transactions to be discussed are contextual in style.

Transaction 2 →1 —Initiator (CESF).

Extroverted

Contextual

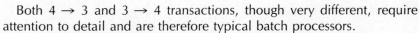
"To ⊡ the ="

This translates as "to signal the match" or "to notice that something is equated to something else." The match may be between an idea and a need—in short, it may be an opportunity. I call this transaction the initiator. It involves taking risks.

There are many situations that involve being alert to a possible match. In general, the transaction has to do with quick reactions, as in certain sports or in social interactions. Car dealers are an interesting case in point. When you, the potential buyer, walk into the showroom, skilled salespersons will observe you until they catch a signal. Somehow, they know when to approach you, and they probably know the car you have your eye on before you do. Statements like "That's the perfect car for you" reveal the effort and skill applied to make the match.

This activity is also typical of the entrepreneur and promoter.

Transaction 1 →2 —Doer (CIFS).

Introverted

Contextual

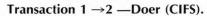
"To = the ⊡"

"To match the signal" is a responsive role, perhaps best exemplified in tennis, where the signals are tactile as well as visual and some body action must respond to and match the sensory signal. The same skills are drawn on by the farmer, shepherd, and others who work close to nature.

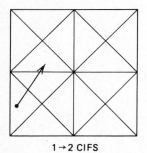

1→2 CIFS

SUMMARY

I've tried to point out the useful keys that can unlock the hidden meanings in the map of capacities. There are three:

1. Be aware of the direction of information flow.
2. Use the pole symbols to construct images or phrases that capture what is actually happening in terms of information-processing.
3. Use all the dichotomous relationships as pointers to the nature of the activity.

Any attempt to grasp the many details presented by trying to memorize all of it would be a totally wrong approach. I wish instead to develop a kind of road sense, an ability to "read" the map. Reading meaning into the map is a very creative and productive process. With practice that process will become easier and increasingly natural and meaningful.

As an interim aid, I have summarized the key elements discussed in this chapter. They may be used for reference purposes.

Examples of Profiles and "Work" Activities

Mode	Profile Name	Work Activity Examples
Intellect Abstract α	Analyst	Science and applied science, applied math and physics, systems analysis, engineering science, law, medicine as diagnosis, trouble shooting (anything involving logic with verbal skill)
	Conceptualizer	Architecture, corporate planning, systems design, conceptual research, management of innovation (anything involving logical structures with visual skill)
	Suspector	Detective service, pure mathematics, military or strategic planning, comptroller (anything involving strategies and planning with visual pattern recognition skills)
	Theoretician	Theoretical physics, intuition-driven research
Verbal People π	Verbalist	Orator, preacher, diplomat, actor or director, writer, english professor
	Critic	Critic, voice teacher, foreign language teacher, translator (anything involving accurate listening skill)
	Perceiver	Counselor, shopkeeper, social worker, business, family law, psychiatrist
	Composer	Poet, lyricist, composer, writer, psychiatrist, artist
Hands Things θ	Implementor	Engineer, experimental scientist, project manager, contractor
	Organizer	Secretary, craftsman, stock clerk, accountant, draftsman, office clerk, programmer, administrator
	Operator	Machinist, surgeon, manager, auto mechanic
	Molder	Sculptor
Body Concrete ¢	Classifier	Politician, administrator, athlete, anthropologist
	Follower	Nurse, musician
	Initiator	Entrepreneur, salesperson, opportunist
	Doer	Dancer, athlete

Basic Personality Profiles

Data Pole		Processing Pole			Verb		Noun
16	→	15		To	⊣Ɛ	the	⋦
15	→	16		To	⋦	the	⊣Ɛ
14	→	13		To	↗	the	⌗
13	→	14		To	⌗	the	↗
12	→	11		To	∽	the	⓪
11	→	12		To	⓪	the	∽
10	→	9		To	△+□	the	⊤⊥△
9	→	10		To	⊤⊥△	the	△+□
8	→	7		To	NN	the	‡
7	→	8		To	‡	the	NN
6	→	5		To	!	the	⊙
5	→	6		To	⊙	the	!
4	→	3		To	°/∣	the	—□—
3	→	4		To	—□—	the	°/∣
2	→	1		To	⊡	the	=
1	→	2		To	=	the	⊡

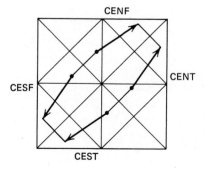

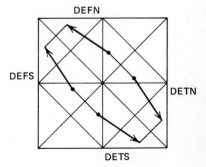

and Mode Orientations

Transaction Name	Transaction Name	
To logically sort structures	Analyst	DETN
To structure logical data	Conceptualizer	DINT
To discover strategies from patterns	Suspector	CENT
To pattern strategies	Theoretician	CITN
To preferentially select associations	Verbalist	DEFN
To associate preferences	Critic	DINF
To make harmony possible	Perceiver	CENF
To harmonize possibilities	Composer	CIFN
To order routines	Implementor	DETS
To make ordered data routine	Organizer	DIST
To label features	Operator	CEST
To recognize signs	Molder	CITS
To dichotomize control	Classifier	DEFS
To control dichotomies	Follower	DISF
To signal matches	Initiator	CESF
To match signals	Doer	CIFS

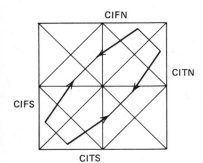

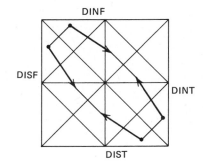

THE STATIC MODEL:
THE MAP OF CAPACITIES

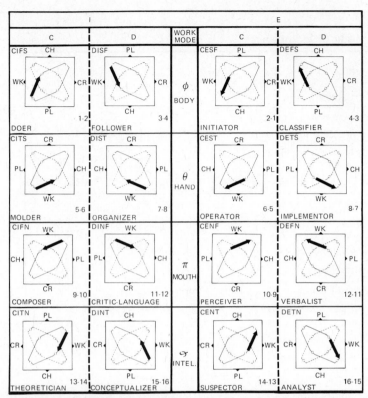

Basic personality profiles and mode orientations. E, extroverted; I, introverted; C, contextual; D, detailed; WK, work mode; CH, challenge mode; CR, creativity mode; PL, play mode; ———, dominant circuit; · · · ·, complementary circuit; a→b transaction shown with heavy arrow.

9

THE PROGRESSIVE AWAKENING OF THE FIELD OF CONSCIOUSNESS

This chapter should help considerably in your understanding of the 16 capacities. It introduces important concepts based on the interrelationships of poles and the resulting development of an information network. These ideas are discussed in the context of child growth and development.

THE STATIC MODEL:
THE MAP OF CAPACITIES

It is fascinating to speculate on how the conscious mind "awakens." The model gives a glimpse that seems to correlate well with accepted models of child development. I include this speculative discussion because it helps clarify the concept of complexity and the bearing it has on interpreting a personality.

Recall that complexity refers to the pole numbers and that the complexity index (1, 2, m, and ∞) is associated with the functions. The pole numbers ordered the poles from the simplest (1) to the most complex (16). The awakening of consciousness in the child is seen as a progressive turning on or activation of poles in the natural order of complexity. As each pole becomes activated, linkages to related poles are formed. Once these linkages are reciprocally established—that is, when there is a link not only from pole x to pole y but also from pole y to pole x—then a channel for information-flow exists between poles. The awakening of consciousness is thus not only the activation of poles but also the establishment of circuitry. We might call this awakening of consciousness the structural development of consciousness.

A second development deals with the information content that is processed and stored in memory as the various poles become activated. This development depends much more on the experiences of the individual: what is experienced and how and where it is filed in memory. I envision this second process as analogous to personal construct theory.

So let us begin at the beginning. A baby has been born. The doctor has just spanked the child, who is now crying and breathing. This is the stereotypical image we have of the beginning of life. The awakening of consciousness surely begins somewhere during the prenatal stage, but, to illustrate the interdependence of capacities, the day of birth will do.

PHASE I (CONCRETE OR GROSS MOTOR MODE)

Level 1

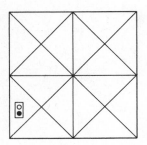

The first pole to awaken is pole 1. This simply provides the ability to recognize a signal, which means that consciousness can register sensation. The various sensory inputs send new signals to the brain about the baby's state of comfort: hungry or satisfied, hot or cold, wet or dry, and so on. With only pole 1 awake, the baby has not yet any skill to interpret such signals. All it knows is that there is a signal, and it responds innately and primitively to it. If it is cold, it shivers; if it's hungry, it cries without any realization of what all that means.

The wiring is such, however, that the linkages foretell what other poles will be affected by the awakening of pole 1. It's an archetypal reaching out. I mean archetypal in the literal sense, the vestiges of evolutionary development that link most basic skills together. For pole 1 the linkages T, X, M, and L establish tentative connections to poles 2, 3, 5, and 9 (see the competition/cooperation matrix in Chapter Seven). I envision these as one-way links, so that information processed by pole 1 can be sent to poles 2, 3, 5, and/or 9, but no processing takes place as yet at these poles. It's very much like installing telephones. Telephone 1 is activated, and wires are connected to reach telephones 2, 3, 5, and 9, but, as these telephones are not yet activated, nothing can happen; no telephone rings, no conversation can take place. The only thing that does happen is that the ends of the lines at 2, 3, 5, and 9 are hot, ready to go.

One can hardly speak of a consciousness when the only capacity alive is that which registers a signal. Until the signal is processed in some meaningful way, one cannot refer to conscious intelligence. That cannot happen until the next step in the awakening process.

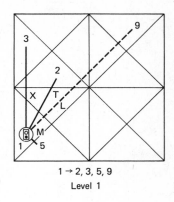

1 → 2, 3, 5, 9
Level 1

Level 2

Pole 2 is next in the hierarchical order and thus the next pole to become activated. In each successive stage, the activation of a pole brings with it the one-way linkages to poles connected through the T, X, M, and L links. For pole 2, these establish links to poles 1, 4, 10, and 6.

Let us take stock of the status at the end of step 2 in the awakening process. Poles 1 and 2 are activated. There is a two-way linkage between poles 1 and 2, a linkage from 1 to 2 and a linkage from 2 to 1. These two poles can "talk" to each other. Poles 3, 4, 5, 6, 9, and 10 are being stimulated but are not yet active, since only one-way linkages exist, emanating from poles 1 or 2. This stage is shown schematically. A completed, active linkage is indicated by a double line. One-way linkages are denoted by single lines.

Level 2 represents a major step forward, for this is the first stage where a transaction can take place (a transaction being a meaningful cooperation between two poles). In this case pole 1 can recognize signals, and pole 2 can match them. The baby can now not only notice a sensation but also recognize that a given sensation matches a previously experienced one. It is as though the baby had learned to say, "I'm crying because I feel uncomfortable in the same way I felt uncomfortable before." This identification of a recurring experience is a quintessential precursor to conditioning. Not only must the signal be recognized, but it is necessary to have the skill to note that it is the same signal. This is the beginning of the very sophisticated skill of identification. But at this level no meaning is attached; there is only a kind of sorting out. "This is like that; the other is not."

To notice and match signals involve processing skills dependent on memory. The growing conscious capability reflects not only the interlinking of poles, but also the fact that the pole-associated memories have an ever increasing repertoire to draw on. Let us look at this in detail at

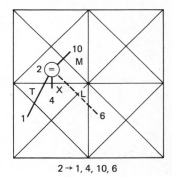

2 → 1, 4, 10, 6

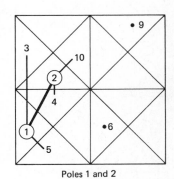

Poles 1 and 2
Level 2

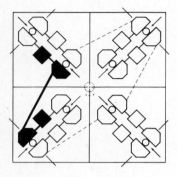

a level that I call metaprogramming. Pole 1 receives a particular signal. It stores that in its memory and also passes it on to pole 2, which transforms the information received to store it in its own memory. At some later time, pole 1 again receives a signal and transmits it to pole 2. Pole 2 can now search its memory, retrieve information based on previous experiences, compare it to the signal just received, and come to one of two conclusions. The first is, "I've had that experience before, it's not a new signal." It might go further than that and say, "The fact that I found the signal high in my memory stack indicates that I've seen that signal recently or many times before." Or, if pole 2 cannot match the signal, it says in effect, "This is a new signal, and I'll add it to my memory as a new entry."

The process can occur in reverse as well. Pole 2 can pull a signal indication from its memory and send it to pole 1 with the request to look for such a preselected signal. Pole 1 thus has been alerted to look out for a given signal. At level 2, then, the baby has considerably more capability than at level 1. It can recognize new and recurrent experiences, and it can anticipate or be put on alert.

Level 3

The baby remains at level 2 until pole 3 comes on line. This is the dichotomizing pole, which adds the additional differentiating skill of pairing signals by positive or negative attributes. It can operate only with the prior capabilities of poles 1 and 2. In this respect, complexity is like Maslow's hierarchy of needs, where level 3 cannot come into play until levels 1 and 2 have first been readied. Pole 3 then adds a new dimension. It says in effect, "Okay, you got a signal, and you tell me that signal is already in your repertoire. I'll tell you even more. This signal is positive; it is useful for survival, and, furthermore, I can tell you that I have filed it as opposite some other signal previously experienced."

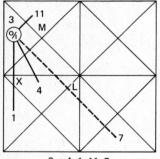

$3 \rightarrow 4, 1, 11, 7$

This is a vastly enriched identification, for it can identify opposing pairs that differentiate between good and bad. By this means, the signal for "hungry" is now related to the signal "satiated," where the value judgment "hungry" is negative ($-$), and "satiated" is positive ($+$). The two signals form a dichotomous pair.

The baby at level 3 is far more sophisticated, for it can now evaluate the value of signals, a vital precursor to self-direction. It knows what's good for it. The state of consciousness at level 3 is again shown schematically. Let us review the status.

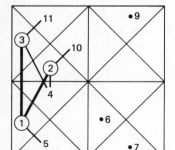

Poles 1 through 3

Level 3

Pole 1 is awake and linked to 2, 3, 5, and 9.

Pole 2 is awake and linked to 1, 4, 6, and 10.

Pole 3 is awake and linked to 1, 4, 7, and 11.

In addition, poles 4, 5, 6, 7, 9, 10, and 11 have been stimulated.

Notice that, even at level 3, only the transactions between poles 1 and 2 are operational, the most primitive transactions labeled the "doer" and the "initiator"; that is, the baby can kick and cry. Poles 1 and 3 are also double-linked, but are not transactions (T), only crosslinks (X).

Additionally, all the poles in the concrete or gross motor mode have been stimulated, and 75 percent (three out of four poles) in the people or verbal mode and thing or fine motor mode have been stimulated. None of the poles in the abstract or intellectual mode is involved as yet, as though that part of consciousness were still asleep.

Level 4

The step from level 3 to level 4 is a major one. Pole 4 now comes on line. It establishes links to poles 3, 2, 8, and 12. This step connects poles 3 and 4 reciprocally and makes transactions 3 → 4 and 4 → 3 operational. The gross motor mode is now operational, and all the poles in the verbal and fine motor modes have been stimulated. There are still no operational links to these modes, so that the gross motor mode must operate in isolation. The intellectual mode is still totally asleep. The child has thus reached the first major milestone of development. One mode is operational at the natural, prelingual level (the primitive sides of the concept and language dichotomies). The child is now at a simple, gross motor stage of development.

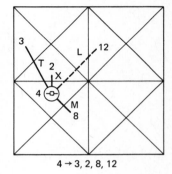

4 → 3, 2, 8, 12

The awakening of pole 4 made major contributions to attaining this milestone plateau. Pole 4 deals with control and feedback. With pole 4 activated the child now notices, matches, differentiates between good and bad, and starts to control things. Thus directed will can now come into play. The child can intentionally cry, or deliberately try to kick a blanket off, or reach for a rattle or into space. It is now a creature whose noises and actions begin to take on interpretable meanings. Now, the child is in a position to start directed experiments. It is not easy at first to find the right signal and control it properly, so it needs to experiment. There is gurgling and whining and screaming and cooing and crying. There is kicking of one leg, both legs, alternating legs; there is grasping and attempts at letting go. And even eye movements are becoming directed. In short, the baby is now at a stage of motor experiencing and experimentation. All this is vital and preparatory for more advanced manipulation and verbal and intellectual skills yet to come.

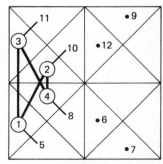

Poles 1 through 4

Level 4

As the capacities progressively increase, the time between stages grows, for there is so much more to do, try, perfect, and integrate. Memories have many more entries, which must be interlinked and sorted out. As the ability to recognize signals grows, more differentiation between sensory and motor signals is needed. There are many more possible combinations, and it takes times to explore the possibilities and to practice the more successful ones. It's a period of debugging basic motor skills and signals, a precursor of motor routines.

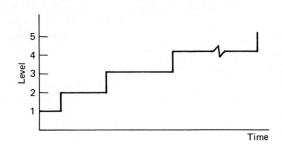

PHASE II (THING OR FINE MOTOR MODE)

Level 5

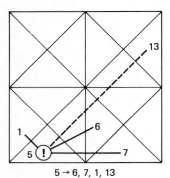

5 → 6, 7, 1, 13

With the awakening of pole 5, the child truly enters a new phase, what might be called the beginning of animalistic intelligence, which is a very important prelingual phase. We shall see the progressive awakening of the fine motor mode, where hand–eye coordination is now built on body coordination to complete the motor development. This also involves the motor part of speech, the muscular control needed for the production of particularized sounds. Other important constructs preparatory to dealing with meanings and concepts develop, largely through the establishment of more sophisticated identification skills involving sorting and ordering through labels.

The step from pole 4 to pole 5 is dramatic. Not only have poles 1 through 4 become greatly enriched through fuller memories and inter-linkages, but the first operational link to another mode is also established. Let us review the details of how that comes about.

	T	X	M	L
One-way linkages from pole 1	1–2	1–3	1–5	1–9
One-way linkages from pole 2	2–1	2–4	2–10	2–6
One-way linkages from pole 3	3–4	3–1	3–11	3–7
One-way linkages from pole 4	4–3	4–2	4–8	4–12
One-way linkages from pole 5	5–6	5–7	5–1	5–13
Double links	1–2	1–3	1–5	
Double links	3–4	2–4		

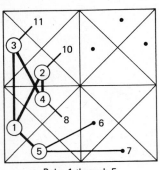

Poles 1 through 5
Level 5

We can see that poles 1, 2, 3, and 4 in the gross motor mode are tightly coupled, and the first operational link from the gross motor mode to the fine motor mode has been established through poles 1 and 5. We also see the first awakening of a pole (13) in the intellectual mode.

These seem to be prerequisites to the appearance of intelligent behavior. The key to that is pole 5, which stands for sign. A sign is much more sophisticated than a signal. A signal, like the light on an elevator button, simply says that something is on or off. A sign, however, is an equivalence. A sign says that some unique something stands for something else. That something else can be quite complicated, like a whole sequence of events. A sign is therefore more like a label or the name of a subroutine. The power of a label rests on the fact that it is an incredible information condenser, like shorthand. A single sign stands for a complex chain of events. Basically, every complex metaprogram in the gross motor mode can be reduced to a single sign stored in the memory of pole 5. It is therefore the beginning of higher-level languages, where one entry of metacode is substituted for many entries of microcode.

This new skill means that the child can now link experiences together into more complex structures. It recognizes mother's face over the crib, sees hands reach out, feels itself being lifted, and so on. These connected sets of sensations and happenings now are linked into a single concept of "mother." It is always the same face, under the same set of circumstances, which produces the wished-for effect. Clearly, the concept of "mother," whatever set of experiences it stands for, must first exist before the word "mother" can take on meaning. Labels, the specialty of pole 5, are therefore the precursors to nouns in linguistic development.

The model makes explicit that the concept underlying a noun, identified as a sign in pole 5's memory, exists long before the child uses the word associated with the sign. You must know the shorthand hieroglyphics before you can read them. Pole 5 is therefore the first step toward language, a culturally acquired, prelingual skill, drawing on experiences perceived through poles 1 through 4. If there is no mother, the concept of mother can't be learned, and ultimately the word mother would be meaningless because the word would map into an empty set of motor experiences.

This is a very exciting stage in a child's growth. The child is suddenly more than a doll-like being. There is a sparkle in the eye—"I know what's happening next"—and a sense of responsiveness builds a link between mother and child. The child is no longer just in its own internal world of signals and experiences. It is now aware of an external environment and its interactions with it; reaching out for a toy over the crib is no longer just a sensual happening but an interaction of doing something with and to the toy.

Before I start discussing the awakening of pole 6, the feature pole, I should point out that there are fascinating parallels in the awakening of modes. Each mode has four poles, and therefore the development of each mode goes through four steps, as we've seen with the gross motor mode. It awakened in the order 1, 2, 3, 4. The fine motor mode awakens in the order 5, 6, 7, 8. What I wish to call attention to is that, in each respective mode (and for the verbal and intellectual modes as well), 1 and 5, 2 and 6, 3 and 7, and 4 and 8 play similar roles in the awakening process. Thus

versus !

in the fine motor mode we tell one sign from another by studying the features within signs. Feature or essence is a more sophisticated comparison than merely to match or not match. We then go to sorting, which is a more sophisticated process of ordering differences. And routines are simply a whole sequence of controls. The awakening of phase II is thus a repeat of phase I, but enlarged in that the set is larger than a complexity index of 2; it is m. We compare not only whether one signal matches another or not; we use contrast to compare many signs. We sort not just positive or negative but a host of things: a marble, a tennis ball, a balloon, a beach ball, and so on. In routine we interlink not only input or output, but a long sequence of controlled events.

It is as though an ambi-syn-anti sequence is at work at every phase. Consequently, we might speak of four as yet unrelated sets:

I) The set "there is": 1 (signal), 5 (sign), 9 (combination), 13 (strategy).

II) The set "compare": 2 (match), 6 (feature), 10 (balance), 14 (pattern).

III) The set "sort": 3 (contrast), 7 (sort), 11 (preference), 15 (logic).

IV) The set "interlink": 4 (control), 8 (routine), 12 (association), 16 (structure).

Put another way, signal, sign, combination, and strategy have something in common in that they are the ambi-syn-anti starting point, each at a more sophisticated level. Similarly, match, feature, balance, and pattern are successively more sophisticated ways of comparing differences. Contrasting, sorting, preferring, and logic are four increasingly more complex ways of discovering order. And control, routine, association, and structure are four more increasingly complex ways of creating interlinkings.

I have given a name to this series of 4-4-4-4 sets. I call them *tasks*. The first task, designated I, is the proposer. The second task, designated II, is the comparator. The third task, designated III, is the evaluator. The fourth task, designated IV, is the gestalter.

F-2

	Task				
Number	Name				
I	Proposer	⊡	!	△+□	⟋
II	Comparator	=	⊙	⟁	⧉
III	Evaluator	°⁄|	Ⴘ	∽	⊏
IV	"Gestalter"	—□—	‡	⊚	⋔

It is my hope that this discussion both underlines the richness of the structure and adds interpretive meanings to the poles. Now with this detour behind us, let us continue with the phase II awakening.

Level 6

Pole 6 has links to poles 5, 8, 14, and 2. This generates double or reciprocal bonds to poles 5 and 2. The latter bond strengthens the bond between the gross motor and fine motor modes. The important link, however, is the interlinking of poles 5 and 6, which makes transactions $5 \rightarrow 6$ and $6 \rightarrow 5$ possible. As I tried to indicate through the ambi-syn-anti parallel, this is the more sophisticated counterpart of the $1 \rightarrow 2$ transaction. That transaction identifies signals. Transaction $5 \rightarrow 6$ identifies signs. A sign is a much more information-rich element to process than a signal. It is roughly comparable to telling which one of six elevators is on its way up as opposed to discerning pleasure or anger from someone's facial expression. Far more information has to be processed in the second case. The capacity of pole 6 to note features—that is, to reduce a host of information to the essential clue—is a powerful aid. What is meant by feature is a reduction of information content to its essential contrasting difference, the very thing a caricaturist does so well.

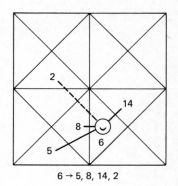

$6 \rightarrow 5, 8, 14, 2$

Pole 6 does its job by reducing visual information to edge effects (contrast of light and dark) and searching for the differentiating sign. Poles 5 (sign) and 6 (feature) thus cooperate to extract visually significant information and to identify it with a message. This provides a child with the important skill of recognizing not only sensory signals, but also contextual situations. The child can distinguish one face from another, danger from comfort, and so on. It is a big step, something like moving from binary arithmetic to advanced geometry.

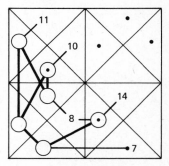

Poles 1 through 6

Level 6

If the child seems interesting in level 5, the proper description for level 6 is that the child is interested. It is interested in everything: what it eats, the toys it has, the people around it. Of course, while poles 5 and 6 are coming into play, poles 1, 2, 3, and 4 keep growing in experience and skill. The body coordination reaches the stage where crawling and walking begin. The growing dimension of the physical world in which the child operates is now matched by the newly awakened skills to be curious and explorative. To enhance that process, hand—eye coordination has to develop next, so that the wonders of the world can really be looked into. This is the development of levels 7 and 8.

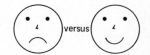

Levels 7 and 8

To save space and time, I discuss successive stages in pairs from now on, for the patterns repeat themselves. Pole 7 links to 8, 5, 15, and 3, reinforcing links among the poles in the gross motor and fine motor modes and establishing new probes into the intellectual mode.

The awakening of pole 8, with links to poles 7, 6, 4, and 16, completes the process. The gross and fine motor modes are operationally connected with reciprocal links. Half of consciousness, the prelingual half, is now

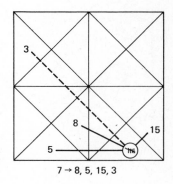

$7 \rightarrow 8, 5, 15, 3$

132

THE STATIC MODEL:
THE MAP OF CAPACITIES

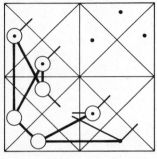

Poles 1 through 7

Level 7

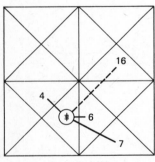

8 → 7, 6, 4, 16

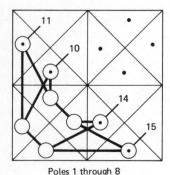

Poles 1 through 8

Level 8

fully awake, interlinked, and operational. All the poles in the verbal and intellectual modes have been stimulated preparatory to their awakening, but no double linkages have yet been established in and to the verbal and intellectual modes.

The prelingual development phases are complete somewhere between ages 1 and 1½. An important part of the last level of that phase is the establishment of the transactions 7 → 8 and 8 → 7. These are the transactions that effect organized hand–eye coordination. These lead to manual skills, which start with the child stacking blocks and feeding itself and ultimately lead to more sophisticated skills such as tying shoelaces, sewing, weaving, constructing, and so on. All are skills that are acquired with lots of practice. Poles 7 and 8 draw on the skills developed previously and bring into play new, more sophisticated and specialized skills, which I describe as sorting and routine. Sorting is a new ordering by some contrasting criterion—size, for instance, with the biggest block first, the next smaller, and so on to the smallest. It is the precursor skill to quantification, or counting. Pole 8 is a new linking together that is sequentially ordered—do this first, that next—well described by routine. It develops first as a manual skill.

Level 8 is a significant benchmark, most apparent from the linkage diagram. First of all, note that the entire field of consciousness has been stimulated for the first time. The last to make its existence known is pole 16, the end point of hierarchical development and complexity. This benchmark is the earliest stage at which the child has any indication of its potential, a hazy vision of what it is to be a complete person.

Second, the prelingual stage is now complete and operational. All the poles in the gross and fine motor modes are awake, and the two modes are operationally linked. There is still a great deal of learning and development ahead, but that should be viewed as part of personal construct theory; that is, memories become enriched through greater content and progressively better internal organization. The point, however, is that the potential to digest prelingual experiences and file them with the proper interconnections at the prelingual level is now established.

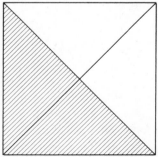

Prelingual, completely conscious.

PHASE III (PEOPLE OR VERBAL MODE)

Level 9

The hierarchically ordered awakening continues now with phase III, where pole 9 awakens first. This is the beginning of what ultimately leads to speech and intellect, and the awakening of pole 9 is a dramatic and sophisticated leap forward. It is the first pole in the intuitive function, the first opportunity for future and imagination to take on any meaning. The child's world suddenly opens to a size beyond reality. Up to pole 8, every skill was sense-dependent and could grow only with real experience. It was a constrained reality. The awakening of pole 9 changes all that. In one big step, the child can suddenly deal with fantasy and make-believe, entertain humor, and deal with abstraction. Yet the pole is relatively simple. It simply dares to combine unconnected elements, to consider what is possible rather than merely what has been experienced. A combination is thus an imaginary sign, a more sophisticated information element because it is more than a signal and more than a real sign. In short, it's as big a step as going from geometry to complex variables.

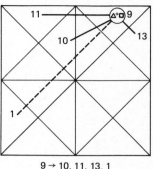

9 → 10, 11, 13, 1

The capacity to combine yet unexperienced elements is at the very foundation of language, for the association of words with experiences is initially a guess for the child. It has heard words in context for quite a while, but the child must invent its own constructs. No one gives it lessons in grammar, so it invents it. A child might well say, "I doed it and I meaned it"—not that it ever heard that phrase, but it invented a construct for itself which it used to compose that new phrase (so "I did it and meant it," comes out that way).

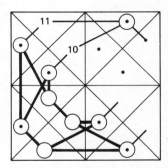

Poles 1 through 9

Level 9

The combining capacity of pole 9 comes into play much earlier than that, of course. The child experiences the auditory sensation of hearing words and the visual sensation of seeing objects. But it has to discover on its own that the two experiences can be combined, that the sound and picture belong together and stand one for the other. This is very dramatically apparent in the case of Helen Keller, who made the connection on her own that the sensations experienced in her hand through her teacher were coupled to objects, such as water, that she had experienced. Language could not develop in her until pole 9 made that important step. This is much easier in the normal child, since pole 9 is only a link away from auditory and visual inputs. In the case of Helen Keller these two inputs, which converge at pole 9, were inoperative. Pole 9 is then the link between seeing and hearing, aided by the complete development and awakening of all poles in and near the sensation function. So pole 9 starts with a whole new world.

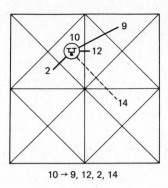

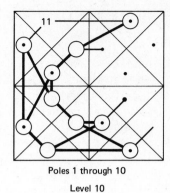

10 → 9, 12, 2, 14

Poles 1 through 10

Level 10

Level 10

These new complex information entities need to be differentiated, just as was the case with poles 2 and 6 before. This differentiating function is carried out by pole 10. Pole 10 is harmony and balance, appropriate for something as complex and unpredictable as combinations of possibilities. Pole 10 provides a spectrum, a qualitative frame of reference that can evaluate whether combinations work, whether things "hang together." Were it not for pole 10, there could be no discrimination. One imagined combination, be it words or fantasies, would be as valid as another. Pole 10 makes it possible to evaluate and judge the rightness or wrongness of a composition. It is the built-in correction that changes "I doed it" to "I did it," "vegebatls" into "vegetables." The discrimination of pole 10 is a far more sophisticated form of contrasting or featuring.

Once poles 9 and 10 come on line, the youngster is ready to experiment with speech and actually starts to speak. She or he also has the capacities now to develop a sense of right and wrong, for pole 10 provides the frame of reference for judging. The child can sense guilt and know it did something wrong before it feels the consequences.

Levels 11 and 12

Growth of consciousness becomes ever more sophisticated. As poles 11 and 12 awaken, the verbal mode becomes completely operational and fully linked to the gross motor mode. The child's speech develops rapidly now. Not only can it use words as signs, but, through pole 12, it can also express associations. Associations develop as the memory of pole 12, organized as associative sets, grows. Words like "family" start to take on meaning, for after all family is a word that is far more than a pointer to an object; it is a pointer to a collection of namable entities.

It is worth remembering that the verbal mode lies in the natural half of the lingual portion of the language dichotomy; that is, once pole 9 opens the door to the lingual half of the language dichotomy, the child

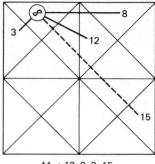

11 → 12, 9, 3, 15

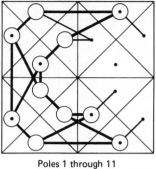

Poles 1 through 11

Level 11

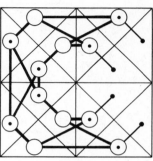

12 → 11, 10, 16, 4

will learn to speak on its own (though not in isolation). Learning to speak is a natural development. In contrast, developing the intellectual capacities (awakening of the intellectual mode) does not happen that easily. Poles 13, 14, 15, and 16 (the intellectual mode) are acquired linguistic skills. We have invented an environment for developing this skill and call it a school.

PHASE IV (ABSTRACT OR INTELLECTUAL MODE)

Levels 13 Through 16

Schools assume that body, hand, and verbal skills preexist. Drawing on those skills, they discipline the child to master intellectual skills represented by the four most complex poles dealing in order with strategy, pattern, logic, and structure.

The higher we move into complexity, the slower the developmental process. Poles 1 through 8 are operational by age 2. Of course, they continue to grow even further. Poles 9 through 12 are not fully operational until age 5 or 6. It is generally accepted that it takes 12 more years (grades 1 through 12) to develop poles 13 through 16, together with greater growth in all other poles. Poles 1 through 4 now evolve into sports, poles 5 through 8 into ever more challenging eye–hand skills, such as sewing or operating a telescope.

When pole 16 is operational, consciousness is fully awake. All transactions and mode links are fully established. The network is quite complex and powerful now.

Actually, the development of poles and modes occurs in overlapping stages. To avoid confusion, this aspect of development was omitted from the prior discussion, but I want to make amends now. A pole is actually not fully operational until all links are established. In the diagrammatical representation, the look ahead (L) link has been omitted, because that additional line would make the diagram unreadable. The look ahead is, however, a very important link. I have therefore chosen to indicate its

Poles 1 through 12

Level 12

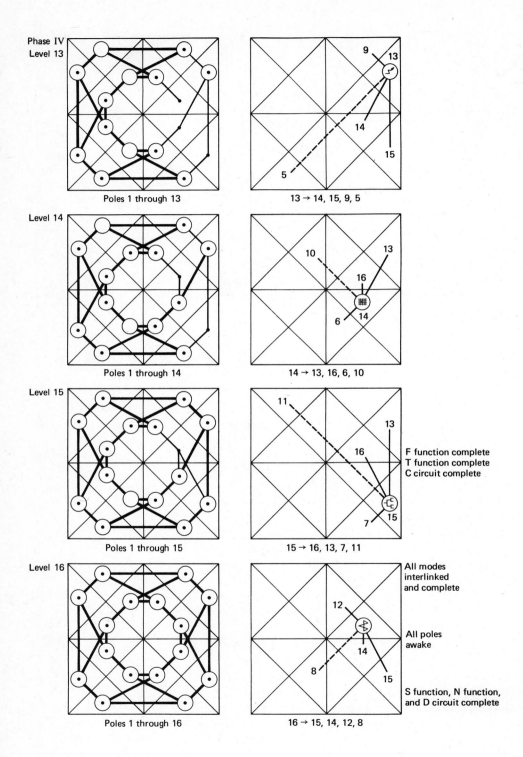

Phase IV
Level 13

Poles 1 through 13

13 → 14, 15, 9, 5

Level 14

Poles 1 through 14

14 → 13, 16, 6, 10

Level 15

Poles 1 through 15

F function complete
T function complete
C circuit complete

15 → 16, 13, 7, 11

Level 16

Poles 1 through 16

All modes
interlinked
and complete

All poles
awake

S function, N function,
and D circuit complete

16 → 15, 14, 12, 8

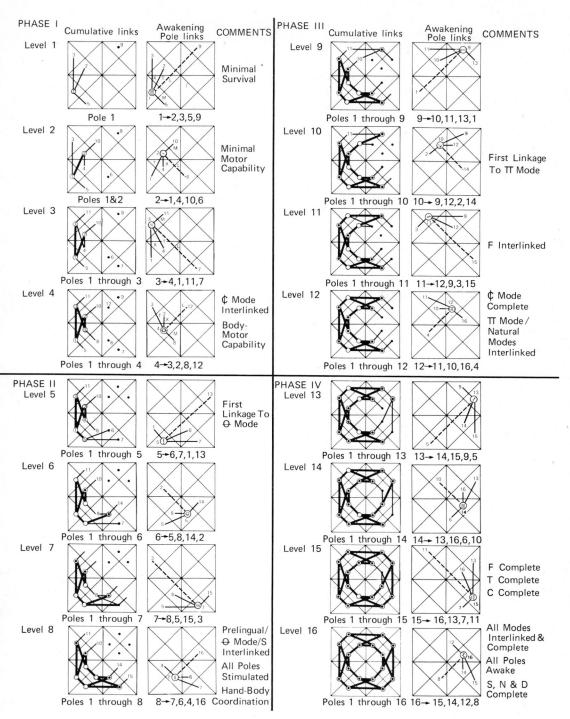

Progressive awakening of poles.

137

existence by a dot inside the pole. When a double L link exists, a dot is entered in the affected poles shown as $\odot$. If you observe the filling in of these double L links by the dots, you would see a second wave of maturation, like a wake of a boat, that follows the development indicated.

If the human being developed in clearly defined stages, personality formation would not be complete until preferences developed among the 16 capacities. The forces that lead to this delineation form the *individuation* process, which is related to the development of the conscious and the unconscious (this is discussed next). But the process starts long before pole 16 is fully developed. The stages of development are thus not clearly demarked and sequenced, but overlap. Some preferences make themselves felt very early in life. For instance, a preferred style (contextual or detailed) can be detected as early as age 5 or 6. Attitude (extroverted or introverted) may also show early definition, but can still change and often becomes differentiated quite late; the more sheltered the environment, the later the delineation. But these observations are beside the point.

The main point of this chapter is to underline the importance of complexity. The ordering of poles has not only personality consequences but also developmental import. A personality $16 \rightarrow 15$ can develop only if all the previous levels have been mastered.

THE DYNAMIC MODEL: THE PROFILE

In Part II we constructed a model of cognitive capacities in a systematic fashion. In Part III we link the organizational structure of the model to an equivalent organization of observable human behavior patterns.

Human behavior is not random—quite the contrary. Perceptive people have developed their own schema for detecting such patterns, the basis for stereotyping as reflected by such statements as, "I've met that type before."

In this section, I attempt to make this intuitive process of classification overt and explicit. The objective is not to classify but to gain insight into a personality by understanding the patterns that exist and follow logically from the model.

10

THE DIFFERENCE BETWEEN A PROFILE AND THE MAP OF CAPACITIES

THE DYNAMIC MODEL: THE
PROFILE

Nothing is quite as fascinating as the process of personality formation. We watch it in our children, and we wonder how it happened in ourselves. Somehow, we know that each of us has a unique personality, although we don't always understand it. In fact, those closest to us are often the most puzzling. Interestingly enough, when it comes to people we hardly know, things seem far less complicated. New people we meet seem like people we have met before, as though there were just so many types in the world. So what is the reality? Is there an infinite variety of personalities, or are there only a few types? And how can we explain either answer?

I try to address these questions one step at a time, for responses involve a number of conceptual considerations that I lump under the heading of *profiles*. A profile can be envisioned as a potential field superimposed on the map of capacities.

There are 16 basic orientations of such fields, giving rise to 16 profile classes. Yet, depending on variations within the gross field and on personal constructs, unlimited variations exist within each class of profiles. The trick is to sort out what is generic from the individualistic differences.

All of us have seen pictures of the body's physiology in anatomy books. Typically, such pictures show the bones and muscles, the nerves, tendons, and organs that are found in everyone's body. Rarely do we see a picture of a middle-aged executive whose body is mostly flab and whose puny muscles reflect the particular state of his physical condition. There is no effective way to show the strength of a particular muscle, certainly not in a quantitative sense. But there should be, for muscle power and body tone clearly make a difference in determining whether a given individual is capable of a given task.

The map of capacities suffers from this same deficiency. It is an abstract picture of what is possible, but not a personalized picture. It does not tell us the magnitude of various capacities or the differences among them. Yet it is these very differences among the capacities that give rise to a unique personality.

One way we might resolve the dilemma is to distort the map of capacities so that relative strengths and weaknesses among the 16 capacities show up as relatively larger and smaller areas on the map—that is, by letting areas on the map represent relative strengths. For instance, we might recognize, as Jung did, that the four functions S, F, T, and N are rarely equal. In fact, Jung referred to a *superior* (strongest) function, two *auxiliary* functions, and an *inferior* (weakest) function opposite the superior function. I have plotted what such a distortion might look like.

N is the strongest function in this illustration of DETN, since the partitioning was such as to allocate the largest area to N. Inevitably then, S is the weakest function, symbolized by the small area allotted to that function. T, in the example, must be the first auxiliary or second strongest function, as noted from the size of the area representing T.

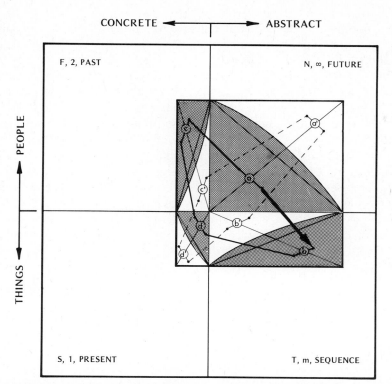

Quantitative extension of model, illustrated for DETN. Style dichotomy is strongly differentiated toward D. Attitude dichotomy is normally differentiated toward E. Focus dichotomy is 66% people-oriented, and approach dichotomy is 80% abstract-oriented; therefore, both are N and T.

I must point out that I could draw a spectrum of profiles with N the strongest function and T the first auxiliary function, differing only in the degree of differentiation; that is, N could be vastly stronger or only slightly stronger than T, depending on how the partitioning lines are drawn. Such a picture could be called a profile of the four-pole model.

If we extend this idea to the eight-pole model, we would have to show the differences in extroverted and introverted capacities, reflecting the dominant style. Such a profile might look as shown.

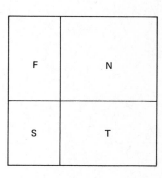

Note that the partitioning is uneven. In this example, extroversion is larger in the T and F quadrants, and introversion is larger in the N and S quadrants, reflecting a D-style tendency. The more dominant the D style, the stronger the distortion, as indicated by the dotted lines.

Finally, if we extend this scheme of visualizing relative strengths to the 16-pole model and observe minimal rules of conformal mapping, we would have a very distorted map. I have labeled each area with the appropriate pole number.

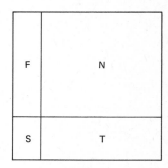

If we measured the areas on the map, we would find for our particular example that pole 16 was the strongest and pole 1 was the weakest, but

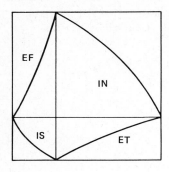

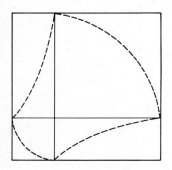

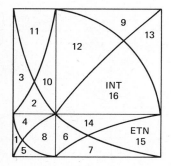

the hierarchy from the strongest to the weakest would not be sequentially from pole 16 to pole 1, the exact sequence depending on the particular profile.

This is a fascinating outcome, for it answers both of the original questions in the affirmative. There can be an infinite number of profiles, depending on the degree to which the map of capacities is distorted. But there also seem to be certain interrelationships resulting from unequal partitioning schemes, which delimit the number of variations possible. In short, there are discernible patterns, although there can be considerable variations in degree within a given pattern.

And this seems reasonable. Clearly, everyone's body is different. Some people have big shoulders and others have long legs. If we take all the observable differences, we also note certain patterns, as though we were speaking of a body personality type. We say, "He's built like a wrestler" or "That's a natural dancer" or runner or swimmer or what have you. Each type has unique strengths and patterns that help us recognize body specialization. And so it is also in the psychological realm.

11

INDIVIDUATION—THE KEY TO STABILITY IN PERSONALITY

The idea is developed here that stability in a personality requires differentiated strengths among the capacities—that is, that part and parcel of a healthy individual is the fact that he or she must have strengths and weaknesses.

THE DYNAMIC MODEL: THE
PROFILE

Embedded in the discussion in the previous chapter are all sorts of subtleties that need to be explored in greater detail. The discussion suggested
that profiles differ from capacity maps in three respects:

1. There are differences in strengths among poles.
2. There is a polar hierarchy.
3. There are discernible patterns.

These assertions raise a number of questions. Must the poles have differences in strengths? Just what do we mean by strength? What forces or
restraints exist that delimit the hierarchies so as to produce only a limited
number of patterns?

These are not easy questions to answer and require a number of detours
that increasingly involve the conscious and the unconscious, a dichotomy
that has been mentioned but not yet discussed. The unconscious is especially difficult to discuss, because, by definition, it is something hidden
from us. We will therefore try to get insights through analogies, and that
will lead us to discuss entropy, a fascinating and important concept.

We will ultimately find that the unconscious functions as a balancing
counterforce to the conscious—the ambi-syn-anti of the personality—that
makes us stable, or psychologically healthy. I address this question of
stability first and other aspects of the unconscious, including entropy, in
subsequent chapters.

A-4

Jung referred to personality formation as the process of *individuation*.
This process can be translated to mean that a healthy, stable personality
results from having made choices among the attributes of the dichotomies.
This is the natural order of events. In fact, the hardest thing would be
ambivalence, not making a choice, not favoring some capacities over
their opposites. Individuation therefore implies a preferential tilting or
one-sidedness. No tilt at all would be the most unstable state, something
akin to a split personality or schizophrenia.

The view that a perfectly balanced system is unstable may at first glance
seem paradoxical. Shouldn't balance be the most stable state? Well, in
dynamic systems—and personalities are dynamic—it's just the other way

D-4

around. Bowler referred to this as equilibration rather than equilibrium.

Equilibration implies a dynamic state, the seeking of equilibrium as an
unending process in which the system is always bringing imbalances into
play. This is a subject well understood in general systems theory and in
engineering and has to do with regulation and control. It is perhaps easiest
to discuss these aspects in a very literal sense through the example of a
governor.

Electricity runs on 60 cycles per second (cps), which is achieved by
regulating the steam turbines that generate most electricity at 3600 revolutions per minute (rpm) (3600 rpm equals 60 revolutions per second
and therefore 60 cps). It is important that these turbines are regulated to

run at exactly 3600 rpm. If the turbine should run at 3601 rpm, all our electric clocks, which are triggered by the 60-cycle frequency, would run too fast.

The irony and the heart of the matter is, however, that to keep our clocks on time, we deliberately see to it that our turbines never run at 3600 rpm. If the turbine does happen to run at exactly 3600 rpm, the governor will see to it that it shifts to a slightly different speed. As a consequence, a turbine's speed hunts around 3600 rpm, sometimes just a little slow, sometimes just a little fast. It is never kept at exactly the right speed.

The reason for this apparent insanity is that the governor gets the signal telling it what to do as the difference between the measured and the desired speeds. That is, the governor gets a constant stream of messages telling it that the turbine is running too slow and to speed it up, probably followed an instant later by a message that the turbine is running too fast and to slow it down. The worst message the governor can receive is a zero message—that there is no difference between the measured and desired speeds—for then it does not know what to do. It must always receive an unambiguous dichotomous signal; otherwise it is blind, because in effect it gets no signal at all.

This phenomenon is not limited to turbines. There are many systems that are made to hunt in order to behave with stability. For instance, jugglers and tightrope walkers are never really in equilibrium. They are always just slightly off-balance, busy correcting for the signal that the system is about to crash.

A secondary reason that makes this constant correcting advantageous for dynamic systems is that the system is more responsive when it is just off equilibrium. We see this dramatically in tennis. The players who must return the serve never stand still. They are in constant motion, not out of nervousness or indecision, but rather to heighten their responsiveness to move to the proper position once the ball has started its path toward them.

Perhaps the most familiar example is driving a car on a straight road. Theoretically, we could keep the steering wheel locked in the straight-ahead position, but that always gives us the feeling that we've lost control of the car. Instead, we find ourselves constantly steering a bit to the right, then a bit to the left, averaging a straight course.

This should suffice to make the point that stability is achieved by always having to make dichotomous choices—either slow or fast, right or left, never exactly in the middle. Put another way, only one or the other attribute of a dichotomy must be in control. A stable system is therefore always tilted, always off neutral. Stability therefore means knowing that there is a dichotomous choice and making it.

Every healthy, normal individual makes these choices. What eludes us is not the making of the choices but the awareness that we made them.

It is the *knowing* that is so difficult, because the process of individuation is so complex, extended, and subtle, masked by the cliché of growing pains. To the growing child, youth is not a search for stability but merely a series of happenings of large and small joys and crises, pains and pleasures. Only in retrospect do we realize that all the forgotten perceptions of, and reactions to, myriad experiences have resulted in a decision about four basic dichotomies. Let us then have a second look at the typical and natural sequence of events in the growing-up process.

THE PERSONALITY ORIENTATION

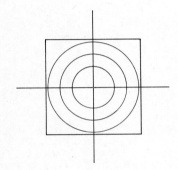

The orientation of a personality stems from the individual's effort to optimize chances for survival in the encountered environment. The individual might be limited in this process by certain predispositions that may be set before birth.

Generally speaking, a child has no biases with respect to the total map of capacities. Every skill is fascinating and possible. The child roams without bias all over the capacities domain. He jabbers away as happily as he uses his hands to dig in the sand. He reasons, reflects, and engages in intellectual challenges with the same zest he applies to body action, be it running, riding a tricycle, or any other activity.

This lack of bias—or, putting it another way, this lack of orientation—continues until a circumstance or experience blocks a personal need. The determinant might be the orientation of his parents or an older sibling. To get his way, the child might discover that he does best when he plays to the parents' or sibling's weaknesses. This is certainly one way the child may stumble across a preferred emphasis in his growing capacities.

It may happen in other ways, quite often through negative experiences, especially in school. He learns quickly that it is our limitations which tell us who we are.

The negative encounter is especially one where the dichotomies start to play a big role. Should some child do poorly in sports, he will naturally drift toward the opposite pole and into more bookish, intellectual directions.

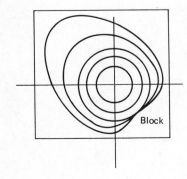

A child's development looks much like tree rings on a capacities map. As she grows, she probes deeper and deeper into what might be called "capacity space." At first there is little bias. Everything is intriguing, and the child grows in experiences in all directions: sharper intellect, improved body coordination, greater verbal skills, and better hand dexterity.

She maintains such isotropic growth until a block is encountered that drives her to explore more actively in the opposite direction. Thus a unique profile is produced that eventually settles into a dominant orientation.

The strengths, or the reliance on innate capacities, start to develop differentially. If there is positive feedback, the process of skewing becomes even more pronounced. It is at this stage that the child develops strong preferences and begins to articulate some meaningful goals, such as "I want to be an engineer." The cultural biases, which we unfortunately build into the development of children, probably come more through the reinforcements than through the blocks. But even the blocks might be induced by pushing a child too hard or by a competitively disadvantageous situation ("I can't ever be as good as my sister").

If we only knew what we do to our kids (and what is going on in their heads), we could probably maintain a child's growth without serious blocks. But even such a lofty goal is not a blessing.

Our society expects a skewing to develop, certainly by the late high-school or early college years. Guidance counselors know how helpless they feel about bright all-around youngsters who do superbly in everything. Naturally, they must go to college, but that only bucks the problem upstairs. College advisors ask them what they want to major in, and they do not know. Everything seems fascinating to them. As a consequence, they change their majors aimlessly, and soon they are accused of being immature or unmotivated.

The truth is that we don't really like well-rounded people. We don't know how to cope with them. One way or another, some sooner, some later, some smoothly, some painfully, youngsters are pushed into a differentiated posture. Some set of capacities, which plots as a skewing on the capacities map, starts to take on a dominant role. When that is well developed in a normal individual, one can speak of a *differentiated* personality.

The individuation process takes place over many years and progresses unevenly. Each period of life is made up of thousands of experiences and little crises that ultimately blur into the single perception of "growing up." The awareness of the key decisions is largely lost. The actual process of individuation is therefore largely unconscious. This contributes to the difficulty we have in understanding who we are.

The unconscious, which plays such a big role in personality development, has been of vast interest to psychology. Most of Jung's writing deals with the unconscious, and he has made important contributions through his work on complexes, symbols, myths, and archetypes. Study of these has helped tremendously in the interpretation of dreams, a widely used means for getting to know what the unconscious is dealing with.

My approach is to get some insight into the unconscious through the structure of consciousness. This approach is more practical for our purposes, for it takes years of specialized training to interpret dreams and to deal properly with the revealed content of the unconscious. In this work we are not interested in the content of the unconscious, only in its purpose, role, and structure. Because consciousness is itself a dichotomy, the unconscious plays a balancing role to the conscious, and its nature can be inferred from its conscious opposite.

It is, however, useful to make the concept of consciousness more concrete, and I do this in the next chapter by using analogies. This detour will lead us to an important conclusion: namely, that the polar hierarchy represents an ordering of consciousness. Those capacities we call the strongest are really only the most conscious. The weakest pole is not really weak, but so deep in the unconscious that it is weak only in its responsiveness to our directions. Strong and weak in a personality therefore translate more properly into conscious and unconscious, with the important realization that we can control and direct only that which is conscious. But who is to say that what we cannot control is a lesser part of our personalities? It is as important, and we can infer its contributions through the dichotomous structure.

12

THE MANY ASPECTS OF ENTROPY

This chapter develops ideas substantiating the view that strength in a capacity is equivalent to highly ordered information and that weakness in a capacity relates to disordered information. These concepts are crucial to the idea of libido-driven information flow as the model for cerebral processes.

The transition from the map of capacities to profiles is a very big step. It is one thing to talk about innate capacities or even their organization; it is quite another matter to derive from those capacities the complex behavior and personality patterns that evolve during maturation.

We have seen that, from general systems considerations of stability, one should expect a healthy personality to show differences in strengths among the poles. But just exactly what do we mean by strengths? That is one question yet to be answered.

We have also pointed out that the tilting that results from the dichotomous choices creates a finite number of patterns that always show a derivable polar hierarchy. But what is the interpretive meaning of such a hierarchy? What does it mean to be highest or lowest?

Related to the hierarchy question is the even more difficult one of how to connect the derived hierarchical patterns to observed behavioral patterns. Without that linking, the incredible order of the theoretical construct cannot help us gain insight into the complexities and functioning of personalities.

And lastly, if we are to deal with consciousness how are we to describe its unconscious attribute which, by definition, is not known? In other words, how can we define and clarify that aspect of the consciousness dichotomy of which we have no awareness?

This chapter tackles all these questions, which are strongly interrelated and are components of a larger conceptual construct that has entropy at its core.

STATIC ORDER

The map of capacities really deals with static order, an order that results from specialization and structure, the same kind of order that is inherent in an organizational chart. It is important to recognize that this order is there regardless of whether anything is happening. Let me put it another way: a library also has an imposed structural order that results from its organization; even at night when no one is using the books on the shelves, that order still exists.

DYNAMIC ORDER

A profile deals with dynamic order, an idea that becomes clear when we think of the system as one that processes information. The system, viewed as a network of poles and interconnecting circuits, is busy with information flowing through the network. Some information enters the network from the outside; some is stored or retrieved from memory; some is being processed by poles; and much is on its way from one place to another.

Order in this sense is anything but static. It is as dynamic as city traffic, and we could describe the state of dynamic order and disorder by how smoothly things are flowing, or by the size of the queues, or by how much disruption has resulted from all this activity. We refer to it as dynamic order, recognizing that the state constantly changes with time. If the degree of order changes, then there are factors that promote disorder and factors that promote order and probably both.

ORDER AND DISORDER

A concern with order and disorder is basic to anything involving information. The forces involved become very clear when we think about a personal filing system or a library. The more you use your files or the library, the more likely that something will be lost or misplaced. Use or activity promotes disorder innately. The more the system is used, the more disorderly it becomes until it ultimately deteriorates to a state of uselessness. This happens unless order is periodically reestablished. That is, effort and energy must be deliberately supplied to create order. There are, then, a natural disordering process that happens by itself and a reverse ordering process that requires energy.

Clearly, the desirable state is order, for that reflects a state of organization that makes it easy to get information. Order is essential if information is to be available. If information retrieval is my goal—for example, if I'm looking for a letter in my file—I expect to find it where the organization suggests it should be. The very last thing I want is to be surprised. I want the very opposite; I want my expectations to be fulfilled. For dynamic use, then, the lack of surprise means order, and order helps information become available and therefore retrievable.

Now suppose that I'm looking for a letter in my files; I go to the proper spot, and, lo and behold, I do get surprised; I find a letter that doesn't belong there. Surely this provides me with a golden opportunity to file it properly. In short, surprise became the alerting signal to help me create order from disorder.

Order and availability versus disorder and surprise, therefore, act like another ambi-syn-anti pair, but now they act as dynamic complements. One triggers the other. If I have a high degree of order in a complicated ordered system, the more I use it, the more disorderly it will become; but then I also generate more surprises, which re-create the order.

ENTROPY

This discussion of order and disorder points to a concept called *entropy*. Entropy is a measure of disorder, a quantitative means for describing a state of disorder. The greater the disorder, the larger the entropy. The greater the order, the less the entropy. It is a term associated primarily with thermodynamics and information theory. The main point I wish to bring out here is that entropy is so useful in describing a dynamic process. While something is happening, I can watch or calculate how the entropy is changing. If the entropy increases, I know that the process going on is causing the order of the system to deteriorate. If the entropy decreases, I know that order is being restored.

But there is much more to entropy. Entropy is a very rich concept that can be linked to availability (thermodynamics) or probability, interpretable as surprise (information theory). Both interpretations can be linked to order.

Even more subtle are the interpretations that explain changes in entropy. A change in entropy can reflect a change in state in a closed system or a change in content in an open system. The latter effect stems from the fact that entropy is an extensive quantity as opposed to, say, temperature, which is intensive (the temperature of 2 gallons of water is not twice the temperature of 1 gallon, but the entropy is twice as much). This aspect has interpretive consequences for esthetics and complexity and through those, to the unconscious, complexes, and archetypes, which are fundamental structures.

But this sounds much too complicated. Let us have a closer, less technical look at these aspects of entropy and its associated connection to the conscious and unconscious.

ORDER, AVAILABILITY, INTELLIGENCE, AND THE SECOND LAW OF THERMODYNAMICS

Let me illustrate the connection between order and availability with a simple example. Assume my car is stuck in a ditch, and I ask several people to help me push it out. Without organization, the people might distribute themselves around the car, with one in front, two in back, and some on the sides, and push vigorously—some forward, some backwards, some sideways; nothing would be accomplished. Their efforts are unavailing for the hoped-for purpose because their efforts would be too uncoordinated and disorderly.

If, on the other hand, I direct their efforts by instructing each to push in the forward direction when I say, ''Ready, set, *go*,'' the car will suddenly break free. Order is needed to make their energy available and their efforts pay off.

Directing this effort, knowing how to structure the coordination of effort, and ordering the effort to produce the useful effect are conscious intelligence. So intelligence is the result of useful ordering.

Let us examine this concept with another example. Consider a new library. Every book has been carefully catalogued and shelved; everything is in place. Chances are very high that, with such perfect order, users will be able to find what they are looking for. The better the scheme that is used for ordering the books, the easier it will be to find things. Because there is order, the reader can always find a given book but, depending on the order, not necessarily the best book.

Suppose the shelving scheme is one where all green books are shelved together in decreasing size. If the catalogue indicates a given shelf location, you might be tempted to look at the adjacent book just to see if that is an even better choice for your purposes. But under this scheme that will be of little use because it is likely that adjacent books will bear no relationship in content to each other.

Now to carry the example even further, assume that the library is understaffed and heavily used. A month later, it will be much harder for readers to find what they want. Some books will be out, some misplaced, some new ones not yet catalogued. The collection has become disordered, and the availability of books has decreased. Only by a consistent application of effort (energy) can the order be maintained. Without such effort, the more the collection is used, the more things will deteriorate into a disorderly mess. This fact of nature is known as the second law of thermodynamics, which states in effect: Left to its own accord, the entropy (that is, the disorder) of any closed system increases.

We have brought out several concepts:

1.   Order and availability are linked.
2.   The effectiveness of the ordering scheme is conscious intelligence.
3.   With use and no outside intervention, order will deteriorate.

OPEN SYSTEMS AND COMPLEXITY

Another aspect of entropy has to do with the *size* of the collection. Let us illustrate the point with the same example. Assume the library was working pretty well. The collection was well maintained and systematically managed. One day, the library receives a $20 million grant to increase its holdings. Clearly, there are new problems. Not only will there be more books in a given subject area, but there also will be more subject areas covered, and possibly even maps, rare books, and other special collections. The expanded size will probably force the library to use a computerized scheme. In short, the increased *content* of the collection will force the library to a new *organizing schema*. This points to the fact that, as information content increases, new organizing schemas are needed.

We experience the same thing with our personal filing systems. Whatever the schema is, there is always a miscellaneous file to cover all those items the filing schema could not accommodate. When the miscellaneous file becomes as large as the file itself, the filing system is useless, and the files had better be restructured.

This is a very important principle, something we might call the increase in entropy due to size or complexity.

ESTHETICS: BALANCING ORDER AND DISORDER

No one is more affected by the various aspects of entropy just discussed than the artist. Be it composing music or creating a painting, artists must make choices among intelligence, complexity, surprise, and information content. If a painting conveys nothing, it is meaningless or dull; if it conveys too much, it is confusing and indigestible. Fortunately, artists can control all the elements of order through their choices of medium, size, color, shape, texture, and so forth.

Artists might set limited challenges for themselves. They may try to produce the most pleasing creation but limit it to a 3 by 4–foot canvas, use only two colors, and restrict the design to only two squares of different sizes. Even with such severe restrictions, it is amazing how many design choices must be faced. Artists really have explored such challenges. Kasimir Malevich's "Suprematist Composition—White on White" in the permanent collection of the Museum of Modern Art in New York City is such an example (one white square placed ingeniously on a square white canvas).

There are many solutions to these challenges, and most have been tried with various degrees of success. For instance, an artist could paint a perfectly regular array of small squares, with just one of the small squares out of place. This always is the problem the artist faces. If his ordering schema is too extreme, too regularized, we don't perceive the work as art. We almost feel as though a machine could have done that. On the other hand, if he carries things too far and uses every conceivable shape, color, and arrangement, we also don't consider it art. It is too chaotic, and no organizing schema can be recognized. It is just a mess. A mess in the same sense that we would not take the rag the artist uses to clean his brushes and stick it in a frame as a painting. It is simply not art, because its design was totally stochastic, created by chance.

What we call art, therefore, falls somewhere between extreme order and extreme disorder. Too much order lacks surprise interest, and too little order lacks an organizing schema. It is as though organization and surprise were opposing forces.

We have already labeled the organizational schema as intelligence. The surprise is properly called information and is also closely linked to entropy. This insight, due to Shannon, is important in cryptography and language analysis. If I write the sentence, "Today t e sun i shining," you have little trouble filling in the voids: "Today the sun is shining." Since you could fill in the missing information, it really wasn't needed information. In fact, the missing letters conveyed no information. That is why you didn't need them. Natural language is redundant in information. If we lose a little, we can usually make it out.

But not all languages are redundant. Information is therefore best described as the *essential surprise*. For instance, in the word "p t" you might guess that the missing letter is "o" (pot). But if I tell you that it is "i" (pit), I have changed your expectation (surprised you) and have given you a lot of information.

Entropy thus measures both the ordering schema (intelligence) and the surprise (information) for collections of small or large numbers of constituent variables. What we call esthetics must find the sensitive midpoint, the optimal entropy. These two ends of the spectrum are psychologically equivalent to the interplay between the conscious and the unconscious.

Consciousness is equivalent to the well-ordered library collection. The unconscious is the uncatalogued (messy) collection. Consciousness reflects the organizing schema; the unconscious, the surprise element.

So the mind is very much like a library with both well-organized and uncatalogued collections. Growing children, as well as students, are constantly increasing the size of their collections (both catalogued and uncatalogued) and periodically reach stages where they need to create new cataloguing schemas to cope with the increasingly large miscellaneous file. This subject interested Piaget, who has pinpointed the stages in very young children when new constructs (organizing schemata) have taken place.

C-3

The point must also be made that the uncatalogued collection is not totally chaotic. If we continue with the library analogy, the point is most easily made clear. Let us assume that the uncatalogued collection is piled up in the order received, a reasonable assumption. Then there is at least a minimal chronological ordering. Sure, someone may will his personal library of old books and backdated magazines, mixed in with current government reports; but even so, there will be a most recent date and nothing will have a publishing date of 2000.

Beyond this general temporal order, there will be clusters of order. A butterfly collector who gave his holdings might have a cluster of material ordered by the subject of butterflies.

The point is that the unconscious too contains intelligence, or complexes, which, however, are embedded in other disordered material that may make it hard to recognize clusters. When they are recognized (and they are constantly browsed through), the material is lifted out and made part of the ordered collection (conscious). The unconscious is therefore a rich source of new material for the conscious.

THE DYNAMIC MODEL: THE
PROFILE

A-4

There is one more ordering aspect in the unconscious that is perhaps the most potent but most subtle of all. It is what Jung called archetypes. There are some basic ordering principles even an uncatalogued collection cannot escape.

Let us assume that someone gave boxes of books to the library to be added to the uncatalogued collection. On unpacking the boxes, a box of diamonds and rubies fell out that had accidentally been mixed in with the books. You can be sure that the box of jewels won't just stay mixed in with that uncatalogued pile of books, because it violates the inherent organizational schema of the existing collection. It has, so to say, a force of its own that we can't escape; so we must pay attention to it and treat it differently from the rest. In fact, we might start a separate section in the library on precious jewels; that is, the embedded complex interacts with the original organizational schema so sharply that it causes changes in the schema itself.

If the complex deals with the structure of the organizational schema itself, as, for instance, books in a library on the subject of computerized libraries, we have a complex that Jung would have called an archetype. An archetype deals with the very structure of which it is a part. It is so fundamental that it is an inescapable part of us all. It is a part of what Jung called the "collective unconscious." Archetypes are the organizational clusters we share in common, the built-in wiring, so to say. Much of this book deals with this. It is the mind speaking to itself about itself. It is thinking thoughts about thinking.

13

LEVELS OF CONSCIOUSNESS

(A Preview of How Levels of
Consciousness Predicate a Profile)

The first three chapters of Part III were designed to introduce concepts we need now.

In Chapter 10 we found that something as simple and rigid as the 16-pole map of capacities can nevertheless represent the personalities of millions of different people simply because the 16 capacities are not of equal strengths.

In Chapter 11 we found that the different strengths associated with these 16 poles cannot take on just any value. For a stable system, the collective influence of the various dichotomies inherent to the organization makes itself felt by imposing restricting relationships on the strengths that poles can assume. Thus a strong pole always gives rise to a weak one and vice versa. So even if we allow for different strengths of poles, the dichotomous structure underlying the 16-pole model delimits the possibilities according to certain structural rules. Pole strengths thus assume some predictable hierarchical order.

In Chapter 12 we found that strength is an important variable in the dynamic model and that we need a clearer understanding of what that variable represents. Strength, order, entropy, and consciousness were then linked, suggesting that they are all related. Specifically, high pole strength goes with high order, low entropy, and high consciousness; and low pole strength goes with low order, high entropy, and low consciousness. We can therefore redefine the strength variable as levels of consciousness. This is the crucial variable that makes personalities different from one another, even though all draw on the same capacities.

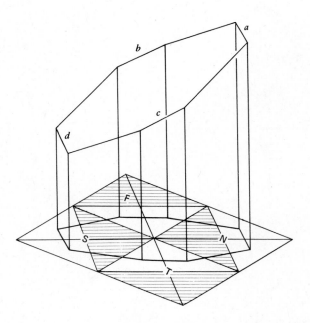

When we think of how a unique personality processes information, we must envision not only the map of capacities, reflecting unique organizational relationships among the capacities, but also unique levels of consciousness assignable to these 16 poles.

Incorporating this new variable, the level of consciousness, would thus produce a very complex diagram, something in three dimensions. Such a diagram is shown as it might look for a particular profile. Even with levels of consciousness shown for only eight poles (those in the C circuit), the diagram is too complex. We need to find another graphic or symbolic way to represent this new variable.

Instead of dealing with one three-dimensional figure, my approach is to use two two-dimensional diagrams and define rules for mapping the information of one onto the other. One of the two-dimensional diagrams is the familiar map of capacities; the other is what I call the *entropy diagram*. The entropy diagram tells us the appropriate level of consciousness for each pole in the map.

This two-step representation might be visualized as:

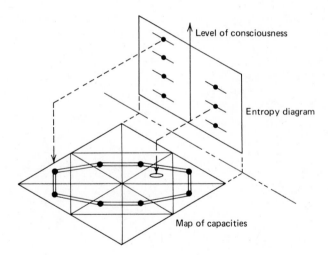

The entropy diagram (with a negative entropy scale—i.e., higher up in the diagram means less entropy) tells us the level of consciousness for each pole. All we need then is some scheme for telling us which level goes with what pole, or which pole is at what level, so that we can relate the information contained in the two separate diagrams.

To discover that rule—namely, how to assign a specified level of consciousness to the various poles—is not simple. First of all, the levels of consciousness are not absolute values; they differ from person to person. All we can deal with are relative values. But even with a relative scale there is a highest and a lowest level of consciousness.

In the transposition to the map of capacities, to which pole do we assign the highest level of consciousness? The answer is: To any of the 16 poles. Each of these 16 possibilities corresponds to what we call a *profile*.

When we include the level of consciousness as a variable, we have transformed the map of capacities from a universal organizing schema of our cognitive capacities into a profile representation. That expands the complexity tremendously. The map of capacities is the same for all of us, but a given profile fits only some of us. The inclusion of levels of consciousness gives rise to 16 uniquely differentiated personality profiles. This is the subject of the remainder of this book.

As we must link levels of consciousness to specific poles, I illustrate the procedure by focusing initially on just one of the 16 profiles. Our reference illustration is that profile for which pole 16 has the highest level of consciousness. This profile will be called DETN. It should be clear, however, that I could have chosen any other pole, and therefore any other profile, for the illustration. Thus the procedure I use for DETN applies to all the other profiles.

In our illustrative profile, the highest level of consciousness is linked to pole 16, thereby defining the profile DETN.

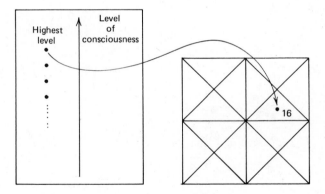

This leaves us with the problem of defining the relationships among all the remaining poles and their relative levels of consciousness. The solution to that problem is truly amazing, for it turns out that the rule for making all the remaining pole-level assignments is invariant; it is the same for all profiles.

I discovered that rule when the model was still at its eight-pole stage through something I've come to call *roles*.

Because the stream of interlinked ideas is so complex, let us jump to the final outcome of the discussion as an overview of where we are headed.

An entropy diagram can be developed that is generic for all profiles; that is, the entropy diagram assigns a unique level of consciousness to every pole in the map of capacities once the pole with the highest level of consciousness is defined. So once we know a given individual's most conscious capacity, we know everything about his or her information processing that can be inferred from the 16-pole model.

The entropy diagram looks like this:

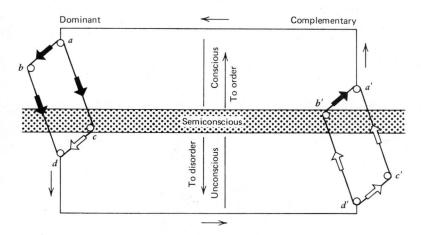

Note that it looks like a circuit in which something is flowing. This something is information. The letters *a*, *b*, *c*, *d* and *a'*, *b'*, *c'*, *d'* represent relative levels of consciousness that follow a fixed hierarchy, with *a* highest in consciousness and *d'* lowest.

The horizontal band defines a semiconscious region separating the conscious region on top from the unconscious region below.

There is a relationship between this flow in the entropy circuit and flows that can be visualized in the map of capacities. The equivalence is illustrated for the case DETN by showing the four flow paths separately from left to right.

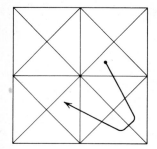 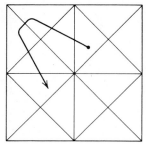 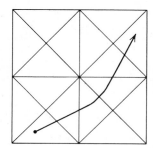 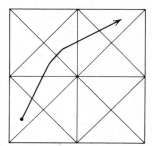

These can be combined as two branch flows, first out of *a*, then out of *d'*:

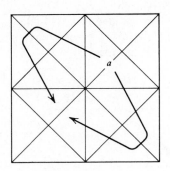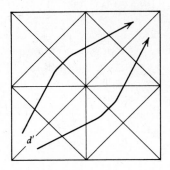

And finally, they can be combined into a single two-path flow pattern.

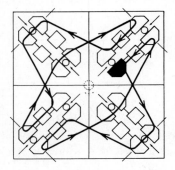

On both the map and the entropy diagram, we see then a natural flow of information in a closed pair of loops emanating from *a* and ultimately returning to *a*. The entropy diagram shows us the levels of consciousness the flow passes through, and the map shows us through what capacities the flow passes.

If we combine the insights of the plots by, say, shading the unconscious regions on the entropy diagram,

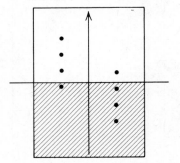

we would also get a shading of unconscious regions on the map of capacities, as shown:

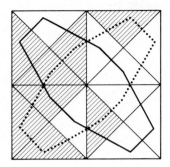

Therefore, some of the information flow and capacities are conscious, and some are unconscious.

It is important to note that this ordered pattern is always the same. All we need to know is the strongest pole. In the diagram just discussed, pole 16 was the strongest. Following are a number of other profiles with the strongest pole noted:

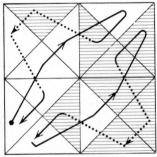

Pole 1 strongest

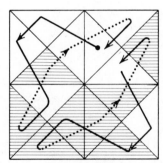

Pole 12 strongest

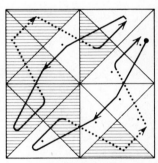

Pole 13 strongest

The pattern is always the same. The entropy diagram produces an overlay of the conscious and unconscious that can take on various orientations. This overlay is a new dichotomy that I call *consciousness*. The different orientations represent what Jung called "manifestations of the unconscious," and each profile has a unique consciousness.

All these outcomes grow out of a single diagram, the entropy diagram, which is generic to all profiles. We need to discuss the diagram in detail and what interpretive insights we can extract from it. Our ultimate goal is to read interpretive meanings into each and every profile; that is, we want to infer from the model how a person with a particular profile processes information. What does he or she do consciously and unconsciously, and what implications can thus be drawn? For these interpre-

THE DYNAMIC MODEL: THE
PROFILE

tations, we find roles tremendously helpful. These too are discussed in detail.

We have, then, several tasks before us:

1. To describe the roles.
2. To describe the dichotomy of consciousness.
3. To describe the construction of the entropy diagram.
4. To describe the interrelationships among the roles, dichotomy of consciousness, and entropy diagrams.
5. To show how these three concepts can be used to construct a profile.
6. To show how we use items 1 through 5 to draw interpretive inferences for each profile.

14

ROLES

Roles are self-perceptions about the various capacities in the map of capacities. For instance, when I asked individuals how they felt about some particular capacity, I would get responses such as "This is very difficult for me," or "I love to do this," or "I never get tired of doing that."

I collected many such responses and found it easy to organize the variously expressed self-perceptions into eight groups such that the essence of each group could be captured by a single key word. I refer to these eight key words as the *fundamental roles*. Amazingly, these eight fundamental roles reflect not only a hierarchical order but also the dichotomous structure of the eight-pole model. I therefore present them here as two ordered subsets, highlighting the oppositional relationships:

Dependable	versus	Erratic
Responsible	versus	Frivolous
Constrained	versus	Free
Difficult	versus	Easy

It is crucial to note that the subset on the left involves descriptors that give the feeling of increasing "uptightness," whereas the set on the right is opposite in character, what colloquially might be called "hanging loose." Put another way, the left set seems to describe levels of control or accountability, as though one were looking for something in a file and the degree of success, reflecting the state of the files, was being described.

The right set of descriptors suggests more a kind of creative spontaneity with differentiated levels of new discoveries. This suggests, using the file analogy, how a person assigned to straightening out the files might feel. He may find the file in such a state that the discovery of surprises that lead to order is a hit-or-miss situation (erratic); or he may have got just the right surprises, which made the job a cinch (easy).

Clearly, there is a connection between these self-perceptions, or fundamental roles, and entropy. The set on the left describes states of increasing entropy, whereas the set on the right describes states of decreasing entropy. One set is therefore associated with entropy production, the other with negative entropy production.

This ordering can be made explicit by assigning letters to the roles:

Dependable	a	versus	d'	Erratic
Responsible	b	versus	c'	Frivolous
Constrained	c	versus	b'	Free
Difficult	d	versus	a'	Easy

We have identified two ordered sets, *a b c d* and *a′ b′ c′ d′*, where *a* and *a′* represent for each set the relatively highest levels of consciousness (low entropy), and *d* and *d′* the relatively lowest levels of consciousness.

The linkage to entropy suggests that we can use these roles as identifiers of the various levels of consciousness of the capacities in the map of capacities. Of course, we do not know the relative levels of the two sets as yet, only their hierarchical order with respect to entropy. But we now have a tool. We can mark the eight levels on the map of capacities as relative indications of levels of consciousness.

I did exactly that with people I had queried about their self-perceptions of specific capacities. I then mapped their responses to these level indicators (*a b c d* and *a′ b′ c′ d′*) and got amazingly patterned responses. A few examples are shown:

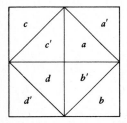 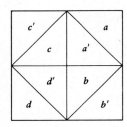 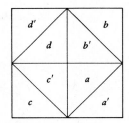

There are several things worth noting:

1. Similar primed and unprimed letters—for example, *a* and *a′* or *b* and *b′*—always fall in the same quadrant. As quadrants represent Jungian functions, this suggests a means for relating functions to levels of consciousness, with *a* and *a′* highest in consciousness. Wherever *a* and *a′* fall must identify what Jung called the superior function.

2. As *d* and *d′* always fall opposite *a* and *a′* and are also lowest on the relative consciousness scale, *d* and *d′* must identify the inferior function of a given profile.

3. By similar reasoning, wherever *b* and *b′* fall must identify the first auxiliary function, and *c* and *c′* must identify the second auxiliary function.

Even more amazing is the pattern of the primed versus unprimed roles. Not only do they fall into opposing circuits (C or D), but also in every case the unprimed role letters fall into the dominant circuit of the particular personality.

Let us look at the case for the reference profile DETN. In the eight-pole model it would appear as follows:

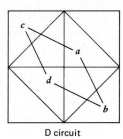 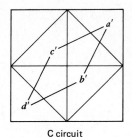

D circuit   C circuit

In the 16-pole model, it would look like this, where the role identifier obviously refers to the superpoles:

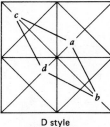 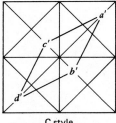

D style
Dominant circuit

C style
Complementary circuit

We recognize the links shown in these diagrams as transactions and note that each transaction falls between unique level indicators. There are eight transactions, falling between:

1.	a and b	5.	b and d
2.	b' and a'	6.	d' and b'
3.	a and c	7.	c and d
4.	c' and a'	8.	d' and c'

As each letter corresponds not only to a level but also to a role, we should also be able to derive self-perceptions about transactions, or *transaction roles*. The combination of key words suggests the following list of new key words. In the last column, another key word is listed, which I call a *mode role*.

We see then that the key words or roles not only reflect levels of consciousness but also suggest relationships among them, leading to transaction roles, which in turn lead to mode roles.

It may be helpful to look at these derived roles for transactions and modes in a different context. Let me consider the work situation of painting a room as an energy flow analysis. Clearly, there is an energy transfer from the painter to the paint. Let us look at the process in detail:

	Fundamental Roles	Transaction Roles	Mode Roles
a and b	Dependable and responsible	Competence	Work
b' and a'	Free and easy	Talent	
a and c	Dependable and constrained	Perseverance	Play
c' and a'	Frivolous and easy	Relaxation	
b and d	Responsible and difficult	Toil	Challenge
d' and b'	Erratic and free	Serendipity	
c and d	Constrained and difficult	Lock	Creativity
d' and c'	Erratic and frivolous	Key	

We must identify an initial state (1) before the painting began and a final state (2) when the room is completely painted. In the initial state the painter is full of vigor and energy, represented by E_1. After he or she, let's assume he, finished painting, he feels tired because of all the work he has done. He's now at an energy state E_2. The difference, $E_1 - E_2 = \Delta E_s$, represents the energy he has expended to do the job. His effort is represented by ΔE_s, where s is the subject.

Theoretically, it is this difference in energy, ΔE, that was transferred from the painter to the paint during the process of painting and must show up as an increase in the energy state of the paint. Let us consider the initial energy state of the paint as E_3. All the paint is in the paint bucket standing on the floor. We can view that paint as having low mechanical potential energy. The job of painting can thus be interpreted as raising the mechanical potential of the paint by lifting it from the bucket to higher elevations, such as the walls and ceiling, until the final energy state of the paint has been raised from E_3 to E_4. That increase, $E_4 - E_3 = \Delta E_o$, represents the energy gain of the paint, where o is the object, and theoretically should equal the ΔE_s transferred by the painter to the paint.

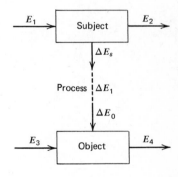

We have conceptualized an energy balance for a working situation that we can generalize as shown:

Let

$$E_1 - E_2 = \Delta E_s = \text{effort}$$
$$\Delta E_T = \text{net energy transferred from subject to object} = \text{process}$$
$$E_4 - E_3 = \Delta E_o = \text{result}$$

where

E_1 is initial energy of subject

E_2 is final energy of subject

ΔE_s is net energy expended by subject $= E_1 - E_2$

ΔE_o is net energy applied to object $= E_1 - E_2 = E_4 - E_3$

E_3 is initial energy of object

E_4 is final energy of object

ΔE_T is energy transferred from subject to object.

Assume $\Delta E_s = \Delta E_o = \Delta E_T$

(T stands for transfer)

Then consider the flow of energy from subject to object,

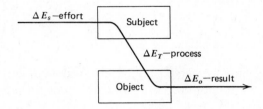

and consider all cases where ΔE_s, ΔE_T, and ΔE_o are sensed by the subject consciously or unconsciously—that is, where there is or is not an awareness of effort, process, and/or result.

We have generated an idealized model that views any working situation in three aspects: effort, process, and result. Which one you notice depends on what you focus on. If the painter's perceptions concentrate on how tired he is getting, he is focusing on effort. If he pays attention to what he is doing, he is focusing on process; and if he looks admiringly at what he has accomplished, he is focusing on results. So which aspect of the work situation is highlighted depends on one's perceptions. Specifically, in this context this refers to whether the painter (1) registers and interprets those signals that tell him his muscles ache or (2) is preoccupied with the routines required for painting (whether the brushes are dry or dripping paint, identifying the border that tells him where to apply paint next, etc.) or (3) deals with an assessment of what's been done already and whether the evaluation is good or bad. Effort, process, and result thus involve different processes of the mind, processing selected informational cues. In this example, internal body sensations were processed, routines were executed, and visual inputs were evaluated. Each can be linked to inputs, transactions, and/or outputs on the map of capacities.

It is interesting to ask what would happen if some of those inputs, outputs, and transactions fell into the unconscious—that is, what the effect would be if the awareness of certain information processing is lost. This situation is analyzed systematically in the following table.

We consider all the eight possible cases, ranging from the subject being aware of the mental processes that assess effort, process, and result, through cases where any two or only one of these three is consciously processed, to the case where there is no awareness of effort, process, or result.

I am suggesting that these eight situations can be linked to the eight transaction roles, as summarized in the table and accompanying descriptions. This is just a different way of looking at common experiences.

Transaction roles listed in order of consciousness levels.

	Awareness			Transaction Roles	
	ΔE_S	ΔE_T	ΔE_O	Dominant Circuit	Complementary Circuit
	Effort	Process	Result		
conscious	✓	✓	✓	Competence	
		✓	✓	Perseverance	
	✓		✓		Talent
	✓	✓		Toil	
unconscious		✓		Lock	Relaxation
	✓				
			✓		Serendipity
					Key

COMPETENCE: Total awareness of *effort, process,* and *result.* Therefore willing to be accountable, able to accept criticism, and able to explain what was done.

PERSEVERANCE: No awareness of *effort,* therefore no sense of getting tired, as, for instance, in hobbies like stamp collecting. Can keep up activity unendingly (almost). Aware of what is being done *(process)* and spurred on by awareness of *result.*

TOIL: Activity that is procrastinated because there is no apparent payoff or it seems not worth the effort. Therefore no real awareness of *result* but high awareness of *effort* and *process.*

LOCK: Activity involved with problem solving. Prepared to put energy into solving it *(effort),* but have no idea how to go about solving it *(process)* or what to expect as a *result.*

TALENT: Natural skill to do something without any real awareness of how it is done *(process).* Merely apply *effort* and it produces *results.*

RELAXATION: Activity done for the fun of it. The *process* is an end in itself. Notice neither the *effort* nor the *result.*

SERENDIPITY: Activity where *result* is achieved without knowing how *(process)* and without apparent *effort.*

KEY: Unknown mysterious phenomenon that is the creative expression of the unconscious. Only through play or dreams is there awareness that the phenomenon has taken place.

THE DICHOTOMY OF CONSCIOUSNESS

When I began to identify the eight fundamental roles that I have introduced in this chapter, I was still working predominantly with the eight-pole model. Empirically, I had found that these fundamental roles, or self-perceptions, mapped onto the map of capacities with the regularity I have described. I found a rational basis for these observations in the 16-pole model.

From the truth table type of analysis applied to the 16-pole model, four dichotomies are derivable, which I call the *dichotomies of consciousness*. In the eight-pole model, similar dichotomies are present that could be viewed as preconscious indicators.

The attribute pairs of the four dichotomies of consciousness or the eight manifestations of consciousness in the 16-pole model are:

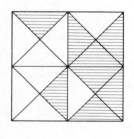 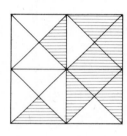 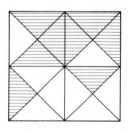 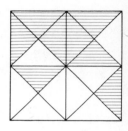

Complements

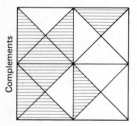 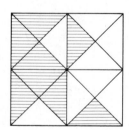 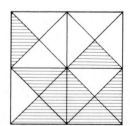 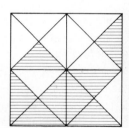

The four preconscious indicators from the eight-pole model are:

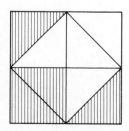 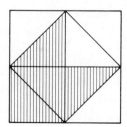 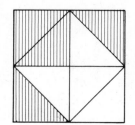 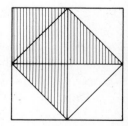

When superimposed, they define conscious, semiconscious, and unconscious regions, indicated by areas without shading, with double cross-hatching, and with single cross-hatching, respectively.

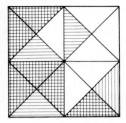 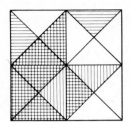 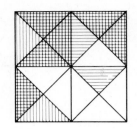 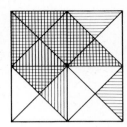

The four dichotomies of consciousness can also be derived from the competition/cooperation matrix. Each dichotomy represents two opposing pairs of poles, together with the poles linked to them from the competition/cooperation matrix (the T, X, M, and L links). If one pair of poles and its linked poles are in the conscious side of the dichotomy, the other pair of poles and its linked poles will be in the unconscious side. Either side of the dichotomy can be conscious or unconscious, depending on which pair of poles is in the conscious.

For the 16 and 15 pole pairs, the links for each pole are first shown separately and then are superimposed on the same diagram. This manifestation of the dichotomy of consciousness pairs poles 16 and 15 versus poles 1 and 2:

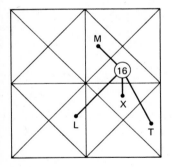 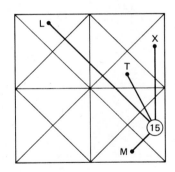 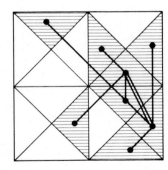

The remaining three dichotomies of consciousness are as follows:

Poles 14 and 13 versus poles 3 and 4:

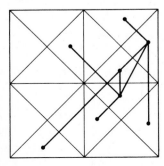 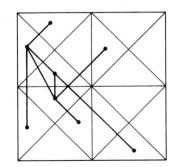

Poles 12 and 11 versus poles 5 and 6:

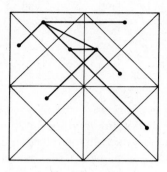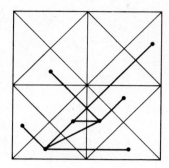

Poles 10 and 9 versus poles 7 and 8:

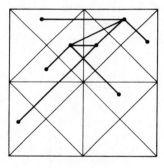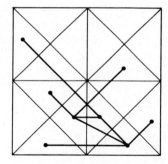

Now let's see what additional insights we've gained from these dichotomies of consciousness, using DETN as an example.

The fundamental roles for DETN are shown, as follows, on the map of capacities:

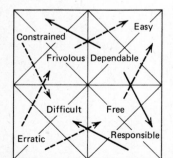

These fundamental roles in turn define the transaction roles and mode roles. For DETN:

Competence and talent, which define the work mode, are in the intellectual mode.

Perseverance and relaxation, which define the play mode, are in the verbal mode.

Toil and serendipity, which define the challenge mode, are in the fine motor mode.

Lock and key, which define the creativity mode, are in the gross motor mode.

The dichotomy of consciousness that pairs poles 16 and 15 (the pole pair for DETN) versus poles 1 and 2 is as follows:

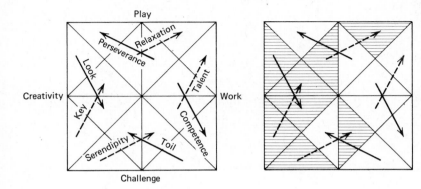

We can see that the mode roles are at different levels of consciousness:

The work mode is in the conscious.
The creativity mode is in the unconscious.
The play and challenge modes are mixed modes, part conscious and part unconscious.

These relative levels of consciousness are generic for the work, creativity, play, and challenge modes. Whether the work mode is in the intellectual, verbal, gross motor, or fine motor mode depends on the particular profile. But the work mode is always the most conscious mode, the creativity mode always the least conscious, and the play and challenge modes always somewhere between the two.

THE ENTROPY DIAGRAM

We have seen that in a given profile capacities have varying strengths described by the fundamental roles, which suggest by means of key words to what extent and under what circumstances an individual can draw on a given capacity. These differences have been linked to the dynamic state of order of the information flowing from pole to pole, where high order is equivalent to a high level of consciousness. The level of consciousness helps us interpret the role that pole plays in a given personality. Noting whether consciousness increases or decreases in a circuit link helps tremendously in identifying the roles of that circuit and of the particular transaction.

The entropy circuit is simply a means of ordering our thoughts so that we can describe in a single construct the myriad ideas that come into

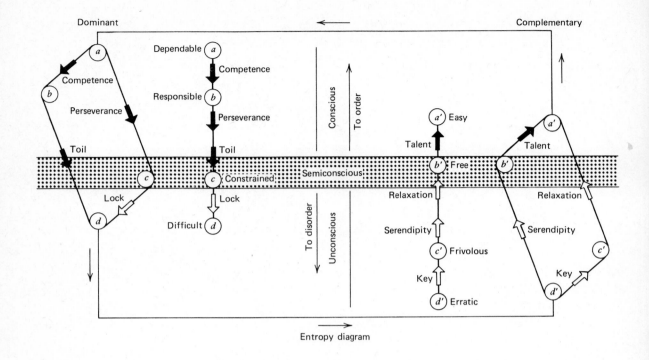

Dominant

Complementary

Dependable a
Competence
Responsible b
Perseverance
Toil
Constrained c Semiconscious
Lock
Difficult d

Competence
b
Perseverance
Toil
c
Lock
d

Conscious
To order

To disorder
Unconscious

a' Easy
Talent
b' Free
Relaxation
Serendipity
c' Frivolous
Key
d' Erratic

a'
Talent
b'
Relaxation
Serendipity
c'
Key
d'

Entropy diagram

play. The circuit is represented by the entropy diagram, which shows where the various poles are on a scale of consciousness.

When you look at the entropy diagram, think of how much of the water destined to go over Niagara Falls is diverted to drive water turbines used to generate electricity. Late at night, when the demand for electricity is low, the excess power is used to pump water back up again for use at high demand times. Thus some of the water circulates first down, then up again.

In the entropy diagram, instead of height representing the potential of the water, it represents levels of consciousness, which is the potential for causing information to flow. On the left of the diagram are two parallel bands of the down flow, the entropy-producing dominant circuit. On the right is the up flow in the complementary circuit, decreasing the entropy and restoring higher levels of order and consciousness.

There is then a flow from the *source* (the top of the falls) at the top of the diagram to the *sink* (the bottom of the falls) at the lowest part of the diagram. This circulatory flow mirrors the flows through the C and D circuits of the map of capacities and shows us at a glance the level of potential, that is, the level of consciousness. The closer we are to the source, the higher the level of consciousness.

The center of the band in the middle of the entropy diagram is the line of symmetry. The band represents a semiconscious region, separating the conscious region on top from the unconscious region below.

178

The eight letters are marked in the diagram at the proper levels; that is, the vertical positions of these letters reflect properly their relative states of "order." Note that *a* is the most ordered and holds the highest position on the order scale and *d'* is the least ordered and holds the lowest position. In fact, you can read off the "order" hierarchy as *a, b, a', b', c, d, c', d'*.

The left circuit, the downside, contains only unprimed letters. This, therefore, represents the dominant circuit in the map of capacities (C or D). The primed letters, in the riser part of the diagram, represent the complementary circuit in the map (D or C).

Think of the division between the conscious and unconscious, not as a sharp border, but as a fuzzy zone where the further you move up from it, the more you are in the conscious.

When we transpose the entropy diagram onto the map of capacities, we are shifting from a general pattern to a particularized case. This is so because the most conscious pole can be any one of 16. *There can be many different profiles, but the entropy diagram will always be the same;* that is, the patterns are the same in all normal, differentiated personalities. Thus this entropy diagram summarizes most of the observations made previously in this chapter. But we can extract vastly more information.

We plot the information contained in the entropy diagram onto the map of capacities by marking the primed and unprimed letters in their proper locations on the map. It is by this simple means that we transform the map of capacities into a profile. It is far simpler than distorting the map. But we must remember that we have superimposed an additional piece of information on the map, namely, order. This order is indicated by the primed and unprimed letters. In circuit language we would refer to this order as *potential.*

The varying levels of consciousness act as a potential field superimposed on the map. This field produces a gradient, which gives rise to a flow. The potential represents what Jung called "libido" or "psychic energy concentration." Libido, or order, is then the driving force that causes information to flow from pole to pole. In a normal, well-individuated personality it reflects the order inherent in the various memories. Poles with well-ordered memories can do efficient information processing and can thus respond to incoming information. The poles, corresponding to collections of cooperating brain cells, can then organize information into meaningful information strings for further processing in other parts of the brain. The potential field results in a transmission of the information string to that pole which, according to the cooperation/competition matrix, would be the most cooperative, namely, that one with which the original pole forms a transaction link. In the example of DETN, information thus flows first from pole 16 to pole 15.

Since the libido at pole 15 is less than that at pole 16—that is, the memory at pole 15 is in a less ordered state than that at pole 16—it becomes increasingly more difficult to do efficient information processing. Errors may thus be introduced, or processing may not be completed, or noninterpretable messages may be produced. As there is lots of parallel processing in the brain, it becomes more and more difficult to compare independently arrived outcomes or to coordinate such output commands. A good example of this is hunting for a word that is on the tip of your tongue. In effect, the sequence of information-processing events that generates the motor commands to physically express the word is not in harmony with those information-processing paths that decide which words to select to express the meaning.

It is much easier to visualize these complex processes as information flows. I refer to such visualizations of information flows as *metaprogramming*. For instance, DETN may be comparing some data that arrived at pole 16 with structures in the memory associated with pole 16. The appropriate structure found in pole 16's memory will be transmitted to pole 15, which then sorts the data according to that structure. Concurrently, the structure is transmitted to pole 12, which searches associative memory for appropriate symbols to capture the meaning of that structure. That information is transmitted to pole 11, which selects words to express that meaning. If the word string assembled at pole 11 contradicts the logical order arrived at by pole 15, we recognize that we're talking (or thinking) nonsense. The resulting tension (conflict) produced between poles 11 and 15 may so distort the libido as to initiate a new information flow. This sequence of events can be pictured as follows:

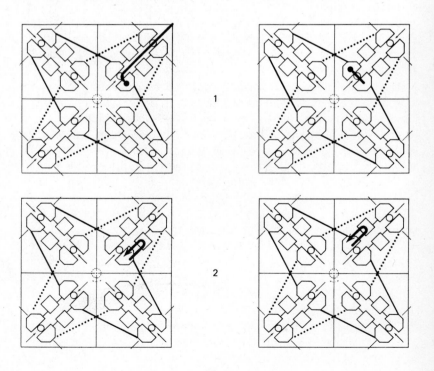

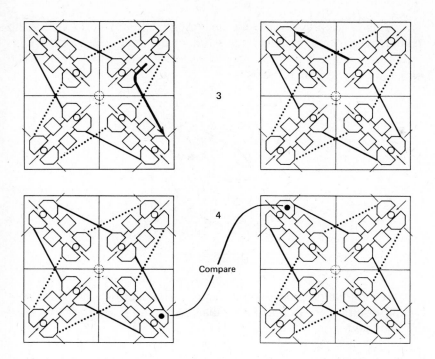

This metaprogram illustrates the information flow paths in a timed sequence and corresponds to transmission in the neural network.

Metaprogram visualizations are thus a shorthand for a sequence of complex information-processing steps.

When the libido represents the natural state of order for a given personality, there is a natural flow, or a preferred information-processing path, that results in a flow from the source (highest libido or potential) to the sink (lowest libido). For DETN this flow is:

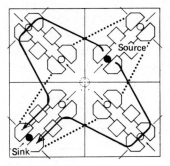

This much of the natural flow of information, all in the dominant circuit, would represent a frustrating or unsuccessful thought sequence, where an idea gets suppressed into the unconscious. It is then the job of the complementary circuit to find a new order that permits a second attempt. This shows as the flow in the complementary circuit, flowing from the sink back to the source:

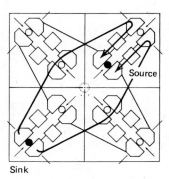

If the information-processing sequence were successful, then an output would result as, for example, articulated speech possibly accompanied by body gesturing.

We see then that the levels of consciousness or potential give rise to a dynamic sequence of information processing, which can be visualized as information flows in the map of capacities.

Because of the natural disposition of consciousness in a given profile, some information-processing paths are more natural for that personality profile than others. For instance, in the profile DETN, the natural potential field is such that information naturally flows from pole 12 to pole 11. This process represents articulating a thought, or speaking. Information flowing from pole 11 to pole 12, which represents listening, is like bucking the tide or swimming upstream for DETN. It takes much more concentration for DETN to listen, and listening is fatiguing. This simply reflects the fact that energy is required to distort the natural potential field to make the flow from pole 11 to pole 12 possible.

In interpreting a profile it is therefore helpful to envision the natural libido-induced flow. This will always be a flow from the source to the sink through the dominant circuit and a restoring flow out of the sink into the source through the complementary circuit.

For all normal, well-individuated profiles, this automatically assigns the natural directions to transactions. As shown for DETN, it makes DETN extroverted in the intellectual and verbal modes and introverted in the gross motor and fine motor modes. Since the work (intellectual) and play (verbal) modes are the predominantly conscious modes (closest to the source), the conscious behavior of DETN is extroverted.

The flows also indicate that N is the superior function (highest level of libido or consciousness and locus of the source). The main flow, shown

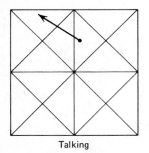

Talking

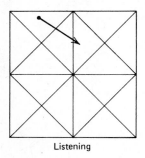

Listening

as a solid line in the diagram, leads to the first auxiliary function, in this case T. The secondary flow, shown as a dotted line, leads to the second auxiliary function, F. The locus of the sink, S, is the inferior function.

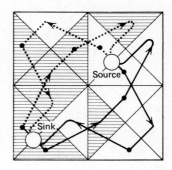

It is useful to remember that the dominant circuit (D for the case of DETN) is the more conscious circuit and the one where accountability is possible. It is also the circuit that with activity promotes disorder; that is, the more we function with accountability, the more we sense the stress produced by it. We get tired and confused, which is the consequence of the increasing entropy. Conscious, accountable behavior shows the wear and tear.

The complementary circuit, predominantly composed of unconscious transactions, is restorative in nature because it recreates order. That part of our functioning for which we do not assume accountability, such as relaxing, daydreaming, and so on, is therefore an important complement to accountable behavior. The complementary circuit is thus that part of the flow which keeps the dominant circuit operational.

15

THE PROFILE

All our efforts to construct the dichotomous model so carefully are now beginning to pay off. Ambi-syn-anti or complementarity can be discovered everywhere. So let us develop a profile step by step. The one I've chosen is again DETN (16 → 15), or the analyst. The profile called DETN is one where pole 16 is the strongest.

The eight-pole model looks like this:

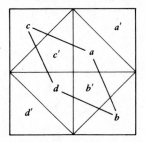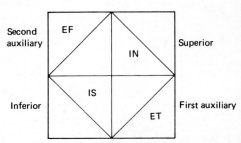

Note that the strongest function is N, the first auxiliary function is T, and the weakest function is S, opposite the strongest function. Also note that the dominant style is D, because the unprimed letters fall into the IN, ET, IS, and EF superpoles.

Next look at this same profile but in the 16-pole model:

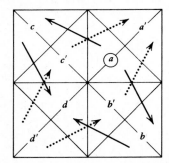

Each pole can now be identified by a number, and the C and D circuits can be drawn in. The letters denoting roles must now be shown between two adjacent poles, because roles apply to superpoles—that is, two introverted or two extroverted poles of a given function. The 16-pole picture appears as follows:

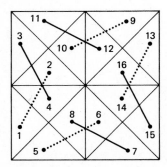

Because we have to develop this particular profile step by step, I show, for the moment, only the unprimed letters; in other words, we'll develop the dominant circuit first.

From the entropy diagram, we know that information flows from *a* toward *d* in two branches: one by way of *b*, and the other by way of *c*. Let us enter these flows with directed connecting lines as shown:

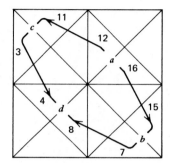

We have now identified four transactions, 16 → 15, 7 → 8, 12 → 11, and 3 → 4. Note that two are extroverted and two are introverted. Also note that transaction 16 → 15 must fall somewhere between *a* and *b*, transaction 12 → 11 must fall somewhere between *a* and *c*, transaction 7 → 8 must fall somewhere between *b* and *d*, and transaction 3 → 4 must fall somewhere between *c* and *d*. These facts help us identify

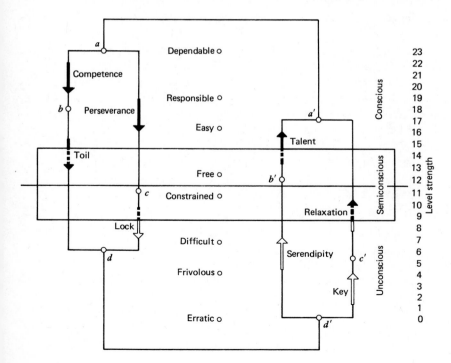

whether a particular transaction lies predominantly in the conscious or in the unconscious by referring to the entropy diagram.

In the transposition I denote a conscious transaction by making the directed line segment heavier. The profile developed to this point looks like this:

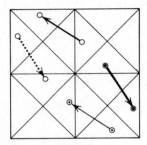

Note that three transactions are conscious. In order of relative consciousness, we have:

16 → 15	Highly conscious
12 → 11	Very conscious
7 → 8	Barely conscious
3 → 4	Unconscious

It helps to see this order if you substitute the transaction numbers with the letters and look at the entropy diagram. Also, recall the discussion of the consciousness dichotomy for DETN from the previous chapter. There the D circuit mapped predominantly on the conscious side except for poles 3 and 4, which were on the unconscious side.

For the dominant circuit, consciousness thus lies predominantly in the intellectual and verbal modes—that is, in the linguistic attribute of the language dichotomy. The personality described by DETN, the analyst, is therefore predominantly lingual. Note also that the most conscious transactions (16 → 15 and 12 → 11) are extroverted and in the D circuit. We know therefore how the dichotomies tilted for this personality.

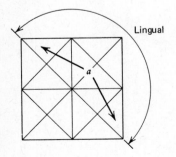

Approach tilts toward intellectual.

Focus tilts toward verbal.

Style tilts toward detailed.

Attitude tilts toward extroverted.

We don't know to what degree this tilting occurs, but we know which way the choices were made during the individuation process.

These are significant characterizing insights for this personality. DETN is very articulate, drawn to intellectual pursuits, and is an extroverted batch processor. Often one can recognize a personality simply by these characteristics, but there is vastly more that we can infer.

Let me complete the transposition by following the same procedure for the complementary C circuit. We skip the eight-pole model and begin with the primed roles marked on the 16-pole map:

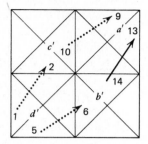

This time the flow is from d' to a' by way of c' and b', respectively. We find again two introverted and two extroverted transactions, but only one, $14 \rightarrow 13$, lies in the conscious.

The next step is to superimpose the two diagrams we've developed, giving us, finally, a picture of the profile. (I've omitted the mode [M] links.)

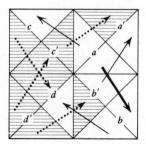

Note that the complementary circuit contributions reinforce the consciousness of the intellectual mode. The primary orientation of this personality is thus intellectual. A corollary of this disposition is that the gross motor or concrete mode is totally in the unconscious. There is therefore not much awareness of body outputs. Such personalities tend to ignore their bodies. This ignoring of the body is compensated only through the unconscious, and therefore it is not uncommon to find such personalities to be hypochondriacs. They don't exercise; they just worry about body deterioration.

The verbal and fine motor modes are what I call mixed modes because they contain both conscious and unconscious transactions. However, remember that for DETN the verbal mode is the more conscious mode ($a \rightarrow c$ is more ordered than $b \rightarrow d$).

It is also worth noting that S is the weakest function and pole 1 is the weakest pole. (I come back to this.)

The complementary circuit reinforces the attitudes of the modes. In this case the most conscious modes, intellectual and verbal, are totally extroverted; and the most unconscious modes, gross and fine motor, are introverted. This is consistent with Jung's observations.

It should therefore be understandable why the profile name is DETN. The name reflects the most conscious characteristics; a D style, an E attitude, and an intellectual orientation involving N and T as the most conscious functions; that is, N and T are the strongest and first auxiliary functions.

There is an alternative way for interpreting the profile name DETN, and this is done through the last three letters. ETN is the name for pole 15. Let us see why that pole should have special significance for a profile description. The most conscious transaction is 16 → 15. We identified that transaction as the analyst. Pole 16 represents the data pole, pole 15 the processing pole. The data pole drives the information-processing system by means of the data it supplies. In this case the data reflect structure (pole 16, $\nleq$), and the driving force for this personality is therefore structure. Unstructured data, unstructured talk or ideas, don't make sense to this personality, who assumes the world has coherence, some orderly scheme. The DETN personality is driven to perceive everything as being part of a conceptual structure. That urge for related order is the motivating force that drives him on.

What *characterizes* a DETN personality is how he processes information. That is pole 15, $\stackrel{\subset}{\frown}$, or logic. This processing or characteristic pole is what the observer sees; it is not what drives him, but how he deals with information. Such a personality would therefore be perceived as a logical, rational thinker. The ETN pole, together with the D style, could be used as a description of his most visible (and most conscious) nature. Thus the name for that profile is DETN.

WORK MODE

$$a \rightarrow b \qquad \text{Dependable + responsible = competence}$$
$$b' \rightarrow a' \qquad \text{Free + easy = talent}$$

In the example of DETN the most conscious transaction, 16 → 15, represented a flow from *a* to *b*, which linked or combined *dependable* with *responsible*. A transaction that involves those two perceptions is properly called *competence*, for competence is that which draws on skills (or capacities) over which we feel we have complete mastery and control. It describes a highly conscious awareness of what we're doing and how we are doing it and thus delineates the areas in which we are willing to be accountable.

For analysts, transaction 16 → 15 thus represents that personality's competence. His or her most salable, accountable skill is the ability to analyze things, whether he or she analyzes the legal intricacies of a situation as a lawyer or medical data as a diagnostician or parts in a machine as a mechanic. His or her competent skill is to analyze.

The transaction falling between *a* and *b* always points to the individual's competence no matter on what capacities *a* and *b* fall. So when the strongest, most conscious poles fall somewhere else on the map, the transaction falling between them still points to that person's competence, though it may represent a very different skill.

The competence transaction (between *a* and *b*) always lies in the dominant circuit and is complemented by the most conscious transaction in the complementary circuit. From the entropy diagram, we see that the most conscious complementary transaction is that between *b'* and *a'*. This transaction links the roles *free* and *easy*; the self-perception of that complementary transaction is described by "this skill comes to me free and easy," a description for something properly called *talent*. For the case of DETN, the talent transaction is 14 → 13, the suspector.

If we focus on the most conscious mode (intellectual), we see that it involves two transactions with the roles *competence* and *talent*. I call that combination the *work mode*. For the profile DETN, the work mode is therefore intellectual or abstract. In his job, DETN is likely to draw on his most conscious skills to analyze and detect. Looking at the facts (they are extroverted), they follow a strategy that focuses on those important patterns that become conceptual clues for arriving at a logical conclusion.

His skill in analysis is tremendously enriched by his suspector talent, which is truly a complementary skill. Competence and talent work hand in glove in an ambi-syn-anti relationship. The application of competence is an entropy-increasing process; that is, competence is applied at the cost of increased disorder. The longer we apply competence, the more the disorder; we tire, we can't go on, our effectiveness deteriorates. The talent transaction, however, is restorative. It discovers order. At the end of a long hard day, we may therefore no longer feel competent to go on, but we sense no loss of talent. Talent doesn't tire. Quite the contrary, it's what pulls us through.

I cannot resist an aside at this stage, for I've seen such dramatic consequences. On occasion, one meets personalities who sell themselves for their talent rather than for their competence. The roles are now reversed. These individuals are paid for their talent and are measured on their performance of it. So they go to great lengths to show off their feats of talent, often overreaching themselves, since talent has no limits. But in the quiet of an office, it is their competence that really produces results. Because the roles are reversed, the competence must deliver to meet the performance promised by the talent. It must deliver even when competence is tired or exhausted. This leads to overextension, working beyond one's limit to the stage of being drained. The mind becomes disorderly, inefficient, even disorganized. The end result, the only way out, is a breakdown or, worse, suicide. This is not idle hypothesis; it is real and points out dramatically why it is so important to operate in natural roles. No father can insist that his child take over as president of the company he built if the son's profile wants him to become a poet. Either there will be a falling out, or the child will pay an awful price.

Understanding the roles of one's capacities is a vital part of survival. That is why knowing yourself is so important. Most of us discover these things by trial and error. The model simply makes the reality of personality overt. But that's enough of a detour for now.

The entropy diagram helps us link fundamental roles together so that we can describe the roles of transactions and modes. So far, I've indicated how that is done only for the two transactions of the work mode, although

Roles

Dominant Circuit (C or D) Entropy Flow: a toward d (a = Strongest; d = Weakest)		Complementary Circuit (D or C) Entropy Flow: d' toward a' (a' = Strongest; d' = Weakest)	
	Pole Opposition		
a Dependable	versus	d'	Erratic
b Responsible	versus	c'	Frivolous
c Constrained	versus	b'	Free
d Difficult	versus	a'	Easy
	Pole Hierarchy		
a Dependable		a'	Easy
b Responsible		b'	Free
c Constrained		c'	Frivolous
d Difficult		d'	Erratic
	Transactions		
$a \rightarrow b$ Dependable + responsible = competence		$b' \rightarrow a'$	Free + easy = talent
$a \rightarrow c$ Dependable + constrained = perseverance		$c' \rightarrow a'$	Frivolous + easy = relaxation
$b \rightarrow d$ Responsible + difficult = toil		$d' \rightarrow b'$	Erratic + free = serendipity
$c \rightarrow d$ Constrained + difficult = lock		$d' \rightarrow c'$	Erratic + frivolous = key

	Modes			
$a \rightarrow b + b' \rightarrow a'$	Competence	+ talent	= work
$a \rightarrow c + c' \rightarrow a'$	Perseverance	+ relaxation	= play
$b \rightarrow d + d' \rightarrow b'$	Toil	+ serendipity	= challenge
$c \rightarrow d + d' \rightarrow c'$	Lock	+ key	= creativity

we want to look at all the other modes as well. A look at the table of roles should make more sense now.

PLAY MODE

Second in the hierarchy of consciousness are transactions that fall between a and c and c' and a'. The respective roles are:

$a \rightarrow c$ Dependable + constrained = perseverance
$c' \rightarrow a'$ Frivolous + easy = relaxation

The latter could properly be described as fun or *relaxation*, the former as *perseverance*. These describe two transactions that become active when we play, and they define what I call the *play mode*. Think of a typical hobby, be it stamp collecting or playing golf. We do it because it's fun. We find the activity relaxing, and we don't take it too seriously. If someone suggests that we make our living that way, well, that would spoil all the fun. It is an activity we do for ourselves. It comes to us easily, but we don't want to be accountable, at least not accountable to anyone but ourselves. That is the easy and frivolous aspect. But we also tend to get lost in our hobbies. Time seems to mean nothing. We get caught up in our hobbies as though they had a hold of us, and so we persevere.

Play is a vital complement to work. All work and no play does make Jack a dull boy. This complementarity is a second-level ambi-syn-anti relationship. Industry understands this very well and therefore provides executives with country club facilities. Play not only restores the capacity to work, it also complements it. Many a problem, sweated over all day, is resolved on the golf course.

What I find most regrettable is that this insight about the complementarity of play for more productive work is applied only to the most expensive labor. Industry has rarely recognized that someone on the production line needs play as much as the executive. Quite the opposite is in effect. Goofing off is not tolerated; this is a short-sighted, counterproductive outlook on the part of management.

The complementary relationship of work and play holds true for every profile, whether the work mode is intellect or brawn, people or things. The lack of egalitarianism is a prejudice not defensible by theory or observation.

The orientation of play vis-à-vis work follows a predictable pattern. We have seen that for DETN work is in the intellectual mode and play in the verbal mode. This orthogonality of work and play is essentially always that way in the normally developed personality. It is one of the patterns to look for to identify a given personality. It manifests itself in the DETN personality in a number of varied but consistent ways. Play is verbal, be it a love for gossip or music. There is a somewhat irresponsible fascination with people, as though one were playing with their lives. DETN types therefore tend to be matchmakers or kingmakers, who use their insight into people as a hobby. They like social affairs, but this liking rarely leads to deep relationships. It's just a way of rummaging in talk and people, of making contact and being amused.

I cannot emphasize the orientation relationship enough. The play mode always lies perpendicular to the work mode and only on one predictable side. There are a number of ambi-syn-anti relationships involved that make the play mode complex, if not confusing. This is so because play is a mixed mode, partly conscious and partly unconscious. Two aspects are important: one involves the conscious transaction, perseverance; the other involves the unconscious transaction, relaxation.

Perseverance, the conscious part of play, provides an important supportive skill to work. It is so closely tied to work that it becomes a routine part of the job. In the case of DETN perseverance is transaction 12 → 11, the verbalist. For DETN verbalizing is an important auxiliary skill supportive of work. In the mind the analytical process plays itself out as word thoughts. It helps DETN to grasp what he or she is thinking. It is also a sequential, logical expression of the thought processes, which are also sequential. Verbalizing is a perfect complement. As a consequence, DETNs are not only intellectually powerful, they are also articulate. They write clearly, express themselves well, and can lecture well on material they have thoroughly thought out. In fact, they would rather speak than listen, because transaction 12 → 11 is extroverted, running in the wrong direction for extracting meaning from words, which would be listening. When they are serious (accountable), they therefore prefer reading to listening.

The other transaction in the play mode is free plus easy, or *relaxation*. For DETN this is transaction 10 → 9, the perceiver. It manifests itself as a frivolous interest in people and conversation—the kind of thing that makes gossip fun, leads to a large circle of acquaintances, makes one want to read the social columns and obituaries, in short, to keep up with the people world and stay in touch. When relaxed, the personality projects a gregarious image, as the transaction is extroverted. This is a very useful skill for the analyst, for it helps relate an abstract problem to its human context. In other words, the unconscious component of play, relaxation, complements the work mode, which might otherwise tend excessively to abstraction. The way relaxation manifests itself in DETNs is, for instance, that as they focus on the problem to be analyzed, DETNs do not lose sight of the client's needs and wishes. In fact, they may perceive certain concerns in the client that form important clues to approaching the problem. Clearly, this is important for the lawyer and the diagnostician. In the case of the physicist, it manifests itself as connectedness to colleagues—knowing what they are doing, keeping in contact, and preserving those relationships by acknowledging their contributions.

Relaxation, an unconscious transaction, is completely outweighed by its opposite, toil, which lies in the opposite (challenge) mode. Toil is conscious, relaxation is not. For the case of DETN, therefore, the interest in people is half-hearted. The predominant orientation is set by the characteristic pole ETN, which is thing-oriented rather than people-oriented. The frivolous interest in people can therefore be misleading. It is just that, frivolous. When DETN is serious—that is, consciously busy—he or she really regards people as things that can be shuffled, directed, manipulated, and applied.

Because play is a mixed mode, it has tremendous variations. Some DETNs are heartless manipulators of people, and others seem genuinely personable, warm, and caring. I mention this for two reasons. The model gives many clear answers at the extremes of conscious and unconscious. One really can speak of a typology. But it is far less specific in the middle range. It can only be alertive, not determinate, because the boundary that divides the conscious and the unconscious is fuzzy and because within a given profile there is a spectrum or range of personalities, depending on the degree to which the personality is differentiated, that is, on how much the dichotomies are tilted. So one should be cautious and resist drawing absolute inferences from the model. However, the general pattern outlined is stereotypical.

Relaxation is part of a mixed mode (the play mode) between work and creativity (a mode discussed later). It forms, therefore, a complement to creativity as well as to work. In the complex creative process, relaxation is the key activity where creative solutions worked out in the depth of the unconscious become recognized. Put another way, relaxing is a requisite for finding out what the unconscious has worked out creatively. Nowhere is this process more dramatically evident than in Watson's description of the discovery of the double helix. The pattern was repeated over and over again: intensive conscious work, ultimately leading to such frustration that there was no other choice but to give up and relax. It was always during this period of relaxation that a new idea percolated to the top and became the trigger for a flurry of activity for the next cycle. Relaxation, then, is the process through which the unconscious makes its creative findings known.

E-13

CHALLENGE MODE

The challenge mode contains two transactions:

$$b \rightarrow d \quad \text{Responsible + difficult = toil}$$
$$d' \rightarrow b' \quad \text{Erratic + free = serendipity}$$

The former is described by *toil*, and the latter by *serendipity*. Toil is a conscious transaction, though barely so. Still, it outweighs relaxation, an unconscious transaction in the play mode. The *challenge mode*, as the play mode, is a mixed mode and therefore complements both the work and creativity modes.

For DETN, the toil transaction is 7 → 8, the organizer, in the fine motor mode. DETN can draw when he must (challenged). But he procrastinates using the fine motor mode to support his work. DETN can organize and use his hands (or a pen) to organize, but only when there is no escape from it. DETN will clean his house, order his files, and file his tax return only when things become unmanageable or a deadline stares him in the face.

The other transaction in the challenge mode is serendipity, an unconscious transaction. For those in contact with the unconscious, it becomes a precious skill that seems to work only when nothing is at stake (erratic and free). To activate it requires an extremely relaxed, devil-may-care attitude. For DETN this is transaction 5 → 6, the molder. Serendipity is a tinkering activity with an artistic flavor and could be sculpting, photography, sketching, gardening, building, cooking, or any other fine motor activity. The activity is too deep in the unconscious to relate in any significant way to work but is a crucial part of the creative process. You recognize the activity when things just seem to pop into your mind. You can't count on anything significant happening, but, if you are in touch with your unconscious, you will recognize it when it happens. In the case of DETN, it is likely to be an identification or recognition that triggers the lock transaction.

CREATIVITY MODE

The *lock* transaction represents the recognition of the problem. That's half the battle, knowing what it is that needs to be solved. The other part is the *key* transaction, finding the solution. Both these transactions are deep in the unconscious and together form the *creativity mode*:

$$c \rightarrow d \qquad \text{Constrained + difficult = lock}$$
$$d' \rightarrow c' \qquad \text{Erratic + frivolous = key}$$

Even for those in close touch with their unconscious, it is difficult to know exactly what is going on. There is simply a general awareness that something important is happening. For DETN, the creative mode has a gross motor (concrete) orientation, primarily involving the body. It is therefore important that the DETN profile not deny body activity during the creative phase. This can take many forms consistent with transactions 1 → 2 (doer) and 3 → 4 (follower). Playing an instrument, dancing, conducting, caring for someone, and playing tennis would all be creativity-promoting activities.

It is interesting at this stage to stop and realize why it is so difficult to create an environment supportive of creativity in the work setting of the analyst. Be it a physics lab, a lawyer's office, or a diagnostic clinic, it seems incongruous to associate with that setting a music room or dance floor, a place to nurse a pet, or a tennis court for use during working hours. Yet, for the analyst, creative problem solving is part of work.

OTHER ASPECTS OF THE UNCONSCIOUS

Even in a given profile, there can be tremendous interpretive differences that depend on the degree to which an individual is in contact with his or her unconscious.

In general, people whom we perceive as "uptight" tend not to acknowledge even the existence of the unconscious. They are convinced they don't dream, and their behavior patterns are deliberately controlled. For such personality extremes, the role of the unconscious is to provide the necessary balancing compensation in what seems to be mysterious ways. To the outsider, it is exhibited as irrational, inconsistent behavior that one learns to circumvent by not bringing up those sensitive areas.

Such an attitude toward the unconscious is unfortunate, for it literally produces half a personality. The natural transactions in the unconscious take on unnatural aspects. For instance, relaxation is thwarted and may become active only as an escape, as through drinking. Serendipity tends to be regarded as an irrational embarrassment and is ignored or suppressed. Lock and key, the transactions of the creativity mode, lie unutilized. There is simply no productive creativity. Precious capacities and skills are never allowed to contribute to the effectiveness of the personality, so any detailed analysis of the contributions of these capacities to the personality is futile. Therefore, delving into the unconscious transactions contribute no insight into these people other than the recognition that the personality is incomplete.

The two exceptions are the weakest pole and, related to it, the least conscious transaction, identified by the role key. In both cases they are always the opposite of the strongest pole and strongest (most conscious) transaction.

For DETN the weakest pole is pole 1 (opposite pole 16), the signal, in the sensation (S) function. DETN is simply insensitive to sensation. He may not notice that his socks don't match or that the hostess has been sending signals for more than an hour that she wishes the guests would go home. In general, anything that triggers sensations is either missed or, if unavoidable, upsetting. If the car or the typewriter or the copying machine breaks down, DETN just cannot cope. A trivial occurrence becomes a catastrophe.

I refer to the opposite of the strongest (most conscious) transaction as the *hidden agenda*. In the case of DETN, with the characteristic trans-action 16 → 15, the hidden agenda is transaction 1 → 2, the doer. A personality with the profile DETN who is not in contact with his unconscious tends to be driven to do things, which gives him a certain restlessness.

At the other extreme is a personality in touch with his or her unconscious. We perceive such a person as at peace with himself and very rich in skills and interests. The capacities and transactions now can play out their natural roles and enrich the personality.

A great deal of specific information can be extracted from a profile simply by systematically interpreting roles and orientations. The interpretive repertoire grows ever richer with experience. Every individual who has been recognized as a DETN and interpreted through the profile makes it easier and more meaningful to interpret and recognize the next DETN personality.

Experience also helps deal with the shadings of a given profile. Initially, a DETN in contact with his unconscious seems radically different from a DETN operating only on the conscious side. But the example clarifies the differences and the similarities, especially once one has encountered DETN profiles somewhere between the extremes.

It is useful to mention in this context that style also creates shadings in personalities that initially may seem confusing. A DETN personality who is very strong in D seems very different from a DETN personality where D is only slightly more dominant than C. But experience will point out the typical DETN nature of both extremes.

Finally, an extreme one-sidedness in consciousness usually goes hand in hand with an extreme one-sidedness in style. This is not surprising, since the dominant style, in this case D, is predominantly conscious. Therefore, the C nature of DETN can emerge only if the unconscious is reasonably operational in the personality.

IV

APPLICATIONS
OF THE MODEL

We are working on a number of interesting problems for which the model should provide some valuable insights. In this part I discuss only the most obvious applications. These are: profile interpretation, interpersonal relationships, creativity, human factors, and artificial intelligence. Because of its tentative and speculative nature, I have moved the discussion of the last topic to Appendix B.

I am also working on applications in test instruments and in related topics in semantics that fit this context but where presentation at the present stage of development would be premature.

16

PROFILE INTERPRETATION

The map of capacities and the entropy circuit are generic. Both show invariant relationships developed through the model; the map deals with capacities, inputs, outputs, and memories; the entropy circuit deals with roles and levels of consciousness.

The combination of the two, in one of 16 possible ways, generates a profile. Each profile is unique at two levels of interpretation. Level 1 interpretations grow out of procedural formalisms such as interpreting the temporal aspects of functions or whether the complexity index leads to a nature that makes things simpler or more complex, interpreting how strengths and weaknesses manifest themselves, and interpreting what the source and hidden agenda tell us.

LEVEL 2 INTERPRETATIONS

Level 2 interpretations grow out of personal constructs and therefore go beyond type. These are interpretations that map the global descriptions of level 1 to the context of the individual. Thus, depending on the interest, training, experience, and activity of the subject, one can fit a descriptorlike analysis to the context. If the context is medicine, the analysis becomes diagnostic. If the context is financial data, it becomes financial. Nothing helps level 2 interpretations as much as experience. Each new subject whose profile has been determined through an interview adds to the level 2 interpretive repertoire. It is this level of interpretation that makes the profile analysis meaningful to the subject—something that can only happen through interviews.

Profiles determined through tests, even computer analyses, are cold and mechanical and at best capable only of level 1 interpretations.

Level 2 interpretations deal with a second personalized aspect that is quite different from the fitting to personal construct. Level 2 deals with the spectrum within types that results from various degrees of differentiation. Some personalities are highly differentiated with respect to various dichotomies; others are not so extreme. Some are sharply differentiated in all dichotomies, and some in most but with a few notable exceptions. These far more subtle differences give each personality a unique coloring. Some of these can be discussed as classes.

Perhaps most dramatic is the effect of differentiation on consciousness. If an individual operates one-sidedly on the conscious side, suppressing or refusing to acknowledge the unconscious attributes, the profile takes on an extreme sharpness that produces a hard, unyielding, extreme personality. By contrast, a profile reasonably balanced between conscious and unconscious attributes yields a much softer, more integrated profile, a person in harmony and at peace with self and surroundings.

The effects of balance between opposing attributes are not always wholesome. Depending on the dichotomy, they can yield a sense of wishy-washiness, indecision, and discomfort.

Sometimes, the lack of differentiation can be linked to two profiles, one receding and the other emerging, as though the personality were in the midst of shifting from one profile to another. This is especially noticeable in cases where attitude is shifting from introverted to extroverted. The phenomenon is not difficult to decipher. Usually, one finds that there were signs of extroverted behavior as a young child—for example, the class clown in primary school—followed by an inward turning, expressed by, "I always used to think of myself as an extrovert until I got to junior high." Usually one finds a perfectionist authority figure lurking in the background. A typical example might be the youngster who tries to please daddy by washing the car. The father, instead of praising the child, only comments, "Here's a spot you missed." This instills the feeling in the youngster that he can't do anything right, and he might become increasingly introspective. In some profiles this leads to introversion. But in the adult, faced with the perfectionist's criticism, a new confidence might develop based on his accomplishments, and the original, natural extroverted profile begins to emerge anew.

Closely related to this example is the persona effect, which often produces two profiles. This usually involves *style* rather than attitude, but it is certainly not limited to style. A typical example is a person growing up in a household dominated by a sharp D style. There may be threats such as if you're not at the dinner table at 6 o'clock sharp, you don't eat. If your room is not neat and your homework not done, you don't go out. With those kinds of absolutes, the child learns to behave as a D type just to survive. This acquired style takes years to throw off. Only when the person has created some psychological distance from the parent ("My dad, I love him, but he was a pain") does the natural C style have a chance to emerge freely. This shifting in profile is often quite traumatic.

Both of these examples are easier to interpret if there is some awareness of age. There seem to be several factors at play. The more innately capable an individual, the longer it seems to take to complete the individuation process. The child who meets his limitations early develops a sharp profile earlier. This means that the brightest students seem to have the hardest time figuring out who they are, and this shows up as a lack of differentiation in profiles as late as their thirties and in some cases even later.

The stressfulness of the environment also has an effect. Those from understanding, supportive, comfortable environments seem to develop sharp profiles much later than those who had to develop a street sense to survive or who for other reasons were thrown out on their own.

Persona effects, of course, also cause a delay in the settling-in of a sharp profile. When an interview yields two potential profile candidates, as is not uncommon, it certainly helps in level 2 interpretations if one knows whether the person is 18 years old, nearer to 35, or closer to 60.

A-4

Age also influences differentiation in later years. Jung made specific references to the phenomenon. It is most easily clarified through the consciousness dichotomy. Most people are still building careers in their thirties and forties. There is a sense of "it's up to me" to reach the top or at least the next goal. Such drive and such orientation toward performance and achievement are bound to emphasize accountability and thus consciousness, possibly at the expense of the unconscious. But there comes a time when people make peace with themselves: "I've made my mark," "I no longer need to prove anything to anybody," or "That's it for me, I don't want to be president." Unfortunately, this "arriving" is sometimes called the midlife crisis. But it's no crisis at all. It is the beginning of something very wholesome, natural, and beautiful. It is a time for people finally to explore the unconscious side, because they are no longer so uptight about controlled behavior and accountability. This activation of the unconscious side of the personality, the very opposite of the conscious profile, could be perceived by others as a personality shift. There is indeed a fascination with what earlier would have been called "extracurricular activities." The engineer might suddenly become very involved with people or philosophy, not just frivolously with his grandchildren, but as a serious interest too long neglected. The mathematician or physicist may turn to music or religion, as did Einstein in his later years.

Such shifts in profiles should be regarded not as a change in profile but as a reaching out. There is a beautiful cyclic phenomenon at play here. The child starts out undifferentiated, fascinated by everything without bias. Then, with adolescence and through the career-building years, a sharpening of preferences, a skewing, must develop to create an identity and a differentiated personality. But this skewing is again rounded out later in life, creating a softer, more tolerant, more all-encompassing personality. It is as though life were a balancing act: it starts in equilibrium, gets exciting as the pole is about to crash because of excessive tilt, and then, just in the nick of time, recaptures the balance, relieving the tension and excitement with a sense of stability.

Level 2 interpretations are the most satisfying and meaningful. They are helped by background and knowledge and require some degree of perceptiveness. Experience helps; so the more you do it, the better you become. This is as true for the psychiatrist as for the layperson. But with the aid of level 1 interpretations, the nonprofessional can learn and put new-found insights to good use.

What the layperson cannot do—and this is a very serious danger—is to deal with or, worse yet, not even recognize abnormal profiles. That is in the realm of the professionally trained psychiatrist or psychologist.

The model deals only with the "normal," "healthy" profile. It is a natural profile, easy to identify in accordance with the model in a person who functions normally. The best advice I can give is to quit if you find it very difficult to identify the profile. You may have stumbled onto something with which you are not prepared or equipped to deal. Just quit. Don't give any explanations, for anything you say may be harmful. Just say, "Sorry, I can't do it." Don't suggest that the person seek professional help, for you really aren't qualified to say so. All you know is that you can't fit the responses into a profile, so keep the burden on yourself where it belongs. It is you who has failed, not your subject.

This is a dilemma. The ultimate purpose of using the model ought to be to obtain insight about ourselves. But to learn of all our dimensions, others, with different strengths and personalities, serve as important models for us. Insight into others thus deepens insight into ourselves. It also helps us to develop tolerance and understanding. Therefore, it is natural to try to discover what makes others tick, to uncover their profiles. And yet, as I have tried to emphasize, there are dangers in doing so. So use judgment in the subjects you select. Use "normal" as your shield, not in the scientific sense but in what feels normal. Pick people you are comfortable with, not persons with behavioral extremes. Exercise caution and lots of common sense.

LEVEL 1 INTERPRETATIONS

Level 1 interpretations are the deadly part but the most important starting point. Their algorithmic nature serves as the key alerter to what to think about. This is no minor matter. The differences among personalities are so varied that, without a structure, any interpretation becomes somewhat overwhelming. The procedural semantics help make the task more focused by addressing the question of how an individual processes information. Level 1 interpretations are therefore the necessary first step.

The recommended procedure is to map the entropy circuit onto the map of capacities and to map the map of capacities onto the entropy circuit. Each has its unique assets. The map and the entropy circuits and the corresponding mappings for the profile DETN, the analyst (16 → 15), are illustrated.

The major advantage of the completed entropy diagram is that it clearly delineates the levels of consciousness. It shows which capacities, memories, inputs, and outputs play the dominant conscious roles and which ones do not. The completely labeled map of capacities has the advantage

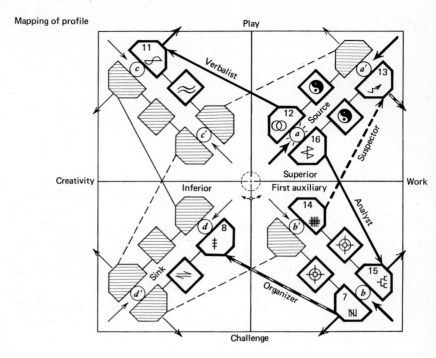

Mapping of profile

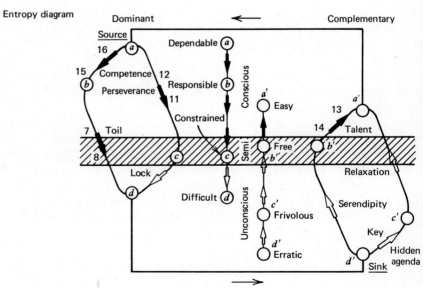

Entropy diagram

Profile identification for DETN.

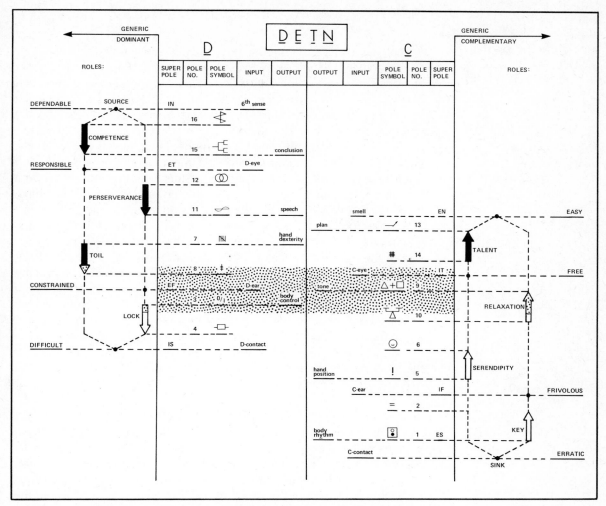

of making complex relationships clear. Functions, output pairings, modes, and orientations are visually explicit.

The Work Mode

Zeroing in on the work mode and the dominant circuit quickly identifies the *characteristic transaction*. There are several points to be noted.

The most conscious transaction, *competence*, is called the characteristic transaction, because it characterizes how the personality deals accountably with information. It gets at such things as "That's the way my mind works" or "What makes me tick?"

APPLICATIONS OF THE
MODEL

The characteristic transaction is most likely to map into the individual's career activity; people tend to have jobs whose demands match their characteristic transactions. The descriptors, especially those generated by the appropriate symbolic phrase "to _____ the _____" are global and need to be interpreted in context. It is therefore most helpful to know what the person does for a living.

These insights are enriched by the mode, because many jobs are also global. For instance, a lawyer might act very much like a personal counselor (people-oriented), legal logician (abstract-oriented), or a procedural technician (e.g., processing an estate which is thing-oriented). The mode helps identify more precisely the subject's approach to the profession.

A closer look at the characteristic transaction identifies the driver pole (beginning of the transaction vector) and the characteristic pole (arrow end of the transaction vector). The labels of these poles are significant. The driver pole identifies the capacity that drives the person's thinking. It is known by the subject, for he knows what is most important to him in processing information and what he looks for in data (seeing what he wants to see, hearing what he wants to hear, etc.). The perception is internalized and therefore hidden from others. What others note in the individual is the characteristic pole, which identifies not the data but how the individual processes the data. When we say, "We judge you by your actions" or "You are what you do," we are really looking at the characteristic pole.

Identification of those two poles also defines the superior and first auxiliary functions. This is not always clear in many of the Jungian references, but it is unambiguous in this model. The driver pole lies in the superior function; the characteristic pole lies in the first auxiliary function.

Another benefit of this analysis is that the source is known. The source is always the superpole of which the driver pole is a part. The further one moves in flow away from the source, the less ordered the memories, and the less efficient and reliable the subject is in processing information.

With the superior and first auxiliary functions identified, conclusions about temporality and complexity are possible, since each function has a unique temporal reference and complexity index. As to the latter, the transaction direction thus suggests going from one complexity index to another. This is the tendency to make things either simpler (moving to a smaller index) or more complex; that is, the individual tends to make a given problem smaller or larger. As to temporality, it is sometimes more useful to look at the inferior function, which is always diametrically opposite the superior one. The temporal aspect associated with the inferior function has little or no meaning for the subject.

The characteristic transaction also automatically identifies style and attitude. The characteristic transaction always lies in the dominant circuit. It therefore determines all the attributes associated with C or D style, which can be summarized thus:

D Style	C Style
Detailed	Contextual
Focuses on one thing at a time (a batch processor)	Focuses on many things concurrently (a time sharer)
Sequential processor	Parallel processor
Slow and thorough	Quick and sketchy
Rigid in crises	Responsive in crises
Clock-driven	Rate-driven
Punctual	Punctuality is not important
Speech or left brain hemisphere dominant	Esthetics or right brain hemisphere dominant
Speaks as though reading from a written page	Speaks in darts and dashes
Exacting, narrow scope	Inexacting, broad scope
Easy recall of word labels	Imprecise word labels ("whatchamacallits")

Attitude is determined by the arrow (toward the characteristic pole). If the flow is to an external pole (i.e., if the characteristic pole is extroverted) the personality is extroverted. Extroverted personalities give relatively more credence to external realities than to their inner instincts. They therefore tend to be realists and are fact- or data-driven. Extroverts are also more action-oriented, as is clear from the entropy diagram. They have more outputs in the conscious domain; there are four conscious outputs for extroverts, three for introverts. They naturally impact their external environment more deliberately.

Remember that competence is generically the most conscious transaction, with full awareness of effort, process, and result. The characteristic transaction is therefore not only controllable, but also consciously intended and directed. It is that activity where the subjects are the captains of their ship, in full control of their will. It is therefore the one transaction where subjects are not only willing to accept criticism, but also where they can do something about it, either by defending themselves or by responding to it by changing what and how they do things. They will also be aware that they get tired (entropy production).

One can gain some insight by noting the pole numbers of the characteristic transaction. Low numbers point to prelingual and natural attributes; high numbers point to lingual and acquired ones.

The *talent* transaction always lies in the same mode and has the same attitude as the characteristic or competence transaction. It is always in the complementary circuit.

Talent is not a willed or consciously directed transaction. It is a by-product of activating competence. It therefore carries with it a spontaneous feel, well expressed by the pole roles free and easy. If competence (dependable and responsible) is the pilot, talent is the copilot. It adjusts itself to the pilot's lead, supporting actions and initiatives.

Talent and competence always form a converse pair when it comes to the complexity index. Thus, if competence makes things more complex, talent makes things simpler. It is this that often makes a job that draws on talent boring. It's just too easy, too simple, and therefore uninteresting.

Nevertheless, talent is an important complement to competence. To recognize just how, the transaction must be interpreted through its poles. For instance, if competence is conceptualizing, then the talent is the pattern envisioning that makes the conceptualizing possible.

Taken together, competence and talent constitute work. The notable difference is that talent, unaware of the process, cannot take criticism. Talent just does something without really knowing how. Even the subject is often unaware of the process until it is pointed out.

The Play Mode

The play mode is a mixed mode; one of the transactions is conscious (perseverance) and the other is unconscious (relaxation).

Perseverance is the second most conscious transaction, as can be seen in the entropy diagram. It is, in a very literal sense, the helper of competence. If competence were the surgeon, perseverance would be the assisting nurse. The pole roles, dependable and constrained, make this amply clear. The helper can be depended on but is constrained by the lead signals from competence (surgeon). It can never take the lead; it can only support.

Perseverance is untiring, because it is unaware of effort. That is fine in a hobby activity, when perseverance acts independent of competence. It then teams up with relaxation as play. But when it teams up with competence, it's another story. It may go on long after competence has quit and ultimately becomes draining. This typically happens with workaholics, who keep going through the motions of work without really getting much done; they just wear themselves out. They would be far better off applying perseverance in the service of play.

Perseverance complements work because it has the same attitude. The play mode always has the same attitude as the work mode. Extroverted in work therefore means extroverted in play. I believe the popular assumption that extroverted is the same as aggressive stems largely from that.

Perhaps the most important characteristic of perseverance is that it lies on the opposite side of the source from competence. It is as though libido were flowing concurrently out of the source into the competence and perseverance branches. Therefore, perseverance carries with it a simultaneity with competence. For instance, for analysts, perseverance is verbalizing (12 → 11). While the analysts are logically sorting structured data (competence being 16 → 15), they are also thinking in words. A kind of inner voice talks to them. It's quite different for DINTs (15 → 16), who cannot talk until they have finished conceptualizing. What occurs as a concurrent perseverance process for DINTs is imaging; instead of thinking in words, they think in pictures.

Relaxation, being an unconscious transaction, does not contribute to conscious work, as do talent, perseverance, and toil. Rather, relaxation is part of a very different phenomenon, whose purpose is to restore the capacity to do conscious work. It lies in the complementary circuit (the entropy-reducing circuit), whose function is to restore order. Relaxation is therefore recuperative. Normally, the transaction plays an active role only when we stop working, that is, when we goof off or relax.

It is my contention that the importance of relaxation is terribly under-valued. It is that which we grudgingly permit during working hours only in response to organized pressure and then only in small doses. We therefore schedule coffee breaks and permit some time in the lounge, again mostly during break time. Yet, relaxation is run not by the clock but by the intensity of work. Workers whose job on a particular day demands very active information processing will produce so much en-tropy that their effectiveness is bound to decrease. They will need more and more frequent periods of relaxation to restore order. Rather than taking such a functional view, we treat relaxation as a fringe benefit. The more highly paid the position, the more we permit relaxation. Put bluntly, company presidents can play golf any time they wish, but programmers under pressure to produce more lines of code cannot. As a consequence, we simply must expect more programming errors. This is a short-sighted view.

I enter into this discussion to make the point that relaxation is really part of an ingenious self-regulating system that works best when left to itself. The self-regulation can function only when it operates in an un-conscious environment, that is, if accountability is removed. A coffee break is not very relaxing if it is necessary to keep looking at the clock to see whether the 10 minutes are up.

The same counterproductive forces are at play in other social inven-tions. For instance, New Year's Eve is supposed to be a happy time. But it isn't for many people, because fun and relaxation cannot be scheduled by external forces. You simply can't say, looking at your stopwatch, "Get on your mark, ready, go and relax *now*." Relaxation works only in its own self-regulating environment. The pole roles are frivolous and easy. It is the frivolous pole that above all needs the lack of accountability; otherwise, it cannot be frivolous.

Relaxation is unique among the unconscious transactions, because it is the only one with an attitude (extroverted or introverted) that matches the work mode. It is this that makes it possible for relaxation to pair up with perseverance to form play.

E-13

In interpreting a profile, which as I suggested should begin with the most conscious behavior, relaxation really plays no part. Rather, it is part of a distinctly separate phenomenon, and it is important to keep this in mind. For instance, if the subject says that he *enjoys* doing so and so, one must always determine whether it is joy in work or joy in play.

The only time relaxation plays a role in work is when work requires creativity. When the conscious task involves problem solving, where the problem can be solved only through a creative idea, then relaxation plays a major role related to work. In interviewing a person involved in creative pursuits—an inventor, a researcher, or an artist—relaxation must be interpreted with a different perspective. It then acts as a kind of counterpole to work. The most dramatic description of this is in Watson's *Double Helix*, a fascinating account of the creative process.

The creative solution is formed in the creativity mode, deep in the unconscious. Because it is unconscious, there is no way of knowing that a solution has been born. It is then that relaxation acts as the messenger. The playfulness of relaxation and its special position between the unconscious and the conscious (see the entropy diagram) make relaxation the first place where creative solutions are recognized. While the individual is pursuing an activity that for him or her is thoroughly relaxing, the idea will suddenly pop into the conscious mind. The key here is relaxing to the individual, not relaxing in an absolute sense. Just sitting in a comfortable chair with eyes closed and feet propped up may not do the trick. It must be the relaxation transaction for the particular profile. For one, it may be talking or even giving a lecture; for another, it may be carpentry; for yet another, it may be taking a shower.

It is useful sometimes to ask people what they do when they relax. The reason they can answer a question about an unconscious transaction is that relaxation is part of a mixed mode. This is in sharp contrast to asking people what they do to be so creative. They can't answer that, because the creativity mode is entirely unconscious.

Relaxation, and the play mode in general, is much easier to identify in extroverts because of the active outputs. It is far more difficult with introverts.

The Challenge Mode
The challenge mode is far less closely linked to the work mode than is the play mode. It, like play, is a mixed mode and lies opposite the play mode. It is generally perceived as a weakness, for it lies far deeper on the consciousness scale.

The conscious transaction is *toil*, the activity that tends to be procrastinated. It is perhaps the hardest conscious transaction to discuss.

Toil acts as though entrance to the transaction were blocked by a high wall. The conscious effort comes from the fact that you first have to climb over the wall. It takes a lot of psychic energy to do that, and people often use the expression, "I've got to get myself psyched up for it." It is this that makes it so easy to put off the activity. Usually, it takes external pressure to activate toil; either you can't escape doing it, or the boss demands it.

The interesting thing about toil is that, although starting it seems so very difficult, once it is started, it is a very competent transaction. It is, after all, conscious. So people who have disciplined themselves to overcome the hurdle are quite good and competent in the toil activity. This can be confusing to the interviewer, for then toil seems like a second competence. But it is far from it, for it is not reinforced by talent.

The complementary transaction to toil is *serendipity*, and it lies far too deep in the unconscious to be supportive. It's a transaction that works like a circuit with a bad connection. Sometimes it works, often it doesn't.

It is interesting to note, however, that people who are in good contact with their unconscious succeed quite well in making serendipity work for them. But there is always a conscious shifting of gears. The subject acts like a different personality. And this is necessary, because serendipity has the opposite style and attitude from competence. An introverted D type may suddenly and deliberately take on the personality of an extroverted C type. It's a fascinating phenomenon to watch, but not very common.

The Creativity Mode
There is little I can say about the creativity mode, since it's completely unconscious. Only through the mapping can we reason it out, and then it may not seem very meaningful. The two transactions in the creativity mode are the *lock* and the *key*.

Nonetheless, one can identify the creativity mode in an interview. It's the mode about which nothing is said. It is the ignored orientation with inactive outputs, the side of a personality that is ignored or taken for granted.

It can also be identified by means of the sink. The sink always points toward the weakness, and people usually know their weaknesses. I use the sink as a prime confirmation that I'm on the right track when I'm fishing for the competence transaction in a profile.

One interpretive aspect of the creativity mode that is fascinating is what I call the *hidden agenda*. It is rare that the subject can identify it, but, if the interviewer points it out, it usually makes sense to the subject.

The hidden agenda is the very opposite of competence. It is the most unconscious transaction, with the role of *key*. It is the unknown source of creative solutions. It is also the counterpersonality, the alter ego. I interpret the hidden agenda as the true motivator of a personality. I view conscious behavior as the complex, torturous actions we have to go through to achieve what the hidden agenda transaction could do alone.

But we have no choice, since the key transaction is not operational. But the concept is important, for it says, in effect, that the sum of the conscious transactions—competence, perseverance, talent, and toil—equals the hidden agenda. It is an example of the duality principle underlying the organization of consciousness; there are always two ways of doing something, but only one is operational for any one individual.

The hidden agenda therefore plays itself out after the fact. Only after all that conscious work has been done and all that tedious effort has been expended, can the true goal be recognized. Only persons in touch with their unconscious recognize that fact. The others are only kidding themselves.

The richness or complexity of the model (depending on your point of view) permits more than one approach to interpreting a profile. For example, one could do it visually, either systematically or dynamically. I want to focus on the latter approach, which I have not emphasized before now.

Dynamic View of Model

By a dynamic view of the model, I mean a process whereby one envisions a libido field and its resultant flows. For me this view of the model has become increasingly powerful, but is difficult to describe because so much of the dynamics is kinesthetically sensed. I feel not unlike a piece of driftwood in a stream, being twisted and turned, pushed hither and yon by the forces that make the river flow. It is a conscious experiencing of the circuit activity of the mind.

One of the advantages of this kind of Gedanken experiment is that inputs and outputs are more integrated with information processing. This is another way of saying that there is a mutual interaction between libido (potential) and information flow. Each influences the other.

Let me give you an example for DINT (15 → 16). Consider an incoming visual stimulus at ET, which is processed and flows toward EF, where it exits as a verbal output. That is a relatively simple flow. But suppose the processing was too incomplete to permit a verbal output. Then the output channel at EFN is blocked, and the information must continue to flow internally for further processing. This causes a shift in libido, which would

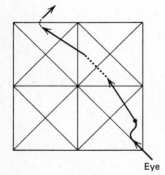

Eye

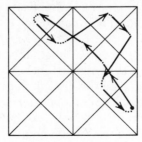
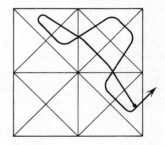

cause the unconscious to play a more active part. The resulting flow may now return the information back toward the source where it can look for additional external (input) information. This would be the case especially if no resolutions were achieved—that is, if no conclusions were reached and the output at ETN were blocked. In this case the information flow may pick up additional visual information and process it by a different loop, resulting in a hand output and producing a new external image that can be processed next.

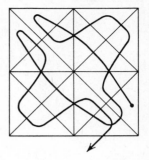

Some of these processes (flows) can take place simultaneously in phased flow relationships, so that, for example, perseverance can trigger serendipity. Such concurrent parallel flows can be very difficult to analyze, but one develops a feel for them that can produce incredible insights.

The tool for keeping track of such complex flows is what I call a metaprogram. I do not intend to discuss that topic here, but I mention it to underline the power that derives from this dynamic (flow and potential) view of the model.

GLIMPSE

Speech is one of the most complex human skills. It draws on every capacity and grows out of either feelings or thoughts. The process is always one where the thought or feeling—the perceived or constructed idea—is translated into a meaning for which words must be chosen, which then are ordered into a proper syntactical sequence that calls forth organic instructions to help the body and mouth produce what we hear as speech.

In this sequence of events, which can be mapped into a transaction sequence on the map (a metaprogram), the body always knows what's happening before the words come out. Therefore, body language must lead speech. For instance, the hands will move before the words are vocalized.

When it's the other way around, the result can be very funny. Occasionally, one sees advertisements on local television where owners, untrained in acting, insist on being in their own commercials. They read the cue cards with a strained and frozen stare, then remember that they should look animated and painfully act out what they have said after they've said it. That reverse procedure is so unnatural that the whole act becomes comical.

I'd love to know whether it's done purposely or not. It may well be an accident that makes the hams think they're great actors, for everyone laughs when they perform.

METHODOLOGY OF PROFILE INTERPRETATION

It would be too tedious and too limiting to give an interpretation of each of the 16 profiles. It would reduce this book to the level of a handbook or catalogue of stereotypes. Such an approach is contrary to the purpose of the model, which is not to limit personalities, but rather to give clues for unraveling the complexity and diversity that do exist.

I therefore suggest a systematic approach that should help interpret a given personality whose profile has been identified. To illustrate the methodology and to create opportunities to bring out certain contrasts, I give a few more examples of specific profiles.

In setting down a methodology, I am aware that not everyone will feel comfortable with my method. I happen to be very visual and therefore find diagrams the easiest way to keep track of details, using the map of capacities and the entropy diagram. The reader should feel free to devise his or her own interpretive procedure.

I mark all relevant details onto the diagrams. Because a specific example is always helpful, I outline the procedure and illustrate it for the case of DINT (15 → 16). The reader should compare these diagrams with the previous ones for DETN (16 → 15):

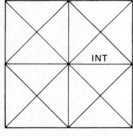

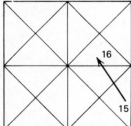

Methodology of Profile Interpretation

Procedure	Example for DINT
1. Look at the last three letters of the profile name. This is the characteristic pole.	INT
2. Find the pole number.	16
3. Identify the dominant circuit, which is the first letter of the profile name.	D
4. The characteristic pole is the processing end of a transaction in the dominant circuit. Find the data pole of that transaction. This is the driver pole.	15
5. The 2 poles identify the competence transaction. The arrow should be on the characteristic pole.	15 → 16
6. Determine the attitude from the second letter of the profile name.	I
7. The transaction in step 5 should exhibit that attitude.	Checks (I)
8. Label the superpole in which the characteristic pole lies as *b* (pole with arrow).	

Methodology of Profile Interpretation   *(Continued)*

Procedure	Example for DINT

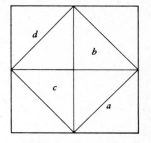

9. Label the superpole in which the data pole lies as *a*.

10. Label superpoles *c* and *d*, with *c* opposite *b* and *d* opposite *a*. The 4 letters should form a diamond in the shape of the dominant circuit.

   D circuit

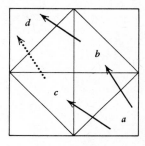

11. Draw in the transaction links of the dominant circuit between all 4 letters such that links from *a* to *b*, *a* to *c*, and *b* to *d* are solid, suggesting conscious transactions, and link *c* to *d* is dotted, suggesting unconscious transactions.

12. Place arrows on transactions as though flow is out of *a* into *d* by way of *b* and *c*:
   a → *b* arrow toward *b*
   a → *c* arrow toward *c*
   b → *d* arrow toward *d*
   c → *d* arrow toward *d*

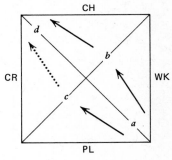

13. Identify modes:
   a → *b* label WK (work)
   a → *c* label PL (play)
   b → *d* label CH (challenge)
   c → *d* label CR (creativity)

14. Transactions in WK and PL should have attitudes as noted in step 6. Transactions in CH and CR modes should have opposite attributes.

   Checks (I for WK and PL, E for CH and CR)

15. Label roles *a*, *b*, *c*, and *d* as:
   a, dependable
   b, responsible
   c, constrained
   d, difficult

   ET, logic and sort
   IN, structure and association
   IS, routine and control
   EF, contrast and preference

16. Label transactions as:
   a → *b*, competence
   a → *c*, perseverance
   b → *d*, toil
   c → *d*, lock
   Note transaction numbers and descriptors.

   15 → 16, conceptualizer
   7 →   8, organizer
   12 → 11, verbalist
   4 →   3, classifier

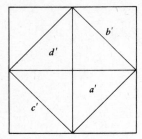

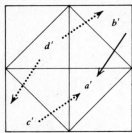

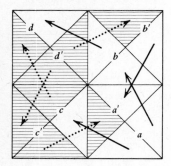

Procedure	Example for DINT
17. Label the superpoles *a'*, *b'*, *c'*, and *d'* by matching *a* to *a'*, *b* to *b'*, *c* to *c'*, and *d* to *d'*, in the same function. Also note the weakest pole opposite the driver pole (step 4).	*d'* = IF (internal feeling, i.e., emotion) Pole 2, match (=)
18. Draw in the transactions of the complementary circuit, with arrows as though flow were out of *d'* into *a'* by way of *b'* and *c'* and label the polar numbers and descriptors. solid as conscious	
b' → *a'*, talent	13 → 14, theoretician
dotted as unconscious *c'* → *a'*, relaxation	5 → 6, molder
dotted as unconscious *d'* → *b'*, serendipity	10 → 9, perceiver
dotted as unconscious *d'* → *c'*, key	2 → 1, initiator
19. Check that arrows in a given mode have the same attitude.	
20. Shade the unconscious poles. The diagram is now complete, and we can refer to it for interpretations. Because of the interrelatedness of all aspects of the profile, it is meaningless to specify a sequential procedure for interpretation. All the following should be noted.	

Summary

Conscious Attributes	DINT
Orientation of work mode	Intellectual
Orientation of play mode	Fine motor
Attribute of applicable dichotomy for work and play modes	Acquired
Strongest superpole (*a*)	ET, rational order
Driver pole	ETN, logic-driven
Characteristic pole	INT, structure and concepts
Temporality	Strong, T and N sequence and future oriented
Attitude in work and play	Introverted
Style: one-sided or balanced	D, detailed, batch
Consciousness: one-sided or balanced	Intellect, D
Procrastinates = toil	12 → 11, writing and articulating

Methodology of Profile Interpretation   *(Continued)*

Conscious Attributes	DINT
Missing dichotomy attribute	Natural
WK characteristic transaction: competence	Conceptualizer

Unconscious Attributes	DINT
Weakest superpole (d')	IF, emotion
Temporality	Weak, F and S, past and present
Hidden agenda	$2 \rightarrow 1$, initiator
Weakest pole	2, match ($=$)
Orientation of CH	Verbal, E
Orientation of CR	Gross motor, E
PL characteristic transaction: relaxation	Molder

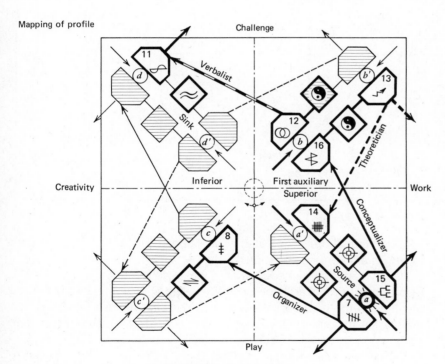

Mapping of profile

Profile identification for DINT.

The completed profile for DINT has been mapped on the map of capacities. The roles have also been filled in on the entropy diagram, where the relative strengths of the superpoles and pole roles are clearly shown

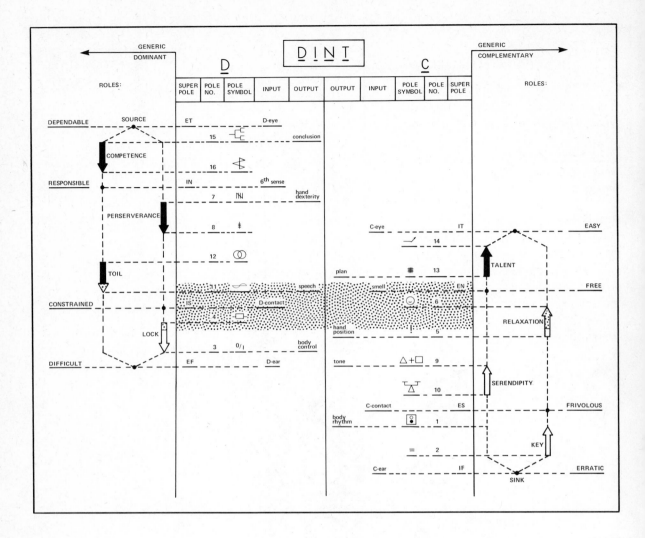

by their vertical order. Something that appears higher up in the diagram means that it is more conscious.

DINT, being introverted, has only three outputs in the conscious domain: conclusions and hand dexterity in the D or dominant circuit and planning in the C or complementary circuit. In contrast, DETN, an extrovert, has four conscious outputs: three in the dominant circuit and one in the complementary circuit.

The entropy diagram makes clearer the concepts of flow in the dominant circuit from the source (superpole ET) to the sink (superpole IF), or entropy production, and of the reverse flow of the complementary circuit, with entropy reduction.

GENERAL DESCRIPTION OF A BALANCED DINT COMPARED TO DETNs*

The characteristic transaction of DINT is 15 → 16, the opposite flow direction of DETN's transaction 16 → 15. Whereas DETN's most visible or characteristic trait is logic, driven by intuition, DINT's seems highly intuitive, driven by logic. DINT is also introverted and so more hidden. It's harder to know what's going on in her mind than in DETN's, which is overtly logical. This is accentuated by the fact that the center of gravity of DETN's consciousness falls between intellectual and verbal. DETN is therefore more verbal and expresses his thoughts, whereas DINT just observes, taking everything in, and says little until she has worked it all out.

DINT deals with the ultimate complexity (pole 16). She seems to spend most of her private time rummaging through her IN memory, reordering its content, and looking for new linkages between symbols and ideas. She is always wondering "How come? Why so?" rather than reaching conclusions. This is typical of the introvert, who takes data in rather than generating outputs. DETN's main transaction, 16 → 15, feeds the output, a conclusion, emanating from pole 15. With DINT, flow is the other way; the visual input enters at 15 and flows to 16, where that information is processed and filed. DINT therefore uses inputs to enrich her internal files, whereas DETN draws on his files to generate an output. DINT is therefore less transparent than DETN.

This visual and private tendency of DINT is reinforced by her talent, the theoretician. An utterly abstract symbolic activity, which reduces all information to patterns, supports her search for structure or conceptual frameworks.

The talent is reinforced by her play mode, which brings hand skill, the skill to express ideas visually, to the visual and pattern dominance. Drawing thus becomes the tool that supports abstract structural and conceptual thought, as is typical of architects and certain scientists. Thus the label conceptualizer, although visual conceptualizer might be more appropriate.

This skill in envisioning is fed by the hidden agenda, the initiator (2 → 1), which acts as the motivator of new ideas and concepts. DINT is therefore always on the lookout for opportunities to apply her concepts to some problem.

This is very different from DETN, who looks for solutions to fit a problem. So he waits till a problem is given and then works out a solution.

---

*I've arbitrarily chosen DETN to be a man and DINT to be a woman to encourage the reader to think of individual personalities.

DINT, on the other hand, is always working out concepts for solutions; in fact, her IN memory is a repertoire of structured solutions. DINT therefore looks for the problem to fit her solutions and thus is the initiator of ideas that fit her repertoire. As would be expected of an introvert, she is therefore less responsive, because she feeds her own need to find application for preworked solutions, rather than focusing on problems of the external world to which she must respond.

Both DETN and DINT are batch processors who like to do one thing at a time, to whom punctuality and the clock are important. They have the same style and work well together.

This is reinforced by the fact that the attitudes of their mixed modes are alike. Only the roles are reversed. DETN's challenge is DINT's play, and DETN's play is DINT's challenge. But the transactions involved are the same. As a consequence, DETN can draw when he must (challenged). But, as described earlier, rather than use the fine motor mode as a supportive tool for his work (as DINT does), he tends to procrastinate. To DINT, organizing and using her hands (or pen) to organize is so very important that it becomes part of her work style. For DETN, such organizing is used only when there is no escape from it. As seen earlier, DETN cleans his house, orders his files, and files his tax return only when things become unmanageable or a deadline stares him in the face. DINT, however, can't work unless she keeps things organized. In fact, the activity of organizing is part and parcel of how DINT does her work.

Let's take a similar comparative look at the opposite mode on the verbal side. To DETN, being in touch with people and articulating thought is part and parcel of his way of working. It's not that way with DINT. Expressing thoughts and dealing with people is a challenge that can come into play only after the work is done or if external pressures force her to address such verbal and people concerns. She can lecture well on subjects she has thoroughly worked out, but she cannot verbalize her thoughts while she is still working on them. Rather, she draws. But both prefer talking to listening.

For both DETN and DINT, the creativity mode has a gross motor orientation, but the lock and key transactions are opposite in attitude. To encourage creativity, DINT therefore must be far more robust and extroverted, engaging in more output-oriented body activity, such as constructing something or physically exhausting herself.

There are many other differences. Although both types are complex, sequential, and future-oriented individuals, DINT tends to make things more complex, going from many to infinity ($T \rightarrow N$), whereas DETN simplifies things somewhat, going from infinity to many. It's therefore far more difficult for DINT to make a decision. There always seem to be infinitely more possible outcomes to be considered before a final conclusion is possible. Therefore, the future always looks rich and exciting.

They differ in weaknesses too. Sensation is DETN's devil; DINT's is feeling, particularly internalized feelings or emotions. It's not that she doesn't have any; it's that she can't control them or express them easily. She is therefore emotionally clumsy and hungry for affection but befuddled when she gets it. She cries and laughs at the wrong times and can be taken advantage of through her emotions. Yet, when totally relaxed and comfortable, she can be very sensitive, even tender. In short, her perceptive skill can work for her serendipitously.

Both DETN and DINT are perceived as complex individuals, intellectuals who, so it seems to simpler souls, have lost touch with the realities of ordinary necessities and basic human intercourse. They seem to live in an abstract world of their own.

CENF AND CIFN

To round out the picture, I give two more examples of two very different profiles, both in the C circuit, CENF and CIFN. I have chosen these two profiles because they form a sharp contrast to DETN and DINT, yet bear the same relationships to each other as DETN does to DINT; that is, the characteristic transaction of CENF, 10 → 9, is opposite that of CIFN, 9 → 10. We thus have one more opportunity to explore contrasts. Again, I assume both are in good contact with their unconscious, thus giving the opportunity to discuss a profile more fully.

There are major differences. The work mode of both CENF and CIFN is people- and verbal-oriented, and both have a contextual style, which might make it difficult for them to work with DETN or DINT. No small part of this is that the C circuit is not the dominant speech circuit, so communication is very different for C types.

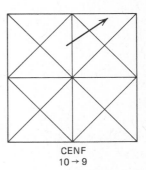

CENF
10 → 9

Both CENF and CIFN love to communicate with people, CENF even more because of the extroverted attitude. Let us focus on CENF first. First, speech is very imprecise, and it doesn't matter what is said. Talk is just another way of reaching out to other people, so that something happens that links them together. What the content is doesn't matter. The hidden agenda is to organize, to somehow bring coherence and sense to the complexity of the people world. But this order is achieved by lots and lots of interactions, by just being with people and interacting with them. For a perceiver, that's all that's needed. The worst thing is to be in a silent, empty world, where there's nothing to perceive. CENF, the perceiver, therefore sees to it that there are interactions so that there is lots to perceive. Since the play mode is oriented toward the experiential (gross motor), it is natural and untiring to experience so many interactions.

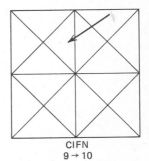

CIFN
9 → 10

This information, taken in through unstructured experiences, is subjected through the characteristic pole 9 to a constant "what if" game. Pole 9 deals with combinations, and thus all sorts of imagined interactions are compared to experiences until an order emerges, which we call insight or wisdom. It is driven by the urge for balance or harmony (pole

APPLICATIONS OF THE
MODEL

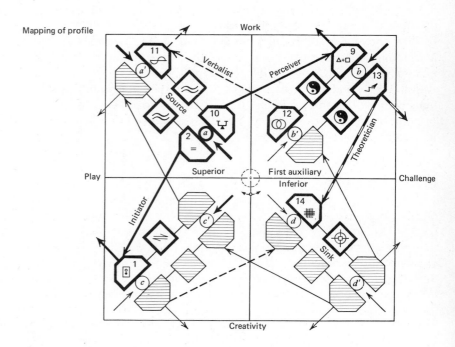

Mapping of profile

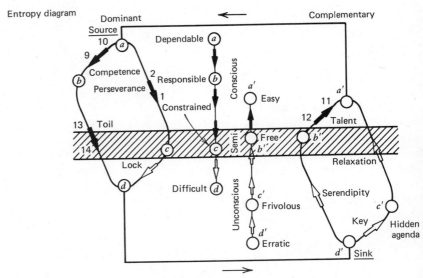

Entropy diagram

Profile identification for CENF.

Mapping of profile

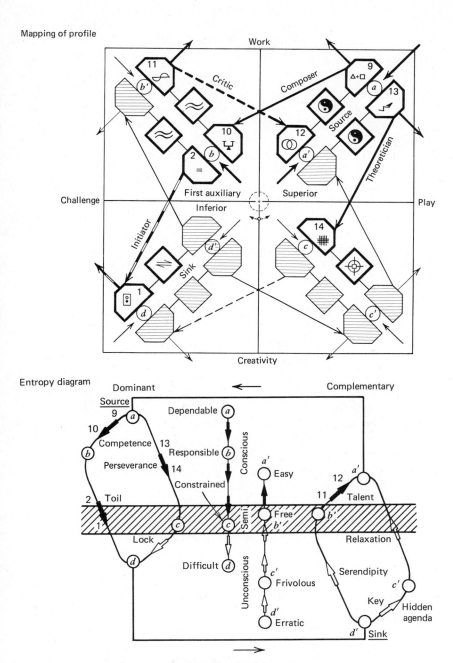

Entropy diagram

Profile identification for CIFN.

10), and order is discovered by determining whether things fit together. The judgment is driven by feeling.

Such a personality seems incomprehensible to DETN. CENF types can't be argued with rationally, for they seem to have no logic (ET is CENF's weakest function). But interestingly enough, CENF's insight is often more reliable than DETN's logic, which can be exasperating to DETN. CENF's intuitive nature always shows. They just know, even if they can't tell you why. Their strongest characteristic is clearly intuition (N).

Let's have a closer look at how CENF comes by her uncanny insights. First of all, CENF deals with both the past and the future. That is a powerful combination, because it links past experiences with future possibilities. CENF doesn't reason out, she extrapolates; she pits experience against logic, and the experience is based on a very rich set of data accumulated in the past.

The perceiver, not being a batch processor, is constantly taking in signals and experiences and embellishing these data with imagined variations (the "what if" game), thus building up an incredible repertoire of memory entries to which a rich sorting of value signs is attached. (Recall the earlier discussion of the IF memory, which suggested that a wavelike value characterization is attached to entries that classify experiences.) "Rightness" is therefore determined not by logic, but by the consistency, fit, or harmony of value signs. It is what is meant by "Yes, that feels right, it hangs together." CENF is thus driven by feeling and is characteristically intuitive. The impression is one of a very active, somewhat scatter-brained, irrational individual with uncanny insight, careless with detail and yet incredibly effective, especially with people. The most basic dichotomy points toward the natural attribute. CENF therefore seems more real and less esoteric than either DETN or DINT, reinforced by the realism brought in through the extroverted attitude.

Though CENF can talk about any subject (a kind of babbling remnant of all the people she has met) and is extremely capable, making decisions easily guided by her insight, she is not an intellectual. Intellect lies in the challenge side. Nor is she gifted with her hands or interested in things. Her world is people—people as they really are, warts and all. CENF is therefore very capable in the real world; she would make a good manager, director, and fit well into a people-oriented business.

CIFN has no trouble with CENF. Both have the same style, the same verbal orientation in the work mode, and the transactions in the mixed modes are identical. But again, the orientation is very different. CIFN is an intellectual, because the play mode (next highest in consciousness) has an intellectual orientation. What CIFN cannot do, or at least not without great effort, is deal with pragmatic reality. Pragmatism equates with S (the here and now), CIFN's weakest function. Nor are external realities important to introverted CIFN.

CIFN, the composer or poet, is intuitively driven. That's where the imagination comes from. But the characteristic pole is IF. CIFN therefore comes across as much warmer than CENF. What shows are his feelings and his sensitivities to values and harmonies. He is therefore emotional, caring, considerate, sensitive. His main activity is to balance combinations or to harmonize possibilities, which can have negative values. CIFN is therefore often a worrier, feeding his own internalized needs. Being verbal, CIFN has no trouble expressing feelings and is often very good, even dramatic and poetic, with words.

One of the subtleties of the art of profiling is to understand hidden agendas. CIFN's hidden agenda is the implementor ($8 \rightarrow 7$), the one who sorts routines or uses routines to do sorting; in short, one who gets things done efficiently. For CIFN, this means he wants a simpler world. This shows up in the complexity index, which goes from infinity to 2—quite a leap. CIFN is thus attracted to the spiritual, be it church, cult, or mysticism, and has a natural inclination to reduce the infinite complexity to a simple do or don't. It is this tendency to oversimplify the complexities to which his intellect is innately attracted that makes the pragmatics of life so difficult. A moral decision, however, is made easily.

I hope these sketches give some indication of the model's power. Remember that the richness of interpretation grows tremendously with experience. Initially, it is perhaps best to plow through all the information in the model more systematically. For instance, there is much I haven't bothered to state for CIFN, and a systematic look at this profile would show that the key dichotomy is lingual. CIFN therefore thinks word thoughts and is gifted in language. CIFN also procrastinates opportunities. He is the one with lots of good ideas that come to him easily, but he almost never gets around to implementing them. And CIFN's creativity is fed by the fine motor mode, the eye and hand, be it doing crafts, gardening, or other hand skills. CIFN finds thinking about philosophical, conceptual ideas relaxing, though this is work for DINT.

DISF VERSUS DINT

I want to describe just one more profile, DISF, because it forms such an interesting contrast to the previous four examples. I want to discuss this profile in a particular context, which is important in human factors applications.

DISF is a profile not uncommon in the nursing profession. It is likely that they will be using computers and other high-technology equipment. Such equipment may well be designed and developed by people with profiles such as DETN and DINT.

DISF and DINT are so different as personalities that major systems disasters can occur, especially if the designer, let us say DINT, assumes that the end user will react to and interact with the system just as he would himself.

APPLICATIONS OF THE
MODEL

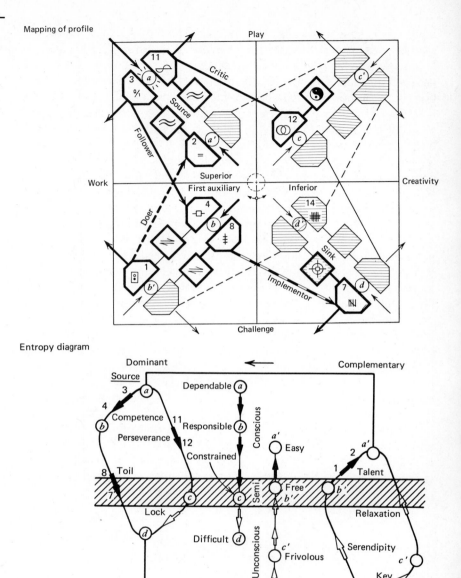

Profile identification for DISF.

Let us first note the differences. Note that DISF, the nurse, and DINT, the designer, have the same style and attitude. But that's about all they have in common.

Let us consider a situation where the designer designs a training program and appropriate manuals for the nurses on how to use the new medical records terminal system. The designer obviously wants to do the best job

DISF	DINT
Concrete	Abstract
Experiential learner	Intellectual learner
Feeling-driven	Logic-driven
Good listener	Poor listener
Makes things simpler	Makes things more complex
Naturally relates to people and feeling qualities	Naturally relates to things and quantification
Auditory	Visual
Past and present	Future and logical sequencing

he can, but his personality causes certain biases, and his orientation is bound to influence his outlook. After all, he designed the system. He loves it and is innately interested in such sophisticated things. It is therefore hard for him to realize that to the nurse this whole business of computers is an alien imposition that only gets in the way of her real interest—people. Therefore the nurses have no love or enthusiasm for the training session in the first place. Second, to the designer the system seems simple. He feels at home with the lingo that describes its functioning. But to the nurse, this new, nonmedical vocabulary is intimidating. In short, the nurse not only doesn't love the computer, she is afraid of it. Such an attitude would never occur to the designer.

Since the designer is primarily concerned with logic and structure, his natural approach to introducing the nurse to the system is to present the system broken down into its logical subunits, probably shown in a schematic diagram. The first thing the nurse sees is thus a complex, abstract picture, which means nothing to her and everything to the designer. The designer is convinced that if he can get that schematic across, everything else will be easy. The nurse, however, having her weakness addressed, feels lost before she ever gets started.

The clever designer would recognize that the nurse is auditory and an experiential learner. Therefore his most effective approach would be to simply get the nurse to have a simple positive experience using the terminal itself. She should be introduced to the system by a simple set of instructions such as "type in your name and push release." The system should be preprogrammed to give some meaningful response. Next the nurse might be asked to type in a patient's name, which should again produce a display familiar and meaningful to her. This way the learning experience would play to her interests and strengths: concern with people, learning by doing, following instructions. At this introductory stage she does not need to know how it works or why. What is most important is to influence her experiential value system (EF) to regard the computer as positive. It also must be simple, because the DISF profile strives for simplification.

There must also be an emphasis on people and the nurse's relationship to doctors and patients. That means that the system itself must be played down. This may not be easy for the designer to do, since he knows far more about the system than about doctors and patients. But he should be alerted to this by an awareness of the personality differences. The list of differences can serve as clues.

For instance, if the designer were selling the system to the administrator, he might well want to emphasize the future potentials of the system. But in an instruction set to the nurse, it is the present and past experiences that matter. He should therefore suppress the urge to expand on future possibilities. What he must concentrate on is building up a repertoire of experiences that relate to present needs.

A workshop should be organized systematically (nurses too are D in style) but its gestalt need not show. Each step in the learning process should be a self-contained unit, hiding the linkages to other learning models. In any learning experience, even though the focus is on the system, people should be brought into the picture, resembling the environment in which the nurse normally works.

A related point involves the fact that the nurse's most conscious mode is body physical. She may therefore prefer to use the terminal while standing rather than sitting. This may not occur to the designer who in his cerebral mode is used to sitting at a desk.

This brief exposition should suffice to illustrate the usefulness of listing opposing attributes of profiles.

And so it goes. Playing the fiddle is very different from nursing, but in terms of the model both draw on the same capacities. So how a given clue from the model manifests itself in a given individual varies from person to person. Put another way, the model tells what patterns to look for, but in what arena that pattern finds expression (e.g. nursing or music,) depends on the unique history and experiences of the individual.

IDENTIFYING THE PROFILE OF AN INDIVIDUAL

The processes and examples of interpreting a profile, given the profile code name, is a necessary first step to applying the insights to real situations. Ultimately, the question of profile identification comes up; one meets a person and wonders what his or her profile is.

The clues from the interpretive analysis then come in very handy. You know that some speak in complete sentences and others jump from thought to thought. You know some can be interrupted and others cannot. You learn to look for these clues and guess the profile and then check whether it fits.

My own preference is to be open and to conduct an unstructured interview that might start with my saying, "Tell me about yourself." Most people respond readily with all the information you need.

To pinpoint a profile, all you need to know is the work mode, the play mode and the dominant style. Since all three are conscious, that is what people usually reveal about themselves. They tell you what they do for

Examples of Profiles and Work Activities

Mode	Profile Name	Work Activity Examples
Intellect Abstract α	Analyst	Science and applied science, Applied math and physics, systems analysis, engineering science, law, medicine as diagnosis, trouble shooting (anything involving logic with verbal skill)
	Conceptualizer	Architecture, corporate planning, systems design, conceptual research, management of innovation (anything involving logical structures with visual skill)
	Suspector	Detective service, pure mathematics, military or strategic planning, comptroller (anything involving strategies and planning with visual pattern recognition skill)
	Theoretician	Theoretical physics, intuition-driven research
Verbal People Π	Verbalist	Orator, preacher, diplomat, actor or director, writer, english professor
	Critic	Critic, voice teacher, foreign language teacher, translator (anything involving accurate listening skill)
	Perceiver	Counselor, shopkeeper, social worker, business, family law, psychiatrist
	Composer	Poet, lyricist, composer, writer, psychiatrist, artist
Hands Things Θ	Implementor	Engineer, experimental scientist, project manager, contractor
	Organizer	Secretary, craftsperson, stock clerk, accountant, draftsman, office clerk, programmer, administrator
	Operator	Machinist, surgeon, manager, auto mechanic
	Molder	Sculptor
Body Concrete ¢	Classifier	Politician, administrator, athlete, anthropologist
	Follower	Nurse, musician
	Initiator	Entrepreneur, salesperson, opportunist
	Doer	Dancer, athlete

a living, and they are likely to tell you their avocation. Either from their speech, demeanor, and dress or with just a few key questions, you can usually establish the dominant style. That's all you need, for those three bits of information can lead to only one profile. For instance, if work is in the concrete mode, play in the thing mode, and style is C, then the source can only be ES and the characteristic transaction must be 1 → 2.

All that remains is a consistency check. But since the profile code name is established, the profile interpretations previously discussed quickly suggest the questions to ask or what to look for. The confirming answer may already have been volunteered. This confirmation procedure is absolutely essential, especially with younger people; differentiation is not always sharp and young people may be more intent on projecting an image than on being themselves.

If your suspicions are confirmed, as they are amazingly often, you can be reasonably sure you have the right profile. If they are not, be very cautious.

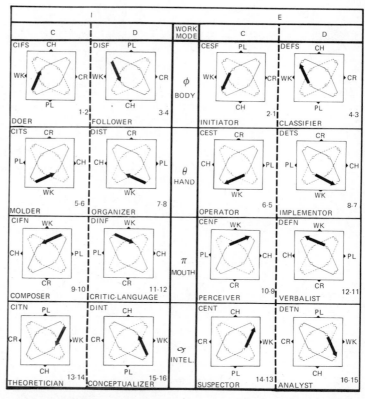

Basic personality profiles and mode orientations. E, extrovert; I, introvert; C, contextual; D, detailed; WK, work mode; CH, challenge mode; CR, creativity mode; PL, play mode; ———, dominant circuit; · · · ·, complementary circuit; a→b transaction shown with heavy arrow.

17

INTERPERSONAL RELATIONS

GLIMPSE

It happens to everyone. There are days in the office when you would have been better off if you had stayed home. The worst is some run-in with your boss when you couldn't afford to lose your temper. But what's worse yet is that you don't know who caused the run-in. You are confused, angry, and hurt.

You come home and your spouse reads "trouble" all over your face, "What's the matter honey?" Your response, one you know isn't deserved, is "Leave me alone! I don't want to talk about it!" and you slam the door behind you. Faintly, you hear a voice from the other side of the door saying with either irony or rancor, "Pardon me, I was just trying to help."

You feel guilty for venting your anger on your spouse, who in turn feels hurt, shut out, misunderstood, and tempted to say, "I won't be treated that way." And your response might range from guilt to resentment.

There is a much simpler way to understand what's really happening. Assume the principal personality here is ET-driven; IF is then the weakest function. Understanding comes through reason, and that takes time. These personality types simply cannot verbalize their feelings until they have been rationally sorted out. They can talk about their feelings once they understand them, but then soothing talk is no longer needed. So one has to accept their ways; there is little someone else can do. Just leave them alone; they'll work it out. Pressure to verbalize their feelings only adds to the stress and shows good intentions without true understanding.

Other profiles respond in different ways to emotional turmoil. Some explode, some sulk, some escape, some brush it off, and some must talk about it, irrational though it may be. It all depends on the profile and the profiles of those around him or her.

The question of what this profile analysis says about interpersonal relationships always comes up. Typically the question is, "Who would make the ideal marriage partner for me?"

Even if there were answers to these questions, to ask them is to take the wrong approach. We are thrown into relationships by circumstances. We don't control them, nor can we control our feelings, needs, and the many other factors that play a role in interpersonal dynamics.

But the model can call attention to like or opposite characteristics, and one can then reflect on a specific situation and see whether such recognition provides helpful insights. For instance, you may have noticed tension in meetings with your new boss. Knowing that your styles are opposite should help you identify some of the specific causes for this tension. Or you may have the feeling in a social relationship that you can't really be yourself, that the other personality seems to make unnatural demands on you. In short, you enjoy the relationship, but it exhausts you. What is it that causes this discomfort, and what can you do about it? Knowing, for example, that the other person's profile makes things more complex and yours makes things simpler may yield some insights into the problem.

What I'm suggesting is that profile comparisons serve as *alerters* rather than as selectors. But this still leaves open the question of whether opposition of some attribute is good or bad.

The more a profile is opposite in attributes to yours, the greater the potential for fascination and stress. The more two profiles share the same attributes, the less puzzling the other person seems. There's simply that sense of "naturally, how else?" But even here, there are two sides of the coin, for the things in common can lead either to a comfortable, relaxed relationship or to one of competition and one-upmanship. And the more two profiles share attributes, the more they share weaknesses as well as strengths. Which is the better relationship—two people who "naturally" fit together but share the same blind spots or two people fascinated with each other, which often leads to stress, but who can help each other overcome their weaknesses?

Let me put this specifically in the context of the structural relationships developed in this chapter. Each profile uses only half the 16 possible transactions, four in the dominant circuit, four in the complementary circuit. In comparing two profiles, there are those that share the same eight transactions, those that share only four out of eight, and those that share none at all. Profiles with similar transactions could be expected to interrelate more naturally than profiles with dissimilar transactions. But which is the better match, and what criteria do we use? Is contentment better than fascination? Profiles with similar transactions are lacking pieces of the map in their relationship with each other, whereas profiles with completely different transactions will have the entire map at their disposal. Is security better than potential?

The factors that affect interpersonal relationships are vastly complex, so that profiles fall far short as a determinant. All you can do is let relationships develop and then use the model as a possible means for understanding some aspects of that relationship to decide whether there is anything you can do to help it.

There are two useful mechanisms for gaining such insights: the polar plot and the mode roles. Before I describe these relationships, however, it is necessary to further explain the tendency to do things *naturally*.

Each profile has a set of transactions that work naturally for that individual under the circumstances described by roles. For instance, under *challenging* circumstances, it is natural for me to express ideas in words: that is, given the right setting, it feels comfortable, unforced, innately right and easy for me to be a *talker*. It is not natural or innate for me to be a *listener* (the reverse transaction). I have to work like a dog to listen. When I do listen, it is never for very long. Before I know it, my mind drifts off, and I quit listening, so that I interrupt or talk over someone else's talk or talk to myself, no longer processing what my ears pick up. Left to my own nature, I will talk (out loud to myself) rather than listen. Nevertheless, I clearly have the capability to listen.

As the competition/cooperation matrix says nothing about direction (it only compares one pole with another regardless of direction), the only clue is entropy, which has a unique direction to it and does not deal with a counterflow in the same circuit. That is, the flow from source to sink in the dominant circuit and from sink to source in the complementary circuit is in one direction only. Each profile involves half of the 16 transactions and only one of the two possible transaction directions between two capacities. If the transaction $1 \rightarrow 2$ is involved in a particular profile, the reverse $2 \rightarrow 1$ transaction is not involved.

This brings me to libido, which I've long related in my mind to entropy flow. It's like a flowing river. If you throw a piece of wood in it, it will naturally flow downstream. That doesn't say that salmon don't swim upstream, but it's an exhausting, sometimes destructive, process. There is something self-protective about such totally energy-consuming processes. We protect ourselves from being drained or mentally exhausted by not swimming against the stream; this isn't to say that we can't, but we would rather do it the easy way. This doing it the easy way seems to be a basic law of nature.

This laziness or finding the easy path, so characteristic of self-organizing systems, is sometimes referred to as the principle of least effort. It seems to me to play the key role in interpersonal relations. If the relationship serves the needs for stimulation and new experiences, then, just as in mountain climbing, it may be exhilarating to expend the energy required. But if the expectation of a relationship is one of a "comfy" feeling, easy communication and mutual understanding, then least effort must be the goal. Equating least effort to compatibility, one can identify stressful and stimulating relationships and effortless and compatible ones most easily by referring to the compatibility table.

The organization of this table involves two key variables, libido compatibility and mode role orientations, that order the 16 possible profiles into a four by four matrix.

It was Larry Miike who first observed that profiles sharing the same source/sink pair share identical transactions. I call such a subset of profiles a compatible group. There are four such groups, presented as rows *A*, *B*, *C*, and *D* in the compatibility table. Note also in the table that groups *A* and *B* are incompatible with each other. The same is true of groups *C* and *D*.

If one focuses on a particular transaction, let us say $12 \rightarrow 11$, that transaction will appear naturally in the other three profiles as well. Trans-

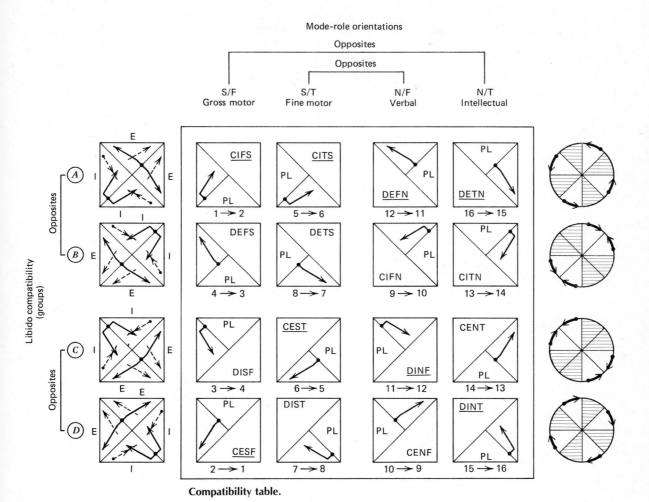

Compatibility table.

action 12 → 11 is talking. Therefore, all profiles in group *A* are talkers, and no one in this group is a natural listener. All the profiles in group *B* then have transactions in the opposite direction, and thus all are listeners. Similarly, all profiles in group *C* have all transactions opposite those in group *D*—that is, all listeners versus all talkers.

All profiles in a compatible group thus have information flowing in the same direction for all eight transactions of each profile.

The four profiles in a group will differ only in roles. Note that the characteristic transaction for each profile in the group falls in a different mode, and that, of course, shifts the disposition of consciousness and thus the roles. Roles thus become a secondary criterion for compatibility.

This difference in mode role and orientation has been used as the organizing principle for the columns in the compatibility diagram. All profiles in the first column, labeled S/F, have their work mode oriented toward the left, that is, in the gross motor mode. All those in the second column, labeled S/T, have their work mode oriented toward the fine motor mode. Similarly the third and last columns have work modes oriented toward the verbal and intellectual modes, respectively.

Each entry in the matrix shows a simplified map, designating for each profile only the source, the characteristic (most conscious) transaction, the name of the profile, and the orientation of the play mode (PL).

The compatibility table also shows for each compatible group a map and polar plot, showing all eight transactions the group has in common. The four characteristic transactions of that group are marked with heavy lines.

The complex interpersonal relationships that can be extracted from the compatibility table in any pair of profiles are most easily explained by means of an example. Using DINT (row *D*, last column) as the reference profile, what can we infer about how DINT relates to other profiles?

COMPATIBLE RELATIONSHIPS

DINT is compatible with CENF, DIST, and CESF, the profiles in its own compatible group (row *D*). All four profiles process information the same natural way (given transaction modes all have the same attitude, as marked at the map on the extreme left). This contributes to easy, comfortable, natural insights into one another. There are no surprises or feelings of strange behavior. Each seems to innately understand the other. All share difficulties with information-processing activities that are not part of that profile group. The following relationships can be observed:

1. Among the four, there are sharp differences in interests because of the differing role orientations. CESF will be most different in focus of interest, representing a profile that is in fact DINT's hidden agenda, or alter ego. They get along well but are active in different worlds.

2. DINT and DIST form a remarkably comfortable working relationship, since the work mode of one is the play mode of the other. They not only understand each other but also enjoy shared work. The most conscious part of their profiles is very similar, with style and attitude the same. They are blind to the same concerns.

3. DINT and CENF form a richer complement to each other, leading to an easy and enriching social relationship. But they form a poor working partnership because the work mode of one falls into the challenge mode of the other. Either one wants to avoid the work interest of the other or they'll compete. But in nonwork settings they benefit by the fact that play and creativity form mode pairs. So they can have creative fun together.

To clarify how to find these relationships in the table let me give a parallel example. Taking CIFN as the reference profile, the relationship discussed in 1 above would be fulfilled by DETS, 2 by CITN, and 3 by DEFS.

INCOMPATIBLE RELATIONSHIPS

DINT (the reference profile) is in group *D*. Group *C* is the opposite of that group; therefore, all the profiles in group *C* use transactions that can be activated for DINT only with great effort. DINT is thus incompatible with DISF, CEST, DINF, and CENT (for the parallel example CIFN, the incompatible profiles would be in parallel order, CIFS, DETN, CITS, and DEFN).

The relationship with any of these profiles is bound to be stressful; it may be fascinating, but DINT has to muster great effort to understand, much less predict, the behavioral responses of any member in this group. They simply have not a single transaction in common. CENT has the same mode orientation as DINT, so their interests may match, but they go about things differently. With DISF there is not even any sharing of interest, since all modes are opposite.

PARTIALLY COMPATIBLE RELATIONSHIPS

DINT's relationship to profiles in groups *A* and *B* are less extreme. DINT will have half the transactions in common with those two groups. In fact, there are specific positive relationships to DETN, CITN, DEFN, and CIFN. For instance, DETN and DINT have identical manifestations of consciousness and therefore empathize well and emphasize or ignore the same things. (This is indicated in the columns of the compatibility table by profile name pairs that are underlined or not underlined. For instance, for the reference case CIFN, CENF would have the same manifestations of consciousness.)

This brief discussion should provide at least a handle for grappling with the complexities of interpersonal relationships. It seems to me that of the many variables involved, group compatibility, mode role orientation, style, and disposition of consciousness are the key criteria, in that order. How they influence a relationship depends on the mutual expectations of the people involved.

GLIMPSE

One of my students, Mary Sue Iannello, managed a small group of social workers involved in foster home cases. Usually, cases came to their attention through the police or a welfare agency as a result of a complaint.

Typically, one of Mary Sue's people would visit the home and might find a whimpering child, a mother unable to cope, neglect, alcoholism, mismanagement, or the remnants of a fight—in short, anything in the gamut of social ills.

Based on what the case worker observed and learned, a recommendation was made to the court, perhaps to place one of the children in a foster home.

Mary Sue had observed that some of her people were superb at the site, relating well to the people and showing excellent perceptiveness that helped in understanding the situation. And there were others who excelled in the documenting and preparing the case for the judge's determination. But only rarely did the same person have both these strengths.

A profile analysis of her case workers showed an incredible C or D correlation with the two skills. With their approval, she not only structured how the work was to be done so that strengths could be best used, she also revamped the physical environment in which they worked.

The C types chose to share a large common room where they could easily chat and compare experiences with one another. They located their desks near the door, where they could meet people, and felt free to come and leave as they chose. The D types got private offices, where they could work in more structured environments, with fewer disruptions and crises. In the process, Mary Sue learned about her own strengths, blind spots, and biases.

She shared what she was learning about the model with her group, so her reorganization thrust became a collective effort. All were happier with the new setup.

I think this model has many implications for management, in both hiring and evaluating managers. The profiles can be used to help managers better understand themselves and their relationships with others. Above all it should give them insights into the people working under them—whether they are likely to oversimplify or to be concerned about future implications—and to explain why a particularly good performer interacts so badly with another good performer.

Managers might also want to take advantage of profile insights when they appoint a special task force. One should be able to predict how smoothly or how poorly people will work together and to what extent the composition of the task force gives some assurance that a variety of viewpoints and perspectives is covered. At the least, the profiles should tell managers what the group's blind spot is.

18

CREATIVITY

Much that is useful has been written about creativity, but I have seen no good theoretical explanation of what goes on, except perhaps Koestler's.

In view of what has already been said about the model, it seems clear that creativity is the product of the unconscious. Creativity therefore works best for those who accept the unconscious side of their personalities, regardless of how they are oriented on the map of capacities. They must operate on their opposite (weak, unconscious) side; for example, thinkers must let their feelings speak (T versus F functions).

It is also clear that creative behavior, since it is unconscious, cannot be directed; it can only be encouraged by structuring the setting to favor unconscious activities. I've experimented some with this and have achieved good results. The trick is to promote the transactions with the roles of lock, key, serendipity, and relaxation. How that is done depends on the profile.

I recall a part-time student who, both on his job and in class, was working on a number of interesting problems but was unable to solve them. Some creative idea was missing. His profile was DINT (15 → 16). It was clear that he had to operate in the gross motor mode, ideally in the C circuit, to activate his creative transactions. We chatted awhile about what he does that might fit that mode. He finally told me that he used to play the guitar but hadn't touched it in years; in fact, he wasn't sure where it was. I told him to find it and that I thought it was the ideal activity for him.

That weekend he found the guitar, which was like finding an old friend. He became lost in playing it and told me that he spent most of the weekend strumming away.

Then came the dramatic results. During the next week, ideas popped into his head in profusion. He worked intensely, solved all his class problems, and made breakthroughs at work that led to two patents.

This is not the only such case, but it illustrates so well the point I want to make. In this case all the elements were right. He had "done his time" working consciously on the problems. He had invested hours applying competence, perseverance, and talent to the point that only toil seemed to be left as the operational activity. And it wasn't getting him anywhere. Clearly, he knew what the problems were, and he had tried many approaches and even knew why they didn't work. He had produced a lot of consciously generated information that led to no outputs. All sank into the sink, and what was needed was a new way of organizing, which is best done by the unconscious.

First, lock had to recognize what the problems really were, then key and serendipity had to come up with solutions. Once they did, he had to be relaxed enough to bring those new insights into his conscious. I could not do that for him, but I could tell him how to structure his activities to encourage lock, key, serendipity, and relaxation to become activated. And it worked.

The recipe for turning on natural creativity varies from profile to profile. A poet ought to work with his hands. A businessman might want to read some science fiction or try to understand physics. And a tinkerer or a mechanic ought to interact more with people.

The last case is well illustrated by a situation I encountered in India. I had an opportunity there to interview Mr. D., who had a prolific record of inventions. An account of that interview appears at the end of the chapter. It is interesting to note that Mr. D. instinctively could operate on his unconscious side as a natural part of his working style. Periodically, he would leave his shop to become socially involved. He'd argue with his wife, talk to people, play with kids, write philosophical books, or read poetry. And it worked.

E-12

The trick seems to be to throw yourself into activities that fit the counterpart of your personality. People like Mr. D. and my student did exactly that and got the exhilaration of that experience.

The irony is that such creative behavior is terribly difficult to carry out in the traditional work setting. Bringing a guitar to the office and playing it all day is just not done. Nor will management look with favor on normally hard-working individuals who suddenly spend all their time cracking jokes in the hallway. Such behavior is too disruptive for controlled, accountable behavior, and yet it's exactly what might be needed for creative problem solving.

Managers thus must face up to the tradeoffs of either having their work environments disrupted or of discouraging creativity. To encourage creativity, they must tolerate and accept unorthodox activities that might stimulate the unconscious side of a personality.

Research labs and universities are far more tolerant of nontraditional behavior. Neither dress nor time is prescribed. And if one of their staff members wants to lie under a tree or spend the whole afternoon in the student pub or on the golf course, it's alright. This is one of the key strengths of these institutions, and it is unfortunate that occasionally someone gets worried and tries to destroy this natural ambiance for creativity.

One of the creative problem-solving methodologies I've found to be effective is synectics. Stripped to its basics, it guides a group through a variety of activities by means of analogies and excursions. It involves a number of useful and helpful "tricks," such as teaching people to be listeners and to assume a positive attitude toward others' comments, as well as keeping records of what surfaces, but basically it is a way for guiding the group through all the modes.

E-8

Synectics provides a structured framework for fantasizing (give me an example of _____ from the world of _____). There is a focus on word labels (give me a book title that captures the essence of _____). Participants are encouraged to act through personal analogy (pretend you are a paper clip and tell me how you feel). There is also a time to catch conflict and paradox, a time to analyze (intellectual rationale), a time to draw, explain, and touch the object. In short, with a group of people representing diverse profiles and the variety of modes to which the participants are guided, synectics enhances the probability that someone will be operating in and drawing on his or her unconscious mode and transactions. It is a kind of shotgun approach that falls into the right patterns.

One observation I have not yet sorted out: there may well be another dichotomy that has relevance to creativity. I have noticed that people with "outrageous" minds tend to live very ordered, structured lives and that people with very ordered minds can tolerate a great deal of disorder around them. It is as though there were some conservation principle of order and disorder at work. If the internal world is to be free to accept disorder, then the external world must be orderly and vice versa. This, I believe, has some implications for those who pull creative ideas out of their heads and for those who discover new ideas in their environments.

Finally, I must make a comment about children, for no one is as innately creative as they. I believe this is because in children the interface between the conscious and the unconscious has not yet become an impenetrable barrier. Nor is differentiation so sharp. As a consequence, their conscious and unconscious are far more balanced and accessible. My experience in courses in design and creativity has been that the operational mode of the child can be reawakened to help the creative process. I've had graduate students feed each other cereal, play games in the dark, talk like babies, and work on the floor. These activities help because they break down the walls that block access to the unconscious. Getting to the unconscious is the key, and this is one way. However, if the profile of the individual is known, the setting can be focused far more easily.

AN INTERVIEW WITH A CREATIVE PERSON

I had an opportunity to interview an inventor, a Mr. D., in India in early 1978. The interview was recorded and transcribed. Subsequently I was asked by Mr. A.M. Elijah, publisher of "The Syntropic Thinker," to add commentary which would relate the interview to the eight-pole model. The interview with my commentary appeared in the December 1978 issue of "The Syntropic Thinker."* It is reproduced below. Commentary appears as normal text. The transcription appears indented, with L for Lowen and D for Mr. D.

---

*"The Syntropic Thinker" Dec. 1978, pp. 19–23. A.M. Elijah, editor and publisher, Institute of Creative Development, Poona, India.

In interviewing a person I draw on everything. So first of all the reader should not assume that the only inputs were those recorded in this transcription. Mr. Elijah introduced me to Mr. D. and, of course, I listened and received visual and emotional impressions. Mr. D. presented a neat appearance, seemed to be sensitive, genteel but not bashful. He obviously was enjoying the limelight and very proud of his achievements. He was open and receptive but not overbearing conversationally. He moved with a slow, deliberate grace—revealing a man who suffers patiently. Quite ceremonially he handed me a book he had written which I could only glance at. It struck me like a self educated philosopher's admiration of the order of science—with a bit of the benevolent teacher–preacher coming out. These are my recollections of that day and the impressions I had prior to the interview. I knew he was proud of his inventions, thought of himself by the label "inventor"—so that seemed a natural starting point. I always try to get people to just start talking about themselves. If it's a subject central to them—they feel at ease almost at once. So I wanted to get Mr. D. to talk about his inventing—but the glance at the book—or something in the prior conversation—also suggested that he was largely self-educated and I wanted to know more about that. These thoughts in my head then gave rise to the opening question. From there on things flowed by themselves.

Prof. Lowen: Can you tell me something about your formal education? I understand you started inventing around the age of thirteen.
Mr. D: That's right. I had the normal schooling. When I started on my first invention I had no technical training.
L: Have you any special training since 1939?
D: No, I did my intermediate studies at College—two years after high school only. I however pursued creative studies on my own.

The response confirmed my general impression. Most meaningful was the phrase "creative studies" preceded by "however." However meant in so many words—"I don't put too much weight on my studies in college"—that confirmed for me that what he knows is largely self acquired, not handed to him by an outside stimulus. As to "creative studies"—there is no such thing in the formal sense. I took it to mean "I search within myself to find answers to my curiosity." The focus is "on my own"—i.e., the I—the internal.

My reaction to his responses—which after all were unforced and therefore revealingly natural—suggested an internal (introverted attitude). What drove him was what was within him not that external to him.

I don't really know what made me ask the next question other than that I wanted a picture of him as a child. There was something beguilingly natural in his anxiousness to be helpful, much as a child tries to please. So I asked:

L: What was the nature of your household? I am trying to form in my mind a picture which says that at a very early age you played with electric wires and phenomena. Where were you exposed to these things? How did you know there was such a thing as a wire?

D: Where I lived there was no electricity, but there was a steamship service. In this steamship there were electrical connections which I studied carefully—how the switches were operated and things like that.

The response did not produce what I was fishing for. It was a rather literal response (suggesting S) but one has to go with what one gets and so I used this opening to explore whether he was visual or verbal.

L: By studying—you mean you observed people? Are you a good observer?
D: I think so.
L: A better observer than a listener?
D: Yes (hesitantly).
L: In other words, you learn more by watching than listening?
D: You are probably right.

His responses indicated that he's visual. Since hands and eyes go together (the focus dichotomy) it was natural to ask for confirmation, and I got it.

L: Are you skilled with your hands?
D: Yes. I work with them—I built the first model of my typewriter myself.

But as is most usually the case—I got more than just a yes. Namely that he built his own typewriter and so it was natural to go with that. I try very hard not to force i.e., steer the conversation—but let it determine its own flow. So I said in effect tell me more about that.

L: Where did you learn these skills?
D: I have no idea of typewriter mechanisms. I had however seen various new typewriters at the Hanover fair. I watched carefully how these were put together and how they worked. I felt these models were too expensive for my country and these would have to be changed. I thought a lot about how to get a typewriter within Rs. 6.000/00 ($750) which cover two languages and two sizes. Ultimately the idea came.

The response again confirms the visual dominance (and therefore a fascination with things) but additionally points—through the statements how they worked, how they were put together—that the observation is guided by logic. There was also a logical quantitative judgement—i.e., too expensive. The response was richer yet. His concerns were externally driven—i.e., cost restraints, effecting some change and then he proceeds to tell me how he solves problems. He ultimately tells me it took time to find the answer and the phrase "the idea came" suggests some unconscious, non-logical process.

The reader will note—that the interviewer has to listen very carefully. It's not what is said—but also how it's said and the listening ear must be receptive to the unexpected. Take whatever is given. Let me review where I stand now. . . .

The focus is clearly on things—i.e., the lower part of the capacities map. The ET pole (logical) and the IT pole (visual ideas) seem to be very active.

"The idea came"—out of the less conscious part—therefore F or N. I have no idea which. This needs to be explored and leads me to my next question.

But there is more to it. My initial assessment was that I'm dealing with an introvert and yet here I find him addressing realistic external restraints through the ET pole. Which is dominant E or I? I must get at that too. So I try to get Mr. D. to describe how he thinks.

L: That's very interesting you said "I started thinking." Can you think back? This is a very complicated process. Is this thinking something that you do—meditating or with a pencil in your hand or while you are working on something—what's going on while you are thinking?

D: I need paper and pencils—when I am thinking—also I need the object I am working on and some necessary tools e.g. I concentrated on developing a typewriter—thought of extending the length of the type bar, of fitting one more type face so as to accommodate two types instead of one. When I recollected that by depressing the shift key of the older typewriter the carriage goes up while in the new one the whole type-basket does down, I thought it would be a good idea to incorporate both in one. . . .

It is noteworthy that his response does not refer to theories—it is rather an experiential description—he recollects not seeing but doing it (depressing the key), i.e., he is reliving an experience and the idea (IT pole) grows out of that. So I had better check on that—since IT deals with images.

L: I follow what you say very clearly . . . but when the idea first occurred to you—that occurred as an image in your mind. . . .

D: Yes.

L: So that again is visual. . . .

He confirms that—so now the profile starts to emerge. It seems to involve the S and T quadrants—primarily—so it is either ET plus IS or IS plus ET. The complementary transaction, ES—IT the less conscious transaction, seems to have IT dominant. The profile might therefore well be DIST. . . .

If this is the correct profile—he would be of D-type and introverted. It clearly matches his eye–hand dominance and fits in other ways. For instance the intellectual activity of writing a theoretical/philosophical book—is a kind of play activity—for the book is really not scholarly researched but rather more narrative, musing on a very intellectual subject. I therefore decided to adopt the DIST profile as a tentative profile. It needs lots of confirmations.

D: I generally get my ideas when I am sleeping—not exactly dreaming yet thinking with my eyes closed—sort of daydreaming. . . .

Now interestingly enough, as happens frequently, I got a very useful response without even asking a question. I simply commented on the visual dominance and somehow this triggered the very useful daydreaming response. Daydreaming is a directed fantasy, an activity of the EN pole. In Mr. D. it can become active only when the visual stimulus is shut off (eyes closed) i.e., it is triggered by internal images of the IT pole. Note that the EN pole is the opposite extreme of the IS pole—the very spot on the map where I would expect creative thought if the profile is as I have tentatively concluded. That certainly is a confirmation. But I must check it. The IS–EN polarity suggests that EN generates possibilities—which get explored by logic driven routines—like taking something apart.

L: But full of images. . . . I want you to think back when you were about 10 years old . . . were you the kind when anything new came in, you got into it and had an urge to take it apart?
D: Yes—I did a lot of that—taking clocks etc. apart and putting them together again.

That now also gets confirmed. "OK" in my next comment says in effect—ok now—I think I've got your profile. Now let me check it out more systematically. The profile says—the inventing is not theory or abstractly driven—let me just check this out.

L: OK? How are you about theory?
D: Yes, I enjoy reading theoretical books on the subject of my interest—this interest brought me here today. . . .

And indeed D.'s response tells me that theory is only a play activity. He uses the word enjoy—not work at and he is selective i.e., he pursues theory only if it strikes his fancy (subject of my interest). I'm quite sure of the profile now but feel I must confirm it systematically. Therefore I ask a question that involves the body. So I decide, for reasons unknown to me, to ask about bicycles.

L: Do you ride a bicycle? Can you think back as to how you learned to ride a bicycle?
D: By trial and failure—no one helped—I maintained my own bicycle.

The response again is revealing (they usually are if the subject is natural and at ease). If "trial and failure" does not describe challenge I don't know what does. Body is his challenge mode. So again the profile is confirmed.

I cannot reconstruct what went through my mind which led to the next exchange except possibly to confirm the same point.

L: With all your interest in what makes things work did you try to figure out what made it work before you tried it?
D: I don't remember.
L: Before using the typewriter did you try to figure out what made it work?
D: I am not sure now—I think I went ahead and used it.

Interestingly enough I also find the responses unfocused, as though D. was saying I don't know what you're asking nor how to respond to it. It was simply a useless exchange except he shows again that his approach is largely experiential ("I went ahead and used it").

For the sake of brevity, I will not analyze the rest of the dialogue in the same detail. Nor is it needed. I'm sure in my mind that the profile is DIST and I'm now searching out new insights and perspectives in a more carefree way. I can afford to get away from the subject. So I ask about the total setting in which he works.

L: I take it you are married and have a family. . . . When you are working on some new invention is it a very private process? . . . Do you just work on it and your wife stays out of your way and lets you do your thing or when you are excited about a new idea you feel you have to tell your wife about it?

D: My family does not appreciate my working—but I talk to them about it—I talk to everyone.

L: Is it useful to you to talk to people about it?

D: Probably yes—more because of my desire to share things with people—to share my knowledge. I have some 15/16 inventions to my credit and want to write one more book—even if my book will be appreciated, as was Leonardo da Vinci's, after 250 years.

He tells me more about his wife than I care to know—(she is clearly D and E). However the digression tells some revealing things. 1) Even though he's visually dominant he does not neglect verbal discourse. This is a healthy anti-one-sidedness compensation important for creativity. He also does not deny his feelings, another healthy move to encourage creativity. He's clearly hurt by the fact that his wife does not share his enthusiasm for inventions, but he goes on and seeks other outlets. "Sharing" is a feeling people oriented activity, and he is a dreamer, he's willing to push his rewards 250 years off in the future, a true introvert—balancing his wife's extroversion. When he can't cope with his wife's attention to reality, he retreats into his inner world. His imagination, N (futures), is active.

L: Were you a good storyteller?

D: Yes—I built my own stories and my children enjoyed them—unfortunately when they asked me to repeat them they were always a little different.

In the exchange about his children, D. tells me that he appreciates (and works at) his creative side, the ability to fantasize (he invents his own stories). One more check. He should be "D"-style.

L: Tell me about your work habits—is your shop laid out in a very orderly fashion—with tools, pliers, screwdrivers in precise places?

D: I tend to be systematic.

L: If a child came running while you were working and said "my kite is caught in the tree?" would you stop working and help the child or say "I am busy now, I'll come later."

D: The latter.

Predictably he tells me in response to a very direct question that he is a D type—the last confirmation I was looking for. He's a systematic batch processor who does not like interruptions.

L: If you are working on something, can you stick with it a very long time?

D: I can work for long stretches at a time on the same problem without feeling the need for distraction.

L: Is your daily life a matter of routine?

D: No—I am rather flexible. The job determines what needs to be done.

L: From your point of view is your wife very rigidly systematic and a disciplinarian?

D: Yes and she is a good manager with money and probably stricter with the children than me.

L: Is there something about your wife's style of working that annoys you?

D: Yes, my wife does not like my inventing and will criticise, will obstruct my working.

L: Do you know why that is?

D: I think that is mostly because of the traditional nature of our womenfolk—she expects me to follow routine, traditions. . . .

L: Assuming you are working a 17 hr schedule—do you set out your priorities and work at them systematically?

D: Let me give you an example—in developing an idea and giving practical shape to it you cannot—at any rate I cannot—work at it systematically. Most of my ideas are obtained during my sleep thinking periods. Sometimes I work on developing some ideas or on improving them and all efforts end in failure. I go to rest and suddenly I am thinking of the trials and I get up and start working and often success comes—it happens.

L: Is it just a matter of luck, you fall into it; so many failures and all of a sudden success comes—is that it?

D: These sort of ideas I cannot plan on; they flash on my mind and I work on it.

L: When that suddenly happens that's an exciting thing, do you talk to yourself about it? Do you feel you have to talk about it to others?

D: Yes, I tell others.

L: You become very talkative but then you go back and work on it and become totally involved.

D: True, I almost forget to eat.

L: So it is very physical? You get very excited and you walk a lot?

D: No.

L: Do you like music?

D: Not particularly.

L: What do you do for relaxation?

D: Working on creative projects is relaxing to me.

In the above exchanges some fascinating comments come about on which I could comment at length, but they are not germane to profiling. They offer however fascinating insights into the creative type. It is as though Mr. D. understood intuitively the importance of the opposite pole. He's not driven. Sleeping, getting away from the problem is a productive complement to working. His outlook about failures is positive. (I almost have the feeling he enjoys his wife's disapproval, it eggs him on.)

L: Thank you, I think I am clear now on your profile. To Participants: Mr. D. is basically in the D circuit as far as the work thing is concerned, but his C circuit is also very active. He uses his capacities more fully than most people, he is not put in a box as much as most jobs force us to be in. If you look back on how he came to be an inventor he is completely self made like a farmer where the farmer is also not a specialist, he has to know everything. His sense of feelings is very good, he observes things, he believes in mystical things. A farmer is a very well rounded individual much more so than a secretary or an engineer who are trained to be specialists. The farmer is much better able to draw on all his capacities and there is a lesser need for him to play as we do golf, bridge etc. Because since he uses all his capacities there is a constant balancing of one capacity against the other so that the ONE-SIDENESS does not scream for this compensation; he is operating in all the modes. This is a very interesting play of the C and D circuits.

It is very difficult to put in print the complexities of the mind. As I was writing this explication so many additional thoughts raced through my mind that I was afraid I'd be writing a thesis. I hope that which I've chosen to articulate is helpful as an annotated analysis of an interview with a very cooperative, honest and fascinating subject.

What should be important to the reader is to understand that the process of interviewing must be a contextual process, irrespective of your nature. It helps to have studied Synectics, an analogical mechanisms technique which among other things teaches you to listen. Listening is all important. The words, the way it is said, is the window to the personality. The trick is to look through the window, and you can learn a lot, not only about the subject of the interview, but about yourself, the diversity of human beings and how pitifully little we understand about human interactions.

Postscript

I'm struck by how different the "in vivo" situation is compared to a post mortem analysis of what went through my head. During the interview, things go much too fast to think everything I've said out in words. In my case the thinking are vaguely perceived impressions, mostly feelings and images. For another interviewer type it's bound to be different. I'm much too busy listening to articulate into words what I sense. It remains symbolic except for the concreteness of the diagramatic profile, i.e., I translate the complexity of perceptions into a profile on the capacities map. It's my shorthand, so to say, I often draw such diagrams while I'm conducting an interview. If the profile attempt is wrong—I start anew with another profile. The tentative profile on paper or in my head is what focuses the bits and pieces I extract from the interview. It's what structures the interview. What I've tried to do here is to verbalize how and from what I arrived at a particular profile.

The other point that must be emphasized is that the interview is not finished until everything on the profile map fits. It is the consistency of the responses to the profile—i.e., the congruence of all aspects of the profile that tells you that you have uncovered the correct profile. This is a vital point for the profile might have been ET–IS, but then play and challenge modes would have been reversed, or it might have been IT and ES with similar results but the D style would not fit. All, and I underline, all the attributes have to fit. One senses this very quickly, because if the interviewer has the right profile most of the questions become leading (predictive) questions to which the response is simply yes or exactly so or how did you know. One sort of feels it as the interview flows that one is converging.

APPLICATIONS OF THE
MODEL

The second post mortem comment I want to make is to state what an extraordinary subject we had. One sees truly creative people only rarely and Mr. D. was an exceptional subject. Exceptional in not only what he made of himself but also in the insights he provided into his inner workings. Though he knew nothing of the model he has done intuitively all that which the model preaches. Operate deliberately on your weak side, use both circuits, develop awareness of your less conscious capacities, be responsive to your inner signals etc., etc. We can all learn from him and I am grateful to Mr. D. for his willingness to have this interview published, for sharing his wisdom and for being so natural and honest during the interview. He is a "Mensch," a whole human being, and that is rare. I thank him and Mr. Elijah for creating the opportunity.

19

ON HUMAN FACTORS

Human factors is concerned with the man-machine interface. There is currently a lot of interest in it, but I'm afraid there is more stress on the factors than on the human. The objective of human factors is to make the human operator feel comfortable with the machine, preferably even to love it. Put another way, if there is a misfit between what the machine demands and what the human operator can deliver, the resulting stress and accommodation should be borne by the machine, not by the person.

That's the objective but rarely the reality. People are incredibly adaptable, but to adapt machines costs money. Industry would spend that money only if adapting machines were less costly than adapting people. Unfortunately, people don't charge for adapting to machines.

It is amazing how unaware we are of things that annoy us. If you stub your toe on your doorstep, you may vent your stress by cussing but leave the doorstep as it is even when you stub your toe repeatedly. In fact, we tolerate far more faults in machines than in people. We criticize our kids constantly and pick on our co-workers, but we put up with the shower that scalds us when anyone flushes the toilet. We put up with the chair that is uncomfortable and with the noise of the dishwasher that really makes us irritable.

So the first thing to recognize on the subject of human factors is our high threshold for tolerating stress. We're simply insensitive to and certainly unvocal about bad design. It is as though we were saying that we'd rather get ulcers or backaches than seem like complainers. That attitude is all wrong. We should complain. We shouldn't tolerate bad design.

In my design classes I usually give students an assignment to record all the misfits they encounter in a day. The lists, once the students become attuned to noticing the misfits, are overwhelmingly long. It almost seems as though designers went out of their way to make life miserable for us. How can this be?

One of my pet theories is that designers design for themselves. They are aware that they design for others, but they really don't understand people. They only know that there are lots of differences among people, but they can't make sense out of them. They see people as:

$$\text{he or she} = \text{me} + \Delta_1 + \Delta_2 + \Delta_3 + \cdots + \Delta_n;$$

that is, everyone else is the same as the designer plus a lot of little differences. As a first-order approximation, designers assume that all these little delta's are almost zero, and thus they omit them. This reduces the equation to:

$$\text{he or she} = \text{me};$$

that is, the designers assume that, if they design for themselves, the result will be fine for everybody else too. As we've seen, that assumes that I'm insensitive to all the things they're insensitive to. If noise in the dishwasher doesn't bother them, it shouldn't bother me. It also assumes that what's important and works well for them will work well for me.

For instance, in writing the instruction manual for some device, designers may find it natural (for them) to explain the effect of all those control knobs by some kind of an array or schematic diagram. But what if my personality is such that I dislike, in fact, find it very difficult to process, such visual information? Is that good human factors? There are unending examples.

I see two possible approaches for improving human factors.

Consumers should become less tolerant: boycott things that don't work, and make their complaints heard.

Manufacturers and designers should understand the profiles of their users. If they made this simple effort, they would find one of two situations.

The user can be anybody; e.g., people who deal with a bank or supermarket. Every conceivable profile can be expected. In that case the product needs options built into it. Redundancy is needed so that opposing characteristics can be accommodated. A touch-tone telephone is a fine example of design that is sensitive to human factors. In dialing a number, the user can follow or even verbalize the numerical sequence, can visualize the pattern that must be touched, or can listen to the melody of the tone. The only thing missing is a different tactile feeling for every button. Nevertheless, considering the dominance of eye and ear as senses, the touch-tone telephone is a very good, thoughtfully redundant design.

If the application points to predictable profiles, then the design must take that preferential skewing into account. At the very least designers should be aware of the personality differences between the user and themselves. If the designers are visually-oriented engineers and are designing a device for a newspaper or a hospital, which is full of word-oriented, auditory-dominant profiles, they should be aware that their judgment of what is "good" must be under suspicion. They need to work much more closely with the user than when they are designing a device for an architect. They might even want to consider using this model to alert them to the differences.

Until we factor personality differences into the design equation, human factors will remain no more than a buzzword.

GLIMPSE

I shall never cease being amazed at the nonsense that goes on in industry. Thousands of dollars are spent to develop a procedure to improve people's

APPLICATIONS OF THE
MODEL

performances or to teach them a new tool that is supposed to increase their productivity. It's really amazing how many managers become excited and unhesitatingly invest $100,000 or more in some such scheme, which ultimately is aborted because nothing comes of it.

The bigger the organization, especially technical ones, the bigger the scale of such nonsense. It goes under various labels: job enhancement, performance evaluations, productivity optimization, performance measures, effectiveness standards, and so on.

All are efforts to quantify dreams. If each programmer could be made to write only one more line of code, for example, the company could save millions!

Totally ignored in such futile efforts is the unrecognized assumption that all workers are alike.

PART **V**

CONCLUSIONS AND AFTERTHOUGHTS

20

STRUCTURAL INTERRELATIONSHIPS

(More On The Key Dichotomy
Of Consciousness)

CONCLUSIONS AND
AFTERTHOUGHTS

Somehow it seems right to end this book about people, so full of technical minutiae, on a philosophical note by discussing the dichotomy of consciousness more fully. If there is such a thing as a king among the dichotomies, it must be that of consciousness, which integrates all the others. It is as though consciousness were the peace-maker, mixing elements without ignoring anything and yet not losing the essential character of each.

Consciousness has ambi-syn-anti embedded in it in very sophisticated ways. The amazing thing is that it emerged from a model of only 16 poles. Therein lies another tale. I had feared that I might have to go to

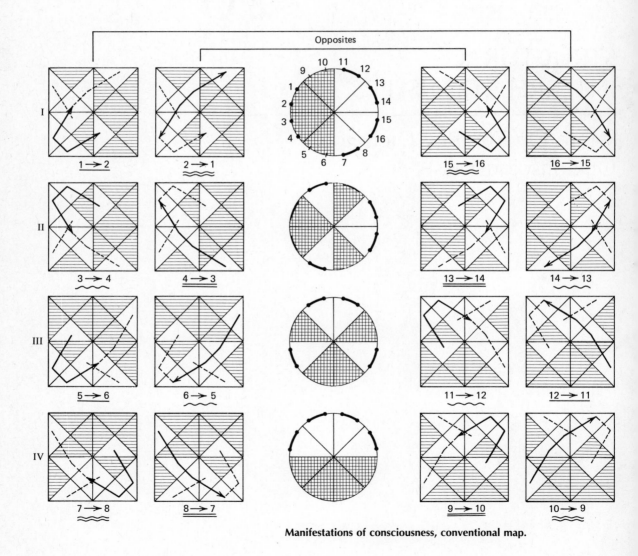

Manifestations of consciousness, conventional map.

a more complex model before any intelligible interpretations were possible. Unfortunately, that would mean going in steps of four; starting with a four-pole model, one would go to a 16-pole model, then 64, 256, 1024, to ever higher complexities until one got to 4^{16}. By that time, one would be dealing with 4,294,967,296 partitioned cells, which is about the size of the cerebral cortex. Could it be that evolution could take place in only 16 steps? This is the kind of crazy question the consciousness dichotomy brings forth.

I know that such speculations are foolish games to many scientists. I agree. They eat up time and lead nowhere in the short term. But the history of ideas is full of such games.

One I cannot escape is the transformations that lead to a representation of the dichotomy of consciousness as the yin-yang symbol. The yin-yang symbol embodies everything the dichotomy of consciousness makes explicit. So let us take a closer look at it.

Three different representations of the disposition of consciousness for the 16 profiles are reproduced. They share the following characteristics:

1. Profiles in a given row, marked I, II, III, and IV, have a common disposition of consciousness.
2. The characteristic transaction for each profile is labeled (e.g., $1 \rightarrow 2$).
3. The two most conscious transactions for each profile are shown with a solid line and the two least conscious transactions are shown with a dashed line.
4. The unconscious cells are shaded as though in shadow.
5. The transactions are differentially underlined to identify profiles of the same group. Those sharing the same disposition of consciousness are hidden agenda pairs.

The three diagrams differ from one another thus:

1. The first shows the disposition on the conventional map of capacities. This representation clearly shows that profiles in a row have the same disposition of consciousness.
2. The second shows the disposition on a polar plot. This schema also shows that profiles in a row share the same disposition of consciousness. In two of the manifestations the yin-yang format appears.
3. The third format shows a transformed map to highlight the yin-yang in all profiles.

This is done in the following manner. One of the attributes of the focus or approach dichotomy, the one marked with the heavy border, has poles numbered in the conventional way of the map of capacities. The re-

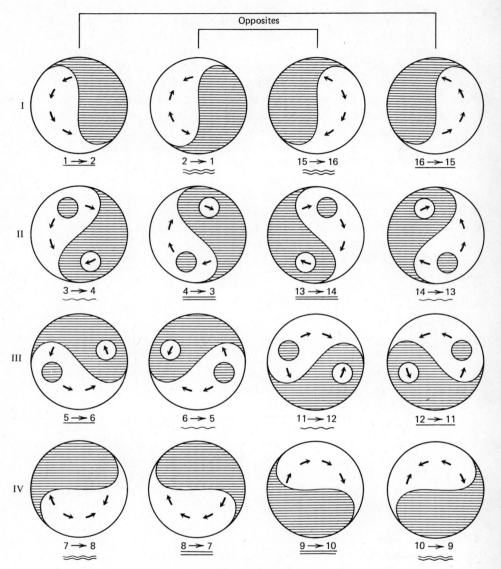

Manifestations of consciousness, polar plots.

maining pole numbers are assigned to cells according to a different algorithm such that opposite poles are located as in a mirror image.

This scheme is a perfectly rational alternative. In the conventional map
the arbitrary convention was adopted to place all external pole numbers
in cells externally located in the field. This positioned opposing poles not
by mirror images but by oppositional attributes. The schema employed

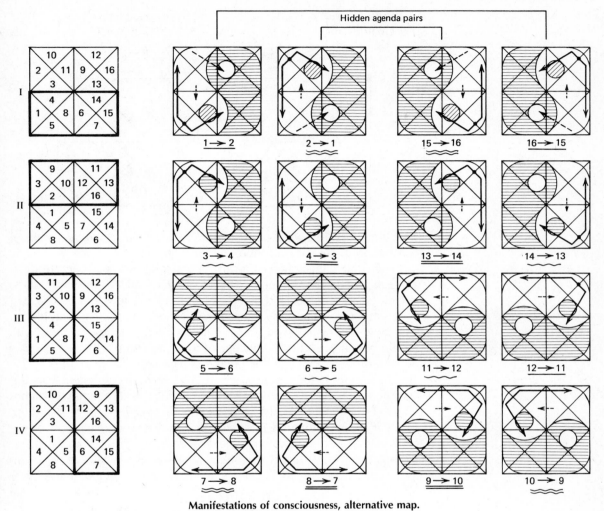

Manifestations of consciousness, alternative map.

here places poles geometrically and symmetrically opposite the field's midpoint:

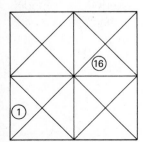 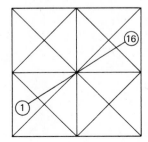

This is not a suitable schema for the map of capacities, which preserved a far greater symmetry for the attributes. For instance, the C and D circuits in these two schemata plot as follows:

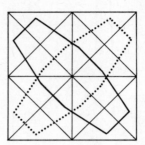 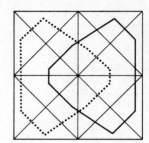

Nevertheless, it is a self-consistent, rational schema, and the results of its application are shown in the third format.

We see that in this schema the yin-yang pattern shows up very strongly. For each profile the unshaded large field contains all the conscious poles, and the shaded large field shows all the unconscious poles. The two circles in these fields show the semiconscious poles for each profile.

Dichotomies lie at the very heart of this model. But it is only now, with the discussion of so many conceptual ideas behind us, that we can see the incredible relatedness that creates such a remarkable whole.

A dichotomy is the result of a partition. Any one dichotomy divides a whole into two opposing parts. When we deal with a family of dichotomies, however, and all the different ways a given pie can be sliced up, we are identifying unifying interrelationships that work together to create the greater whole. Dichotomies taken singly are thus an analytical or organizational tool. But dichotomies taken all at once serve as a synthesizing tool. In this model, then, we looked at both the analysis and the synthesis. Together, they produced this remarkable enrichment I call ambi-syn-anti, where the whole is larger than the sum of its parts—a free benefit, so to speak, that I called complementarity. Nothing plays so vital a role in this than consciousness.

I've just suggested that we get something for nothing, for how else could one interpret the statement that the whole is larger than the sum of its parts? This greater whole is the central idea underlying this model, for it is what makes a human being more than a machine. We are, therefore, talking of the very essence of humanness, which is often more aptly expressed by symbols.

CLUES FROM SYMBOLS:

In trying to get insights into the meaning of subsets of the 16 poles, I've found it very useful to think purely in terms of the applicable symbols.

For instance, I know of no better way to define the sensation function than as ⊡, !, —□—, ‡ —that is, signal, sign, control, and routine. Many of the key words presented in the first table of chapter one were developed this way. Let me discuss a few illustrative examples.

Ehrhardt's identification of "tasks" was the result of pondering the meaning of symbols in the matrix rows:

1	5	9	13
2	6	10	14
3	7	11	15
4	8	12	16

Note that the rows represent pairs of superpoles of the J and P variety. And indeed Ehrhardt's task labels fit the Jungian J and P meanings very well.

The four poles of each mode therefore have specific tasks to do, namely, to propose, to compare, to evaluate, and "to gestalt." These tasks mimic ambi-syn-anti, which stated:

For every thing	=	propose ⎱	
there is an opposite thing	=	compare ⎰	P
and within every thing there are opposites	=	evaluate ⎱	
that can cross-combine to form a new thing	=	gestalt ⎰	J

Another insight grows out of the eight-pole model. It is reasonable to wonder what might be the meaning of polar opposition in that model:

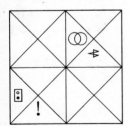
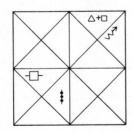
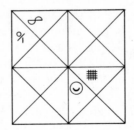
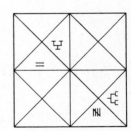

ES is opposite IN, IS is opposite EN, and so on. What might these oppositions tell us? The previous discussion suggests that we substitute pole symbols and extract meanings from their combinations. Let us do just that and indicate the interpretive meanings by new key words or labels.

Such exercises never cease to fascinate me. Not only do they give insight into the richness of the English language in expressing concepts, but they also give linguistic handles to semantic partitions.

CONCLUSIONS AND
AFTERTHOUGHTS

Opposite Superpoles

ES	1	⊡	Literal	versus	Symbolic	◐	12	IN	=	Translation
	5	!				⪦	16			
IS	4	–□–	Prediction	versus	Surprise	△+□	9	EN	=	Expectation
	8	‡				↗	13			
EF	3	°/|	Extreme	versus	"Intreme"	☉	6	IT	=	Impression
	11	⌒				♯	14			
IF	2	=	Value or quality	versus	Worth or quantity	Ⅲ	7	ET	=	Assessment
	10	⊤⊤△				⊏ꞓ	15			

Note that these partitions—translation, expectation, impression, and assessment—are composed of two sides of the entropy coin. The two capacities in each superpole are either in the detailed or contextual circuits; for example, poles 1 and 5 are in C, and poles 12 and 16 are in D. And each partition has superpoles of opposite characteristics: literal versus symbolic, routine versus surprise, extreme versus "intreme," and value or quality versus worth or quantity.

I should explain the coined word "intreme." I could find no existing word to express just what I had in mind, although "nuance" comes closest. I'm concerned with the analysis of data here. An easy example might be grading students in a class. One way of looking at the data would be to simply decide who passes and who fails. That would be an ordering by extremes. But I might also want to look at a finer structure, the As, Bs, Cs, Ds, and Fs, or even finer detail such as how many students got exactly the same grade. Such an analysis of a finely structured order is possible only when one looks at what falls *between* the extremes, and I simply have called this the intreme.

We've identified a good many of the relationships in this dichotomous model of consciousness. There are many more, but the list is too long to develop systematically. Whenever I observe or interview a person, and my attention is drawn to some recurring pattern observable in certain personalities, I try to discover what combinations of poles might be at work. Such efforts often lead to exciting new insights. So I find that one develops a skill equivalent to learning a new symbolic language, and that is what I advocate. It really is like a new language, and one learns it best by using it.

POSTSCRIPT

I've lived with these ideas now for four years. The model was never intended to be born, for I started out on a very different problem, the question of human scale. Now with this work behind me, I find myself drifting back to the original challenge. But I come to the task with a different perspective. I have learned something; in fact, my view has totally flipped.

Four years ago I would have argued vehemently that at its root intelligence requires hierarchical ordering. Something had to be in control. That such an idea would vanish is the biggest surprise to come out of this work. Ambi-syn-anti has become to me a concept so meaningful and powerful that it need not walk in the shadow of hierarchy. It is, as we have seen, an outgrowth of hierarchy and thus even more powerful. I now believe that the difference between managing information and intelligence per se is this very step from hierarchy to ambi-syn-anti as the underlying principle of organization.

I must therefore assume that ambi-syn-anti is basic to all biological systems; that is, control grows not out of power (like a god) but out of the tension of opposite approaches on the way to resolution. Thus I see opposition as a positive force.

The world looks different now, and I like it.

Walter Lowen

AFTERWORD

This is an unusual and personal book. What are we to make of it? Let me, Walter's silent collaborator, give you my evaluation of it by stating what I accept, what are open questions to me, and what further work needs to be done. I disagree with some of Walter's interpretations of the model, but that is entirely consistent with the model itself. But let me go on with my side of the story as I tell you how I reached that conclusion.

In the summer of 1977 a friend of Walter's asked me to read his manuscript, which was at the eight-pole model stage. It was a much more computer-oriented and static model back then, at least in manuscript form. Although it was difficult and took lots of energy to read, the ideas expressed and their potential applications seemed enormous. It was sure to be controversial, but I felt that the inevitable attacks would have to focus on the details, not on the overall concept of approaching intelligence through organizational principles, fleshed out with empirical research and observations, instead of approaching intelligence through examination of the biological workings of the brain.

It was also obvious that, whatever manuscript was in existence, Walter's mind and growing experiences in looking at human behavior were far ahead of whatever he had put down in writing. He needed an incentive to organize his thoughts in writing, and I chose to be that nagging element in his life. I told him that it would take two to four years, and I write this as the third year ends.

The material began to pour out: extension to the 16-pole model, the hierarchical ordering of the capacities, the connection between entropy and the conscious–unconscious dichotomy, and so on. Walter's profile, DINT (15 → 16), tends to make things more complex, going from many to infinity. So every time I made a suggestion, Walter's response resulted in even more questions and more work to do. I, on the other hand, being a CIFN (9 → 10), tend to simplify, going from infinity to 2. So once I determined that Walter had finally produced enough in writing to provide a sound book, our problem became where to stop.

Faced with that dilemma and with my simplifying nature, I was content to write a book that put forth Walter's basic model, knowing that even that already obsolete (in Walter's and my minds) book would be stretching the intellectual capacities of most readers. Putting down in writing less than what could be said did not bother me, because such selective composition is basic to writing. Walter, on the other hand, would never be comfortable with that fact of life, so he ultimately left the decision to me as to the general content of this book. The concepts covered are part of his life and thus are always changing. I am now tired of the theoretical aspects and anxious to prove to myself that the model is capable of doing what I think it can.

A final aspect of our collaboration is that Walter's style is detailed and I am strongly contextual. Our opposite styles have been an advantage in writing this book, particularly since this is Walter's story and my role has been to help him tell it. So he generates the details, and I provide the context. I also find intellectualizing relaxing (it's my play mode), so it has been relatively easy for me to do this in my spare time. His work is my play, which has been a source of irritation to Walter. But I'm getting ahead of the story.

So, what do I accept of the model, and what are my doubts? I accept that this particular organizational approach in classifying human behavior is as good, if not better, than any other. Why? Because the assumptions are not only clearly stated, but they also are separable into assumptions on the particular structure of the model and assumptions on what characteristics are given to each attribute. Each dichotomy is derivable on mathematical grounds and has to fit a specific orientation on the map of capacities. What these dichotomies are and how they relate to each of the other dichotomies are based on empirical observations: Jung's functions (focus, approach, I versus E), brain research (C or D style), and observations of human development (lingual versus prelingual, innate versus acquired). Other theories of human behavior are much more subjective (look at Freud!) or do not state their assumptions as clearly as Walter's does.

Walter's particular inspiration is in turning the static map of capacities into a dynamic model, but it rests in his powers of observation, which must be accepted by the reader just as many of us accept Jung's observations. I am talking about people's self-perceptions, what Walter has labeled the fundamental *roles*. His inspiration lies in connecting these observations to a method of describing the undescribable, the unconscious, through the entropy concept of deterioration and restoration of order. It has been this transposition of the entropy diagram onto the map of capacities that makes it a useful model for observing, predicting, and affecting human behavior.

But it is at this point that I cannot just rely on Walter's personal observations and experiences and need to prove the model's potential applications to my own satisfaction. Walter's observations alone are not enough, for the model tells us that he, too, must have his blind spots. And as far as I know, he alone grasps the intricacies of the model. He has had students immersed in it, but theirs have been momentary fascinations with it in the classroom. And my experience has been primarily theoretical. So pay attention to the potential applications of the model, but be a little skeptical, as I am, of Walter's analyses of specific situations. Let me give you two reasons why I insist on this.

First, even in this limited 16-pole model, we have not finished exploring the possible structural relationships. This places limitations, at least for the present, on its possible applications.

The second reason for my reservations is that Walter's experiences with people, as defined by the profiles of the model, are limited to his circle of peers, primarily the intellectuals and verbals. He has had little opportunity to observe the gross motor and fine motor profiles, for he is never in contact with them professionally or socially except in passing. And these are the profiles—those of the truck driver, the farmer, and the professional athlete—that are deep in the unconscious side of *his* profile. So even experience with these types may not help him, for they are or lie near his hidden agenda, which he admits he may recognize but will never really understand. So Walter's model predicts that his *own* observations are flawed and need other perspectives.

Thus there is a need for validation of the model in its applications. This can only come from experience, and this experience must emanate from others besides Walter. To lay out the basic foundations so that a wider audience can begin to appreciate the model's potential and experiment with it have been the primary purposes of this book. Spreading the word on a personal level has its limitations, and this book explains enough of the concepts so that the model can be useful to a wider audience.

There are three ways of validating the usefulness of the model. The first is building up case experiences, preferably by others in addition to Walter. We are collaborating on such an effort. The second way is to pursue the model's simulative, or artificial intelligence, implications. As Walter has said, most artificial intelligence representations of words are too simplistic. But in this model everything is linked; a word is not only a meaning, it is also a symbol, a particular association with other words, an image, a feeling, and a label. A word therefore must have all these mappings, for a word can awaken in us a meaning, an image, a feeling, an auditory recall, and proper motor responses to express it verbally and through body language. I suspect that Walter will pursue this with computers. The third way is to correlate the organization of the brain as depicted by the model with current biomedical knowledge of the brain. This task would have two purposes: to further refine the model and to use the organizational power of the model to integrate all the scattered bits of information being collected in brain research into a coherent explanation of what all that research means. I hope to undertake this task with some understanding biomedical researcher.

So there you have it, Walter's seminal contribution to the study of human behavior. The irony of this rational explanation of human behavior is that behavior is ultimately shown to be also irrational. But if you now understand enough of the model, you will see that this is not ironic at all, but a natural consequence of being faced with dichotomous choices and having to make them.

Lawrence Miike

APPENDIXES

THE SUBSETS OF THE MIND

(An Integrative Approach, Viewing the
Four- and Eight-Pole Models as Subsets
of the 16-Pole Model)

We start with the fully partitioned map of 16 cells, numbered 1 through 16, and look at various subsets of them. We can associate labels and meanings with such subsets, which are of great help in interpreting the map.

As the map is intended to be a visual crutch, I emphasize the visual representation of the various subsets.

The key interpretive aspects embedded in the map of capacities are first shown through diagrammatic overviews. All the pairings, groupings, and oppositions pointed out by the labeled "tools" reveal structural or organizational relationships, a key consequence of the dichotomous structure of the model. What they tell us is that the power of the mind stems from the interrelatedness of its component parts. The capacities of the mind most often work as a team, much as an athletic team or an organizational team. Each subset represents a kind of committee or strike force, depending on the analogy used. We can't understand the functioning of Congress, for example, without knowing the committee structure and the interrelationships between the Senate and the House of Representatives. Nor can we understand a forward pass in a football game without knowing whether the quarterback and end form an active team. Likewise, we can't interpret a personality's behavior without understanding the subsets of the mind, that is, how capacities work together or separately. The map of capacities is an empty and dead domain without these interpretive tools.

To me, so highly visual, the accompanying diagrams tell the whole story. Not only do they show an ordering of the relationships, but they also have interpretive meanings. Analytically, the map of capacities deals with organization. The difficulty for the user is that the organization is so incredibly interrelated that it is hard to keep the many relationships straight in one's mind. This is why the map is so complex to the beginner and so rich to one thoroughly familiar with it. As an aid in transforming confusion into richness, the diagrams are organized in the following ways.

1. As subsets of 8 and 8, called dichotomies.
2. As subsets of 4, 4, 4, and 4, with opposing and complementing sets of 4.
3. As subsets of 2 out of 16, generally called links, with various interrelationships.

All the unique subsets, each bringing out a particular interrelationship, have been given names so that they can be referred to and differentiated. The names either refer to Jung's nomenclature or were chosen to be as descriptive as possible.

Interrelationships are viewed as either simply static groupings or as involving a flow. A grouping addresses what a subset of poles have in common, that is, what magnified characteristic emerges when the poles in a subset are active and work together as a team. A flow is more specific in that direction becomes important; we are not only dealing with co-operating poles but also asking what happens if 1 feeds 2 or if 2 feeds 1. This directional difference is noted by a vector, a link between poles with an arrow on one end. A link without arrows means flow is in both directions.

The second aspect of the summary diagrams is their interpretations. This is more of an art than a science, but with practice the subsets become ever more alive with meaning.

People always ask how I get the clues to insights in an interview. Well, it is strongly linked to these interpretations. Under each diagram is an interpretive "key word," and my ears are perked to catch them. If someone says, "I like to *analyze* situations" or "I tend to be very *critical*," I immediately catch these key words, and they point to a particular subset of the map. I realize there are a lot of key words, but one learns them quickly as a new vocabulary.

The key words are not exact. There are many others that are just as good. To me the key words suggest a feeling, an image, an idea, or an experience, which in turn brings to mind similar words appropriate to the context. However, they have a very definitive root in the symbols assigned to the capacities.

This process is best illustrated by an example. Suppose the question is on the meaning of the subset 4, 8, 9, and 13. I immediately translate these poles into image or word symbols.

4	8	9	13
$-\square-$	$\ddagger$	$\triangle + \square$	$\longrightarrow\nearrow$
Control	Routine	Combination	Strategy

I note that there are subsets within this subset: 4 and 8, and 9 and 13; 4 and 9, and 8 and 13; and 4 and 13, and 8 and 9.

The last set involves opposite pairs, which tells me at once that the subset 4, 8, 9, and 13 deals with a conflict, a contrast, or some oppositional tension.

I also notice that the subset $-\square-$ and $\ddagger$ involves very similar capacities. In fact, they constitute a superpole. What they share is control, doing the predictable. The other subset, $\triangle + \square$ and $\longrightarrow\nearrow$, does the opposite. It tries to create a new possibility, combination, or strategy. The overall subset therefore deals with predictability versus surprise. Those two opposing characteristics come together in what I call *expectation*. That would be a good key word for the subset 4, 8, 9, and 13. Expectation is our mind set in anticipation of an event. When we read a sentence in a particular context, we expect the predictable. If we are surprised, we may have come upon a pun or a joke.

Each label below each subset diagram grew out of this kind of analysis. So it is literally true to say that the roots for interpretations of the map lie in the symbols for the capacities. They yield very rich sets.

I find a strange fascination not only in the richness of the English language (a second language for me) but also in the word relationships brought out by thesaurus constructions and by the relationships discussed in this Appendix and Chapters 5, 6, and 7. These fascinations contrast sharply with artificial language efforts, be it Esperanto, or the aborted effort in Scandinavia to create a unifying language by committee, or, more current, the present flurry of activity by computer professionals in semantic analysis. Clearly this interest is related to office automation and the dream of dictating a letter into a computer and having the finished, clearly-typed letter plop on someone's desk miles away, with nary a secretary on the scene.

Compared to the mind's way of doing things, this kind of effort seems a hopelessly simple-minded attempt. It might be achieved by brute memory power, but it is bound to be a Frankenstein-like product.

Far more elegant and fascinating are children who, as has been reported in the literature, invent their own language. There is even one case where a child growing up in a multilingual household concluded that each person spoke his or her own language; so she invented one for herself.

That such feats are possible can be rationalized by assuming that language is a structural mirror of the mind, not merely a permutation of bit strings.

In the following few pages, I give a cursory overview of the most basic subsets of the model. It ties the key labels to subsets and diagrams and thus establishes a minimal vocabulary. These and other terms are discussed in far greater detail in Chapters 5, 6, and 7.

E-6

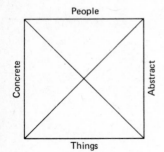

MODES

Modes represent subsets of four capacities each that plot as triangles formed by two diagonals on the map. The subsets are:

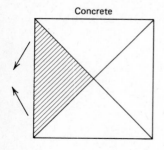

Concrete mode	1	2	3	4	To the left
Abstract mode	13	14	15	16	To the right
People mode	9	10	11	12	Toward the top
Thing mode	5	6	7	8	Toward the bottom

The modes are closely coupled to outputs.

Concrete mode: Gross motor action involving body, arms, and legs for activities like dancing, athletics, and physical work.

Thing mode: Fine motor action involving predominantly the hands for activities that require manual dexterity so important in crafts, art, and music. These activities typically involve hand–eye coordination and play a major role in body language, including the control of head movements and other subtle movements.

People mode: Most closely associated with what Lessac calls *vocal life.* In general, it involves the face, especially the mouth area for the audible production of speech, tone, and voice control, as in singing.

Abstract mode: Coupled to intellectual outputs involving, specifically, strategies and logical conclusions. They are the outputs resulting from abstract thought processes.

It is helpful to see how the particular capacities involved in producing these outputs fit together.

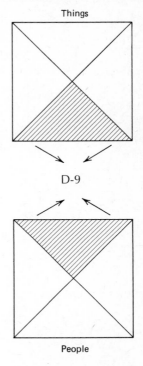

Things

D-9

People

Body				
Hand				
Speech				
Intellect				

Body outputs are served by signal, match, contrast, and control.

Hand outputs are served by sign, feature, sort, and routine.

Speech and voice outputs are served by combination, harmony, preference, and association.

Intellectual outputs are served by strategy, pattern, logic, and structure.

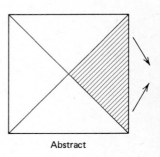

Abstract

FUNCTIONS

Another set of disjoint subsets consists of combinations of capacities or cells that form quadrants in the map. They are called *functions* and fit the Jungian descriptions of them.

Sensation	S	1, 4, 5, 8
Feeling	F	2, 3, 10, 11
Thinking	T	6, 7, 14, 15
Intuition	N	9, 12, 13, 16

The functions are most closely associated with inputs as follows:

S. Contact senses such as touch; involves signal, control, sign, and routines.

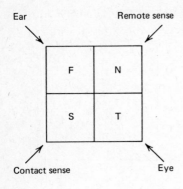

Ear — Remote sense
F — N
S — T
Contact sense — Eye

F. Couples with hearing through the ears; involves match, contrast, preference, and harmony.

T. Couples with seeing through the eye; involves feature, sort, pattern, and logic.

N. Couples with the remote senses, including smell and what is called a sixth sense; involves combination, association, strategy, and structure.

COMPLEXITY

Recall that the capacities are hierarchically ordered and that they develop progressively from the most basic (1) to the most complex (16) capacity.

$$S \quad 1 + 4 + 5 + 8 = 18 \rightarrow 1$$
$$F \quad 2 + 3 + 10 + 11 = 26 \rightarrow 2$$
$$T \quad 6 + 7 + 14 + 15 = 42 \rightarrow m$$
$$N \quad 9 + 12 + 13 + 16 = 50 \rightarrow \infty$$

I have summed the capacity numbers for each function. The sum increases from S through N, suggesting that the combined effect of a set of four capacities becomes increasingly complex as we move from S to N. This suggests that S and F are relatively close at the simple end of the complexity scale and that T and N are relatively close at the complex end of the scale. I have therefore assigned to each function a complexity index, shown in the second column in the following list, consistent with this observation.

S	1	Oneness	Acceptance
F	2	Duality	Opposition
T	m	Many	Complex but finite
N	∞	Infinity	Ultimate complexity

The complexity index is very useful both in interpreting transactions and in breathing meaning into functions.

S = 1 Deals with just-so-ness, acceptance, and pragmatism.

F = 2 deals with dichotomous choices, like or dislike; that is, with value systems and therefore qualitative judgment.

T = m deals with ordering many pieces of a puzzle and therefore with measuring, quantifying, and quantitative judgments.

N = ∞ deals with fantasies, imagination, and possibilities; that is, plays the unending game of "what if."

TEMPORALITY

Consistent with this complexity index is a finding by Mann, Siegler, and Osmond that correlates the functions with temporal orientations.

A-6

S correlates with the present.

F correlates with the past.

N correlates with the future.

T correlates with a sequence—that is, from the past to the present into the future.

DICHOTOMIES

Dichotomies are important symmetrical subsets consisting of disjoint subsets of eight cells each. The unique nature of these subsets is that they do not contain opposite cell pairs. To appreciate the import of this, let me review that capacity 1 is the opposite of 16, 2 is the opposite of 15, 3 is the opposite of 14, and so on. We are especially interested in subsets that do not contain both 1 and 16 or both 2 and 15, and so on, but only one of each oppositional pair. I call such subsets *dichotomies*, several of which are important for interpreting the map.

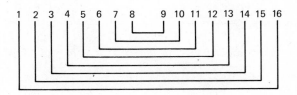

A dichotomy consists of two subsets paired such that the second subset holds all the cells opposite those in the first subset. These opposite pairs of subsets have been given names. The key dichotomies and their attributes are listed. Note the cell opposition.

Dichotomy Name	Attribute Name								
Language	Prelingual	1	2	3	4	5	6	7	8
		↕	↕	↕	↕	↕	↕	↕	↕
	Lingual	16	15	14	13	12	11	10	9
Concept	Natural	1	2	3	4	9	10	11	12
		↕	↕	↕	↕	↕	↕	↕	↕
	Acquired	16	15	14	13	8	7	6	5
Style	Contextual	1	2	5	6	9	10	13	14
		↕	↕	↕	↕	↕	↕	↕	↕
	Detailed	16	15	12	11	8	7	4	3
Attitude	Extroverted	1	3	5	7	9	11	13	15
		↕	↕	↕	↕	↕	↕	↕	↕
	Introverted	16	14	12	10	8	6	4	2
Focus	People	2	3	9	10	11	12	13	16
		↕	↕	↕	↕	↕	↕	↕	↕
	Things	15	14	8	7	6	5	4	1
Approach	Concrete	1	2	3	4	5	8	10	11
		↕	↕	↕	↕	↕	↕	↕	↕
	Abstract	16	15	14	13	12	9	7	6

The four manifestations of consciousness are shown below as four sets of opposite pairs. The conscious attribute is shown unshaded, and the unconscious attribute is shown shaded.

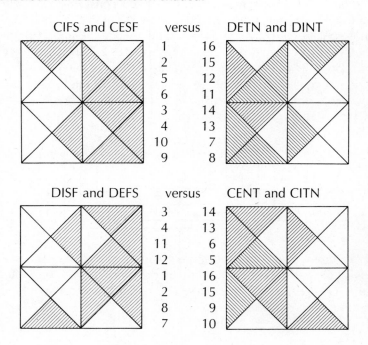

CIFS and CESF	versus	DETN and DINT
1	16	
2	15	
5	12	
6	11	
3	14	
4	13	
10	7	
9	8	

DISF and DEFS	versus	CENT and CITN
3	14	
4	13	
11	6	
12	5	
1	16	
2	15	
8	9	
7	10	

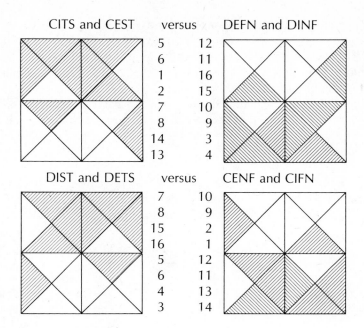

CITS and CEST versus DEFN and DINF

5	12
6	11
1	16
2	15
7	10
8	9
14	3
13	4

DIST and DETS versus CENF and CIFN

7	10
8	9
15	2
16	1
5	12
6	11
4	13
3	14

OTHER NOMENCLATURE

POLES: A capacity is also called a pole.

SUPERPOLE: Poles of the same attitude and in the same function are called superpoles. There are eight superpoles, which also hold oppositional relationships (see the eight-pole model in Chapter 6).

ES	versus	IN	1, 5 versus 16, 12
IS	versus	EN	4, 8 versus 13, 9
EF	versus	IT	3, 11 versus 14, 6
IF	versus	ET	2, 10 versus 15, 7

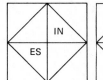

LINKS: Chapter 7 discusses a competition/cooperation matrix that explores shared and unshared attributes among capacity pairs. Those capacity pairs that share common attributes in certain consistent ways are considered linked; that is, they tend to cooperate. The links have important interpretive consequences.

A link can be visualized as a telephone link, that is, a wire connecting two poles that permits information to flow from one pole to the linked one. Linkages thus involve pole pairs that share information. The direction of information flow thus becomes important. This vector characteristic is indicated by an arrow.

There are five significant links to which I have assigned names and interpretive meanings that become important primarily in artificial intelligence models. Regardless, the reader should master the nomenclature to understand libido-driven flow.

TRANSACTION: The strongest link is the main carrier of information. Transactions play a key role in interpreting profiles. There are eight extroverted and eight introverted transactions.

C E:	$2 \rightarrow 1$	$6 \rightarrow 5$	$10 \rightarrow 9$	$14 \rightarrow 13$	Opposite
D I:	$15 \rightarrow 16$	$11 \rightarrow 12$	$7 \rightarrow 8$	$3 \rightarrow 4$	pairs
C I:	$1 \rightarrow 2$	$5 \rightarrow 6$	$9 \rightarrow 10$	$13 \rightarrow 14$	Opposite
D E:	$16 \rightarrow 15$	$12 \rightarrow 11$	$8 \rightarrow 7$	$4 \rightarrow 3$	pairs

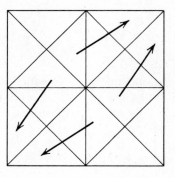 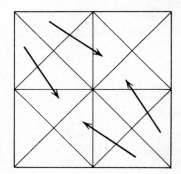

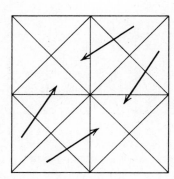 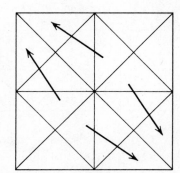

MODE LINKS: Mode links also transmit information; that is, they are channels for libido-induced flow. Mode links always link poles into a superpole. They are:

$1 \rightarrow 5$ $4 \rightarrow 8$ $3 \rightarrow 11$ $2 \rightarrow 10$ $7 \rightarrow 15$ $6 \rightarrow 14$ $9 \rightarrow 13$ $12 \rightarrow 16$

$5 \rightarrow 1$ $8 \rightarrow 4$ $11 \rightarrow 3$ $10 \rightarrow 2$ $15 \rightarrow 7$ $14 \rightarrow 16$ $13 \rightarrow 9$ $16 \rightarrow 12$

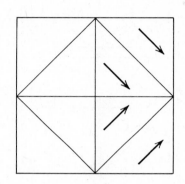 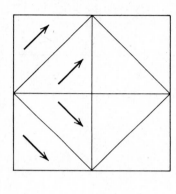

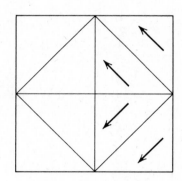 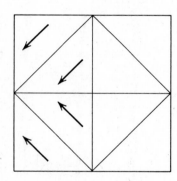

The flow of information must be controlled, and that is done by means of feedback signals flowing in links. In biological systems such feedback normally works to suppress a natural activity. The suppression can result in either positive or negative feedback. Positive feedback activates an action; negative feedback prevents one. The following links serve such feedback functions.

F-7

CROSSLINKS: Crosslinks provide positive feedback. The links are:

$1 \rightarrow 3$ $5 \rightarrow 7$ $9 \rightarrow 11$ $13 \rightarrow 15$ $2 \rightarrow 4$ $6 \rightarrow 8$ $10 \rightarrow 12$ $14 \rightarrow 16$

$3 \rightarrow 1$ $7 \rightarrow 5$ $11 \rightarrow 9$ $15 \rightarrow 13$ $4 \rightarrow 2$ $8 \rightarrow 6$ $12 \rightarrow 10$ $16 \rightarrow 14$

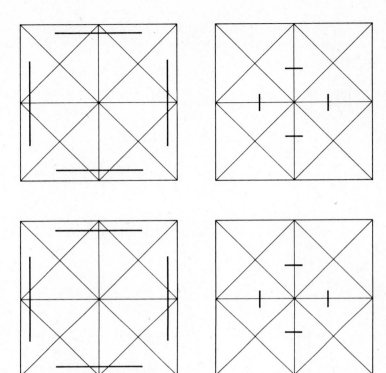

LOOK AHEAD: Look ahead is the weakest link and provides negative feedback. The links are the following:

$1 \rightarrow 9$ $5 \rightarrow 13$ $3 \rightarrow 7$ $11 \rightarrow 15$ $4 \rightarrow 12$ $8 \rightarrow 16$ $2 \rightarrow 6$ $10 \rightarrow 14$

$9 \rightarrow 1$ $13 \rightarrow 5$ $7 \rightarrow 3$ $15 \rightarrow 11$ $12 \rightarrow 4$ $16 \rightarrow 8$ $6 \rightarrow 2$ $14 \rightarrow 10$

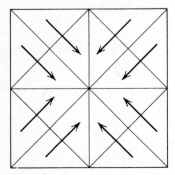

There is one more link that involves memory and serves as both information and feedback transmitters. These links are the following:

$1 \rightarrow 4$ $5 \rightarrow 8$ $3 \rightarrow 2$ $11 \rightarrow 10$ $7 \rightarrow 6$ $15 \rightarrow 14$ $9 \rightarrow 12$ $13 \rightarrow 16$

$4 \rightarrow 1$ $8 \rightarrow 5$ $2 \rightarrow 3$ $10 \rightarrow 11$ $6 \rightarrow 7$ $16 \rightarrow 15$ $12 \rightarrow 9$ $16 \rightarrow 13$

The transactions are by far the most important links for profile interpretation.

SIMULATION

APPENDIX **B**

The concreteness of the model invites speculation on how intelligent behavior might be simulated on a sufficiently powerful computer. Although this subject properly belongs in a separate book on artificial intelligence, I have found that some conceptualizations of such a simulation help make explicit the unique information-processing capacities of the 16 poles. Therefore, I roughly describe here how the 16 poles might operate on the microlevel. The underlying ideas are closely coupled to the ideas outlined in Chapter 20 on the interrelationships among the poles.

My view is that each function (S, F, T, and N) has a language all its own: sensation recognizes only labels, feeling recognizes only dichotomies, thinking talks in arrays, intuition talks in symbols. So I envision four basic building blocks: labels, dichotomies, arrays, and symbols. These are consistent with the complexity index (1, 2, m, and ∞).

The first consequence of this assumption is that memories must be organized to fit these basic building blocks. Therefore, sensation memories store labels, feeling memories have a dual positive–negative storage, thinking memories store information in highly organized arrays, and intuition memories are organized according to symbols. Let me state this another way. S is a dictionary, and N is a thesaurus. T is an indexed data base, and F is a list of antonyms and synonyms. I believe the invention of these linguistic aids is simply a copy of how our minds function.

But assertions such as these are not enough. We must also consider the organizing schema for each function, and I see that as a *coupling*. Labels are coupled to motor functions, to complexes of motor functions, in fact. Thus every label or identifier has a mapping to a complex of muscular activation instructions, what Lessac calls an organic instruction.

The mind–body coupling occurs primarily through the S function. The body always reflects the "present" state of mind. Even if the mind is consciously preoccupied with some future problem, such activity will affect the state of the S registers through transaction linkages; that is, these preoccupations reflect or foretell the body state. The presumption here is that an unsolved problem in intellectual consciousness is likely to produce an S state, or a register state in the sensation function that corresponds to organic instructions that place the body in a state of muscular tension.

I find contemporary slang most revealing. It is full of phrases such as "uptight," "with it," and "hang loose," which are descriptors of both a mental and a body state. The slang can be divided into two groups: those words that describe the body state revealing an unconscious mind state and those words that describe the body state reflecting a conscious mind state. "Uptight" would be an example of an unconscious mind state. The body state reveals the mind state before the conscious mind recognizes its own situation. This is why body language is so revealing, and why others, sensitive to body clues, can often see you more clearly than you can see yourself.

The body reflects a conscious mind state when mind and body work together harmoniously, which is evident when you are dancing while in the mood for it or when your tennis game or golf swing really goes well. It is then that you're "with it."

It has always fascinated me how hard athletes have to concentrate just before an event, be it the high jump or weightlifting, to get psyched up and in the proper state of mind. It is as though they were setting the registers in their heads so that the proper organic instruction would come into play. It is a matter of mind over body.

Thus mind over body is the result of organic instructions from conscious mind states. Body over mind results in body signals or language that reveals the unconscious state of the mind. The interaction of the two must have health implications; this is what Norman Cousins wrote about and what yoga, ulcers, and psychosomatic disorders deal with.

The coupling in the feeling quadrant is linked to like and dislike and therefore to past experiences. I assume that a plus sign is the symbol for like or good for survival and a minus sign is the symbol for dislike or bad for survival.

The coupling for the arrays in the thinking function is to the eye; the representational structure is organically inherent in the structure of the retina, which is basically a hexagonal array.

The coupling for the intuition function's symbols is to archetypes, which have many representations. To me, a visual type, graphic symbols are the most helpful. I envision a list such as $\bigcirc$, $\bullet$, $\square$, $\triangle$, and so on, where the symbols must be interpreted as archetypes. The circle thus stands for earth, warmth, and mother. The dot denotes the center or the self; the square stands for an inanimate object; the triangle represents authority, power, the hero, the father.

I'm mindful that only a few of these basic organizing units are needed for a rich set of representations. The combinatorial nature of elements generates thousands of representations from a dozen units.

Of equally basic import is my conceptualization that these structures and representations serve to identify nouns, adjectives, and relational prepositions—in short, objects, qualifiers, and relationships. Verbs are represented by so-called metaprograms, or transaction sequences. Thus nouns are stored data, and verbs are stored programs that simulate a particular flow of information through the model's network. For example, the verb "to analyze" is simply stored as transaction $16 \rightarrow 15$. With only 16 transactions (actually, many more if I include the other links), a vast vocabulary of verbs can be constructed.

It is important to recognize that, even though the schema is envisioned as universal, the coding for each representation can be unique. In short, each has its own personal construct. It is therefore not surprising that verbal communication is often so difficult.

An important feature of such a conception for simulating intelligence is that *everything is linked*. A word is not only a meaning, it is also a symbol, a particular association with other words, an image and thus an ordered set, a feeling with positive and negative classifiers, and a label with sensory—motor connections. It is essential that a word has all those mappings, for a word can awaken in us a meaning, an image, an auditory recall, and proper motor responses to express it verbally and through body language. As a label, we recognize a word through all our senses. It must therefore have its appropriate representation in far more than just one memory. Language cannot be just list processing. Quite the contrary, it integrates all our capacities. To me, therefore, most artificial intelligence representations of words are too simplistic.

I see our unique linguistic capacity as pervasive in the total organization of the brain and not in a specialized corner of it. Language is not an accretion, but an integration. It draws on every capacity; it is a systems consequence. Any word thought, every phrase and every word, has not only one but many representations in the mind. If it is heard, one can reconstruct and preconstruct its sound, and therefore it can be felt by reexperiencing the motor sequences that produce it as a sound. Each word has a physical motor translation to which we also attach a pain or pleasure value. We may like words such as "moon" and "love" because the execution of the necessary organic instructions feels good and pleasant. We may have negative feelings about words such as "screech," because the required motor state is unpleasant. But it goes much further than that. We see words in many ways. We can visualize what a word represents. We can see the shape of the motor connections to words. The mouth feels round when it is shaped to say "ball," and it feels stretched when we activate muscles to say "steeple." Thus the act of speaking also awakens shapes that link to the eye. A word is not only visualized as a label, the image for which it stands, but also as a motor experience in itself. This is particularly true of prepositions and prefixes. "Before," "behind," "below," "next to,"—all are tied to the thinking function matrix, which visually makes the relationship explicit. It ties words to visual experiences. And words are also symbols, the means for associating one word with a class of related ones. All this pervasive involvement of capacities is active even before reading and writing skills are learned.

Complex as this may seem, it is only the beginning of a meaningful simulation. There must also be the interplay of the C and D circuits. The words and the syntax and even the semantics may be provided by the D circuit, but there must also be context. All linguistic processing therefore takes place in a context provided by the C circuit. It also falls upon the C circuit to serve as a filter. It cannot permit all information to enter the D circuit; otherwise we couldn't stick to a subject. This is particularly important because the D circuit is a sequential batch processor that must be protected from interruptions. The C circuit provides both context and focus so that the thread of thought is long enough to permit the relatively long time required to string a set of words together.

The conceptualizations I have painted in very rough brush strokes must be regarded as pure speculation. They are an invention of the mind, not the result of experimental evidence. However, there are some encouraging validations. I've gone through the Gedanken experiment of how such conceptualizations would hold up for a deaf and blind person. Could such a person learn a language? And sure enough, if the proper links are activated, there is sufficient circuitry in place for other senses to take over and create all the requisite mappings to represent linguistic thought. This mechanistic approach could have far-reaching implications.

Let me apply these ideas to the functioning of the poles.

Poles 1 and 5 are envisioned as time-ordered, single-entry lists of signals and signs. They are coupled through their respective memories to motor experiences, handled by poles 4 and 8.

Similarly, poles 3 and 2 organize dichotomous relationships in a dual-entry (positive and negative) memory, linking each entry to a binary value system. Poles 11 and 10 do a similar coupling but with the aid of wave characterizations that can handle a spectrum of positive and negative values.

Poles 6 and 7 and poles 15 and 14 have a matrix organization with a shiftable origin and reference grid. The reference grid is linked to motor functions at pole 8.

Poles 9 and 12 and poles 13 and 16 are linked to relational memories. I envision poles 9 and 12 as associative memories, where elemental entries are assigned to supersets, each under an archetypal symbol. Meaning is extracted from intersections of those supersets. Poles 13 and 16 are stored in memory through structural linkages.

I've made some effort to explore the format that bit strings might take to handle all the required mappings. I've concluded that adaptations of computer representations can work, provided certain flags are postulated. But it is not appropriate to go into such detail here. What is important is that one tries to think about the four basic building blocks, the couplings, and the form of the memories, as one tries to envision the functioning of the 16 capacities.

To make these ideas more specific, let me go a bit deeper.

I assume a bit string, called a word, is the representation of information at any one time in the complex circuit. When I say information flows from pole 15 to pole 16, I mean that the ordered bit string is transmitted from pole 15 to pole 16.

There must then be a register, at each end of the transmission link, that holds the word. The receiving register can also act as a buffer to temporarily hold information until it can be processed.

At any one instant there is thus a state that can be envisioned as information frozen in time, showing what bit strings are held in every register at that moment. An instant later the state will have changed because information will have been transmitted from one register to another, so that registers now hold different bit strings.

This change from one state to another must be orchestrated in some orderly manner; there must be a conductor who synchronizes all this activity. I envision this conductor as a central clock that determines the cycle time. It may well be that some brain waves are the physical manifestations of the clock cycles.

I envision this clock to be like an old-fashioned grandfather clock, with a clock dial showing time and a pendulum showing rate. The C circuit sees only the pendulum; the D circuit sees only the dials. Both are triggered by the same cycle time—the tick-tock effect.

The organization of each of the 16 poles is very similar to one another. Each contains a powerful central processor (CPU). However, each CPU operates with specialized software that reflects the unique capability of that pole: one does logical sorting, another specializes in pattern analysis, and so on.

Each pole also has a number of connections to peripherals, specifically to inputs, outputs, preprocessors, memories, and various transmission channels. These transmission channels are the links that provide connections to other poles, specifically the links of transaction, mode, crossover, and the look ahead.

For each possible path through which information can flow, be it to or from memory, input, output, or some other pole by way of a specific link, there is a preprocessor that acts as a filter, as a buffer, and as a register.

The buffers act as temporary memories in which queues can build up. This is particularly important for links between the C and D circuits. Since the D circuit batch processes, sizable queues can build up for information coming from the C circuit.

The organization of a pole may therefore look something like the following, which is for the EST pole:

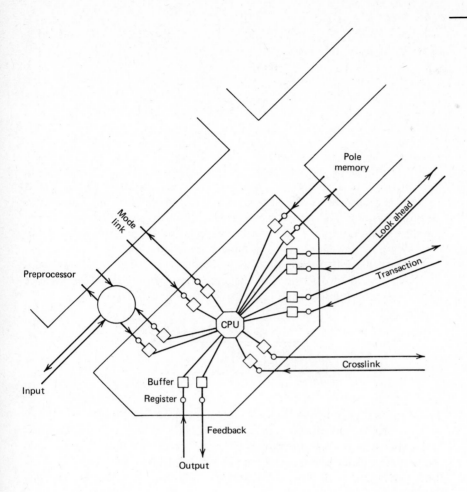

Information therefore can be channeled to flow in many different directions. The information on where to send a bit string is contained in the operation code (OP code), which is part of the word.

OP code	Information bit string	Flag

←————————————————— Word ——————————————————→

The central field is the one that carries the information content and is the one most revealing about the various poles. As mentioned earlier, four languages are involved, one for each function. The information field is therefore divided into four subfields, one for each of the four building blocks: symbols, arrays, dichotomies, and labels. The remaining field is used for flags that carry out special functions.

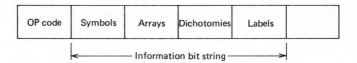

OP code	Symbols	Arrays	Dichotomies	Labels	

|← Information bit string →|

The representation for each bit can be binary—that is, 0 or 1, indicating the presence or absence of a particular bit—or some more sophisticated system. It is an academic point, since any system can be transformed into another system. The richer the representational system, the shorter the bit string. As computers run on binary representation, it is sensible to envision any simulation as using binary representation.

One needs only a positional assignment in the field to interpret the unique content of a string. For instance, one can envision the symbol field as something like this:

○	·	Δ	□	⋈	†
1	1	0	0	0	1

which says that only the symbols ○, ●, and † are involved.

This information must be combined with information in the array subfield, which determines how these symbolic elements are to be combined. For instance, should the symbol be Ȯ or ⊙? Clearly, very complex symbols can be built, or the symbol string can be used as stand-alone components.

All these speculative conceptualizations about representations of information become more meaningful when they are linked to the organization of memories, for it is in the organization, through what I referred to earlier as couplings, that operational insights are gained.

Let me discuss these memory organizations one at a time. Since memories are shared, eight unique memories must be discussed.

THE S MEMORIES

The simplest memory involves poles 1 and 4, where signals are linked to motor commands. It can be envisioned as shown.

The memory shown represents a unique personal construct. A particular string in memory can point to either a signal or a motor command. Thus each string represents a unique label for either a unique signal

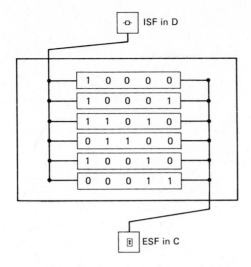

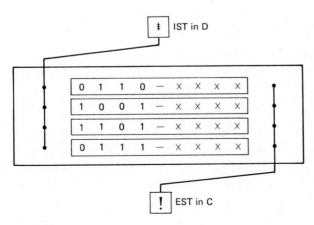

received through the senses or for an instruction set to the motor system as to which muscle to tighten or relax. Therefore, a label can be identified either from or as a signal, or from or as a body state.

A common example of the coupling occurs when we are startled. Unexpectedly, someone touches us on the shoulder, and the whole body is shocked into a new motor state. There are innumerable other examples, including body language, pointing and gesticulating, and tapping to music; all are linkages between signals and motor control.

The information can flow in any number of ways. A signal may recall a body response, or a body response may recall or suggest a signal. Or a new body experience may be stored as a new label, such as when we learn a new skill.

Closely related to the memory involving poles 1 and 4 is the memory involving poles 5 and 8, EST in C coupled to IST in D. It is envisioned as shown.

This is a more complicated memory. The left portion looks just like the 1 and 4 memory; labels for signs are coupled to labels for routines. These labels should be regarded as names of subroutines, which are sequential programs of a series of motor commands. The label is then an organic instruction; for example, "tie a shoelace." The program shown schematically in the right portion of the memory is then the sequence of motor instructions needed to carry out the organic instruction to tie the shoelace. It is as though the 5 and 8 memory were a multipage version of the 1 and 4 memory.

I use the word "label" here as an identifier. Its only restriction is uniqueness. There is no classification requirement per se on the label. We do think of labels by classes, but such an organization is imposed on labels by other components of the information field of which it is a part, such as association with other labels through symbols or by connections to images or feelings. There is therefore no inherent order to labels, nor is one needed, for no demands are made on labels other than that they serve as identifiers of experiences. To know whether a given experience or signal was just like a previous experience or signal, all one needs to be able to do is compare a string in the register to any of the strings in memory. Either one finds a duplicate (previously experienced) or does not. In the latter case one knows that it's a new signal or experience.

Whatever inherent order there may be to labels must come from the motor link. Surely, there are families of organic instructions that relate; certain movements in dancing are related to conducting, for example, and walking is related to running. Basically, though, I view the S memories simply as lists, typical of the oneness of S.

THE F MEMORIES

The memory of poles 3 and 2 connects EFS in D with IFS in C. The complexity index of F is 2, and thus the F memory is dualistic. It is the simplest level of ordering, where ordering is achieved by opposition. For every positive entry, one may therefore expect a negative entry. F memories are therefore memories that assign a positive or negative value to labels or whatever information comes to F. Basically, positive or negative relates to like or dislike or to useful or harmful for survival. It can be assumed that somehow the system state knows that hunger or cold is negative and that satisfied and comfortably warm is positive. The value assigned relates to systems equilibrium and tolerance levels. The FS poles assign a positive or negative value to incoming information, and filing is carried out accordingly. Therefore, one expects to find a positive or negative assignment in the F field.

I show a $+$, a $-$, and an xx position. The x indicates in which field the $+$ or $-$ is to be assigned. Is it the label, the array, or the image representation that is to be judged? The xx position identifies the S, F, T,

or N field and the $+$ or $-$ position, depending on whether the entry 0 or 1 indicates like (10), dislike or opposite (01), no opinion (00), or both (11). Entries valued "like" are stored in the positive half of memory, and entries valued "dislike" are stored in the negative half. A paired entry position is thus created, which enters not only value judgments, but opposition as well. Big and little, black and white, wet and dry, and all such antonyms are filed in opposite registers in memory.

One can envision the organization as follows:

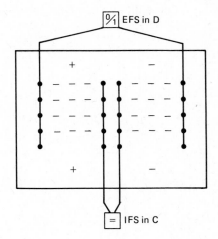

The organization of such a memory permits matching and opposition, the respective processing capacities of poles 2 and 3. The pole can interrogate memory and, by comparison, ascertain whether a given set of information has been experienced before, whether it was judged positive or negative, or what the opposite experience might be.

The 11 and 10 memory connects EFN in D with IFN in C. The FN memory is similar to FS but more elaborate. Instead of a simple dichotomous classification, FN deals with a spectrum of value judgments. I envision these judgments as represented by wave forms, roughly suggested by these examples:

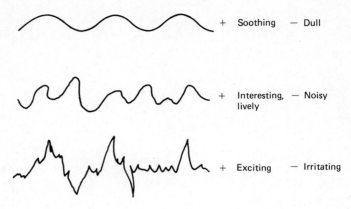

+ Soothing — Dull

+ Interesting, — Noisy
lively

+ Exciting — Irritating

Whether these characteristics are actually represented by waves or by parameters characterizing waves, such as frequency, amplitude, or regularity, is academic. Whatever the representation, a spectrum from pleasing to aggravating values can be described.

A suitable memory and its field representation might look something like the following diagram:

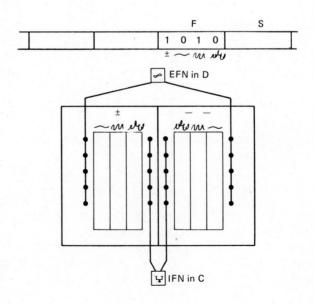

The wave form can be used to store the value assigned to past experiences or to assess which of several retrieved items are more suitable to match an expected value (preference) or to fit to another wave form (harmony).

THE T AND N MEMORIES

To complete this section on simulation, four more memories, two in the T quadrant and two in the N quadrant, remain to be described. I find myself in a peculiar dilemma. First of all, we are dealing with more complex processing functions, so the memory organizations are bound to be more complex. The situation is, however, far worse. Because T and N are my strongest poles, I have done far more work on these constructs than on the previous four. In a way, I already know too much to give a simple explanation. So let me proceed somewhat differently here.

First, let me give the diagrammatic representations of how I visualize the remaining memories.

The 7 and 6 memory has ETS in D with ITS in C:

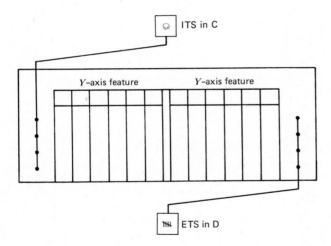

The 15 and 14 memory has ETN in D with ITN in C:

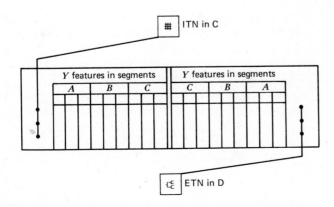

The 9 and 12 memory has ENF in C with INF in D:

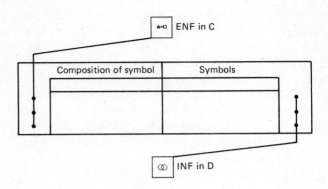

The 13 and 16 memory has ENT in C with INT in D:

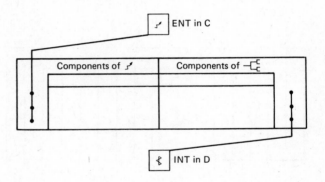

Clearly, matters are getting vastly more complex. So let me merely list those conceptualizations I have arrived at as consistent with the simulation.

The T memories reflect the structure of the retina. I envision this as a hexagonal, honeycomblike grid. Crucial to this grid is a set of reference axes with shifting origins. The origin can be located at the center of any one of three adjacent hexagons or at the intersection of the three. When the reference axis is in the center, information is processed as a grid; that is, there is or is not a visual entry in any given field position. The entry can represent a visual image or a mathematical abstraction. Either way, symmetry, shape, position, and so on, can be ascertained.

Fascinating effects can be simulated through the shifting of the origin. It can simulate eye saccades, holding moving objects fixed in the field of vision, or tracing an object. Because shifting axes requires eye movement, a motor function, the image analysis is also linked to sensory or S functions. Eye–hand coordination and sensing a shape are common examples of this coupling.

When the axis shifts to the intersection of three adjacent hexagons, processing shifts from field analysis to edge analysis; that is, information processing uses the edges of the hexagonal array as logic paths. The eye then serves as a visual decision tree rather than as a pattern of fields. The basic structure of the retina thus provides the organizational frame of reference for pattern analysis or logic processing simply by shifting the origin.

The N simulation is even more complex. First one must ask, Where do the symbols come from and how are they linked to archetypes? I envision an archetype as a hard wiring, with each archetype representing a linkage to a part of the brain, including the more primitive parts. One might think of each symbol as a building block in the architecture of the brain. More complex symbols are then constructed out of the cooperation between N and T. In short, complex symbols are assembled, with the aid of T-supplied patterns, from the basic symbols or symbolic building blocks. This structuring or assembling of complex symbols also gives the N poles the power to deal with structures.

Symbols thus play two major roles. By themselves, they reference the organization of the hard-wired brain itself through the basic symbols with all their archetypal overtones. Working together with F, they serve as labels for sets and subsets, the basis for associations and meanings. Working with T they provide structural and logical relationships. I assume that the basic building blocks are universal, reflecting a shared organization of the brain. This would make Jung's concept of the collective unconscious tractable.

I envision the compositional functions of symbols working in conjunction with F or T as personal constructs and therefore unique to each individual. A clear example of this was suggested by Ehrhardt, who invented a specific construct of how the conception of Saturday might be represented in two individuals' N poles. His example assumes that each symbolic entry can be equated with a label in the S pole and that membership in a set is regarded as membership in a fuzzy set. The following diagram illustrates how a single concept may be understood by two individuals.

F-2

Personal Construct	Key Word	Conscious	Associations	Unconscious	Associations	Symbol
A	Saturday	No boss	0.8	Freedom	0.8	
		Outdoors	0.8	Self	0.6	
		Social day	0.9	Energy	0.8	
		Sleep late	0.4	Fun	0.7	
		Car	0.3	Alive	0.6	Sun
		Sports	0.6			
		Dates	0.9			
		Dancing	0.7			

Personal Construct	Key Word	Conscious	Associations	Unconscious	Associations	Symbol
B	Saturday	Stay home	0.9	Family	0.8	
		Relax	0.6	Rest	0.7	
		Kids at home	0.8	Warmth	0.8	
		Television	0.4	Security	0.6	◯
		Cozy	0.7	Love	0.7	
		Sports	0.4			Mother
		Car	0.3			
		Chores	0.5			

The organization of memories bears a strong relation to complexity. Low-complexity poles have simpler memory organizations that permit processing to go on more quickly. A natural consequence of this is that low-complexity poles are drawn on more frequently in support of the processing activity of higher poles, but not the other way around. This relative activity situation is further complicated by the fact that, categorically, poles in the C circuit process information more quickly than poles in the D circuit. This is most easily discussed at the extremes.

Poles 1, 2, 5, and 6 are the four simplest poles in the C circuit, and their opposite poles, 16, 15, 12, and 11, are the four most complex poles in the D circuit. One can therefore expect poles 1, 2, 5, and 6 to be able to carry out many processing activities while poles 16, 15, 12, and 11 are busy carrying out a single processing function. One would therefore expect a relationship among these poles that describes the supportive functions of simpler poles to more complex ones.

Let me describe a typical cerebral activity to illustrate what I'm talking about. In articulating a thought—expressing an idea as a sentence—the whole sentence is composed in our heads as a single process. We usually know the whole sentence before we say it. That is why we can be interrupted and still finish the sentence. To compose the sentence, we need to focus in on its structure (pole 16), the rules of grammar (pole 15), the meaning we want to convey (pole 12), and the words we chose to convey the meaning (pole 11). So the process of articulating one sentence requires the undivided attention of these four complex poles.

While this is going on, poles 1, 2, 5, and 6 are used dozens of times. Signals are constantly registering (pole 1), such as sensing that you mispronounced something or knowing, while you are speaking, that what you are saying is really not what you mean or even that you are lying. The matching activity (pole 2) is constantly being drawn on in service of the activity of the more complex poles, checking that the sequence of words matches the logic and word selection plan. The word selection plan can't even take place unless poles 5 and 6 suggest a whole slew of labels that suitably express the essence. For instance, while I'm writing this sentence, already structured and composed in my mind, I can, as I get there, decide whether I want to use the word "mind" or "head" or "consciousness" or "by poles 12 and 11."

The whole process is a bit like an assembly line. While the main conveyor moves slowly along in the main composing task, there is a flurry of activity going on in subassemblies, all in support of the main assembly. It's never the other way around.

This discussion should be sufficient to emphasize that complexity is not just an interesting aspect of the model, but a very fundamental aspect of the organization of consciousness. Without a hierarchy among the poles, the mind could not function as effectively as it does.

REFERENCES

A. BOOKS ON OR BY CARL G. JUNG

1. Evans, Richard I.   *Jung on Elementary Psychology* Dutton, New York, 1976
2. Fordham, Frieda   *An Introduction to Jung's Psychology* Penguin, Harmondsworth, 1968
3. Jacobi, Jolande   *The Psychology of C. G. Jung*, 8th ed. Yale University Press, New Haven, Conn., 1973
4. Jung, C. G.   *Psychological Types* Princeton University Press, Princeton, N.J., 1976
5. Jung, C. G.   *Man and His Symbols* Dell, New York, 1976
6. Mann, Harriet, Siegler, Miriam, and Osmond, Humphry   "The Many Worlds of Time"   *The Journal of Analytical Psychology*, Vol. 13, 1968, pp. 33–56

B. DERIVATIVE TYPOLOGIES BASED ON JUNG

1. Malone, Michael   *Psychetypes* Dutton, New York, 1977
2. Myers, Isabel Briggs   *The Myers-Briggs Type Indicator*, Manual 1962, Consulting Psychologists Press, Palo Alto, Calif.

C. BOOKS RELEVANT TO PERSONALITY

1. Gesell, Arnold   *First Five Years of Life* Harper & Row, New York, 1940
2. Graves, Clare W.   "Deterioration of Work Standards" *Harvard Business Review*, Vol. 44, No. 5, September–October 1966, p. 117

REFERENCES

3. Gruber, Howard and Voneche, Jacques, Eds. *Essential Piaget* Basic Books, New York, 1977

4. Luscher, Max *The Luscher Color Test* Pocket Books, New York, 1971

5. Maslow, Abraham H. *Motivation and Personality* Harper & Row, New York, 1970

D. *BOOKS RELEVANT TO MODELS OF THE BRAIN*

1. Andreae, J. H. *Man-Machine Studies* Department of Electrical Engineering, University of Canterbury, Christchurch, New Zealand, July 1979

2. Bannister, D., Ed. *Perspectives in Personal Construct Theory* Academic, London, 1971

3. Boden, Margaret *Artificial Intelligence and Natural Man* Basic Books, New York, 1977

4. Bowler, T. Downing *General Systems Thinking* Elsevier North Holland, New York, 1981

5. Chomsky, Noam *The Logical Structure of Linguistic Theory* Plenum, New York, 1975

6. Koestler, Arthur *The Act of Creation* Dell, New York, 1964

7. Metzner, Ralph *Maps of Consciousness* Collier, New York, 1971

8. Lessac, Arthur *Body Wisdom: The Use and Training of the Human Body* D.B.S. Publications, New York 1982

9. Lessac, Arthur *The Use and Training of the Human Voice: A Practical Approach to Speech and Voice Dynamics*, 2nd ed., DBSs Publications, New York, 1967

10. Lorenz, Konrad *Studies in Animal and Human Behavior*, Vol. II, translated by Robert Martin Harvard University Press, Cambridge, Mass., 1971

11. Pattee, Howard H. "The Complementarity Principle in Biological and Social Structures" *Journal of Social and Biological Structures*, Vol. 1, 1978, pp. 191–200

12. Readings from Scientific American *Progress in Psychobiology* W. H. Freeman, San Francisco, 1976

E. *SOME UNUSUAL REFERENCES RELEVANT TO MY CONSTRUCTION OF THE MODEL*

1. Alexander, Christopher W. *Notes on the Synthesis of Form* Harvard University Press, Cambridge, Mass., 1964

2. Cirlot, John Eduardo *A Dictionary of Symbols* Philosophical Library, New York 1972

3. Cousins, Norman *Anatomy of an Illness as Perceived by the Patient* Norton, New York, 1979

4. Dreyfuss, Henry, Ed. *Symbol Sourcebook: An Authoritative Guide to International Graphic Symbols* McGraw-Hill, New York, 1972

5. Floyd, Keith "Fields within Fields within Fields" *Of Time and the Mind*, No. 10, Winter 1973–1974 World Institute Council, New York.

6. Jesperson, Otto *Language—Its Nature, Development and Origin* George Allen and Unwin, London, 1922

7. Miller, George A. "The Magical Number Seven Plus or Minus Two (Some Limits on Our Capacity for Processing Information)" *Psychological Review*, Vol. 63, No. 2, March 1956, pp. 81–97

8. Prince, George M. *The Practice of Creativity: A Manual for Dynamic Group Problem Solving* Macmillan, New York, 1972

9. Sagan, Carl *The Dragons of Eden* Ballantine, New York, 1978

10. Shannon, Claude E. *The Mathematical Theory of Communication* University of Illinois Press, Urbana, 1959

11. Snow, Charles Percy *The Two Cultures: And a Second Look* Cambridge University Press, 1969

12. Elijah, A. M., Ed. *The Syntropic Thinker* Institute of Creative Development, Poona, India, December 1978

13. Watson, James D. *Double Helix: Being a Personal Account of the Discovery of the Structure of DNA* Atheneum, New York, 1968

F. UNPUBLISHED STUDENT PAPERS AT STATE UNIVERSITY OF NEW YORK, BINGHAMTON

1. Michael Aigen *A quadripartite model of conscious systems*, 1978

2. Steven P. Ehrhardt *Communication, learning and an organization of the 16 poles of the Lowen model with respect to the role each plays within its mode*, 1979

3. Mary Sue Iannello *The implications of Dr. Lowen's model of consciousness for management theory*, 1977

4. Kenneth David Ridley *Neurophysiological correlates of the Lowen consciousness model*, 1977

5. Donna H. Rhodes *The holographic hypothesis: a paradigm for the systems age*, 1980

6. Matthias D. Stec *Lateral Cerebral Asymmetry and its relationship to the Lowen model of information processing along poles*, 1980

7. Eugene Surowitz personal communications, 1980

AUTHOR INDEX

SUBJECT INDEX

DATE DUE

GAYLORD			PRINTED IN U.S.A.